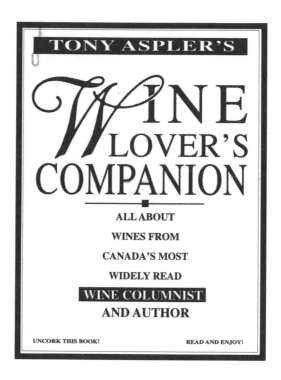

TONY ASPLER'S

WINE LOVER'S COMPANION

ALL ABOUT

WINES FROM

CANADA'S MOST

WIDELY READ

WINE COLUMNIST

AND AUTHOR

UNCORK THIS BOOK!   READ AND ENJOY!

TONY ASPLER'S

WINE
LOVER'S
COMPANION

ALL ABOUT

WINES FROM

CANADA'S MOST

WIDELY READ

WINE COLUMNIST
AND AUTHOR

UNCORK THIS BOOK!   READ AND ENJOY!

McGRAW-HILL RYERSON
Toronto   Montreal

First published in 1991 by
McGraw-Hill Ryerson Limited
300 Water Street
Whitby, Ontario
L1N 9B6

1 2 3 4 5 6 7 8 9 0 A P 0 9 8 7 6 5 4 3 2 1

Canadian Cataloguing in Publication Data
    Aspler, Tony, 1939-
        Tony Aspler's Wine lover's companion

    Includes index.
    ISBN 0-07-551242-4

    1. Wine and wine making.   I. Title.   II. Title:
    Wine lover's companion.

    TP548.A76 1991   641.2'2   C91-094483-0

SENIOR SUPERVISING EDITOR: LENORE GRAY
DESIGN: SHARON MATTHEWS
COVER PHOTOGRAPH: WEINBURG/CLARK THE IMAGE BANK CANADA
AUTHOR PHOTOGRAPH: KEN FAUGHT, TORONTO STAR

Printed and bound in Canada

To those men and women
around the world who make wine
that sings in the glass.

ABOUT THE AUTHOR

Tony Aspler is the most widely read wine writer in Canada. He has been active on the international wine scene since 1964. As a consultant and wine judge, he makes frequent trips to the vineyards and wine fairs of Europe, and is recognized as the leading authority on Canadian wines.

His previous books include *Tony Aspler's International Guide to Wine, The Wine Lover Dines* and *Vintage Canada*. He is a wine consultant to restaurants and hotels in Canada and the United States.

Tony Aspler has lectured extensively on wine in Canada, and has been accorded international honours for wine writing. The wine columnist for *The Toronto Star* since 1981, Aspler has also contributed to *Toronto Life, City & Country Home, Wine Tidings, Canadian Business, Food Service & Hospitality, The Wine Spectator* and *Wine & Spirit*.

Contents

ILLUSTRATIONS

TABLES AND CHARTS

Acknowledgements

People who care about wine are only too willing to share their knowledge — and their cellars — with you. It is anathema for the true enthusiast to open a fine bottle and consume it alone. To quote American writer Clifton Fadiman, "A bottle of wine begs to be shared; I have never met a miserly wine lover."

I have pursued the grape around the world for over twenty-five years and if and when I catch it I will always owe a debt of gratitude to all those who have enriched my knowledge and experience along the way.

My list of "thank you's" would sound like an Oscar acceptance speech, so I will encompass all of my friends and colleagues who have wittingly or unwittingly assisted me in this enterprise with the following toast:

To winemakers at home and abroad, my fellow scribes and the wine-drinking public whose questions are the most penetrating of all; may I wish you sunshine in plenty, rainfall at the right time and an endless vista of fine vintages to grace your days.

However, I would like to thank *The Toronto Star* for giving me a platform to express my thoughts on my favourite subject. Many of the ideas offered in this book had their genesis in *Star* columns I have written over the past twelve years.

I would also like to thank Konrad Ejbich who read the manuscript and kept me on the oenological and grammatical straight and narrow with his insightful comments and suggestions.

Introduction

Pinned to the notice board above my desk is a quote by Albert Einstein. It reads: "Everything should be made as simple as possible, but not simpler."

Good advice for any writer.

Wine can be simple or it can be ritualized into the gustatory equivalent of Newtonian physics. It depends on how you want to approach it. In the following pages I have tried to demystify the subject for those who are interested in the process and the product but who are constantly being put off by arrogant waiters, confusing wine lists, ill-informed store clerks and loquacious wine snobs. The emphasis here is on the practical — how to buy wines for current drinking, for laying down and for matching with food.

You won't find much about soils and sprays, pHs and new theories on cold maceration techniques. There are other writers who have dealt with these aspects more competently than I can. What I offer is an easy reference guide to what you might expect a wine to taste like, which producers are reliable and how to get the best out of the bottle you buy.

I have also avoided touching on the subject of wine and health. Suffice it to say that no-one to my knowledge has ever contracted typhoid, yellow fever or cholera from drinking wine. The same cannot be said of water. In fact, Roman legionnaires on the march were issued a litre of wine a day. They used it to sterilize their water and to dress their wounds.

Wine is the most natural of medicines whose benefits to the heart, digestive and nervous systems have been well documented by many medical institutions around the world. Were it not for the ghost of Prohibition past (and present), wine would be more routinely prescribed by doctors today than it is, in place of such ubiquitous chemicals as aspirin and Valium.

I am more interested in what wine does *for* you than *to* you. It is the most convivial of beverages which, since biblical times, has been a boon and an ever-constant companion to the civilized mind. I am convinced that there is no better way of problem-solving than for the parties to meet over a well-chosen bottle.

If, as a result of perusing this book, you get bitten by the grape, regard it as a benign affliction because there is no known cure. I know. I have all the symptoms.

Cheers!

The Fruitful Grape

ANATOMY OF A GRAPE

Grapes are the only fruit on this planet that become more interesting after they have been squashed under foot. That's when they start to ferment, and fermentation — the conversion of perishable grape juice into enduring wine — begins with the act of crushing.

One single grape berry can tell you a lot about how wine is made and why it tastes the way it does. As an experiment, take

CROSS-SECTION OF A GRAPE BERRY

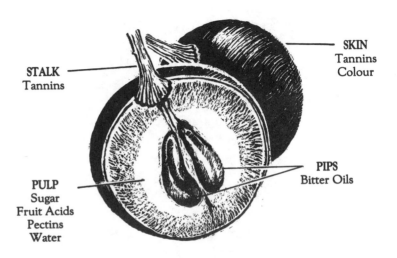

STALK
Tannins

SKIN
Tannins
Colour

PIPS
Bitter Oils

PULP
Sugar
Fruit Acids
Pectins
Water

1

The action of the yeast will convert grape-sugar into alcohol and carbonic gas in almost equal proportions. If the gas is allowed to escape the wine will be still. If it is trapped the wine will have a sparkle. The higher the sugar content of the grapes the more potential alcohol in the wine.

Colouring Grapes

There are a few varieties of black grapes that actually produce coloured juice. These are called teinturier and are used to add colour to inexpensive red wines. They are grown in hot climates, especially in the Southern Rhône, Languedoc-Roussillon and Midi regions of France. The best known are Teinturier du Cher and Alicante Bouschet.

two berries, one black and one white, each with its stalk still connected. They can be ordinary table grapes for our purposes. Notice on the skin the waxy bloom that you can polish off. This substance attracts and holds wild yeasts that float in the air. When the grape is crushed and the yeast adhering to the skin comes into contact with the sugar-rich juice inside the grape, a fermentation will start — at a warm enough temperature — converting the grape-sugars into alcohol.

Now slice both berries in two from the stalk down. Inside you will see the pulp and the pips. Rub a finger across the inside surface of both black and white grapes and you will notice that in both cases the juice is colourless. Taste it and you will get an immediate impression of sweetness.

If grape juice has no colour how do we get red wine? The pigmentation is in the skins of black grapes. The skins have to macerate with the juice in order to leach out colour. For a rosé it's a matter of hours; for red wines the process takes a few days to several weeks depending on the grape variety.

White wines can be made from black grapes simply by pressing their juice without allowing any skin contact. These wines are called by the French *blanc de noirs* (white wine from black grapes), and you will see the term on champagnes that have been produced from the black Pinot Noir and Pinot Meunier varieties.

Now press the pulp out of the black grape and chew on the empty skin. It will taste slightly bitter. The stalk will taste even more bitter, but the worst of all is the pip. That astringent, dry, woody taste is a compound called tannin. Since tannin exists in the skins, stalks and pips of grapes, its concentration in red wines will be much greater than in whites because of the maceration process required to extract colour. There are also wood tannins which can be introduced into wine being fermented and matured in oak barrels.

Tannins produce that harsh, rasping flavour (like overly strong, cold tea) in young red wines. Although they may taste offensive when young, tannins give red wines their ageing potential. It takes a matter of years for these tannins to soften up and eventually, if left long enough, they will precipitate out with colouring matter as sediment in fully mature reds. In certain years, such as 1975 in Bordeaux, wines were produced with such concentrated tannins that they may never soften up before the fruit dries out.

Grape Stats

*A grape is
80% Water
10 – 12% Sugar
(glucose and fructose)
depending on the
amount of sunlight
during its growing
period
5 – 6% Acids, trace
minerals, pectines
Skin = 11% in weight
Pips = 2 – 6% in weight
Pulp = 83% in weight*

Certain grape varieties are more tannic than others. For instance, Cabernet Sauvignon with its small berry size and thick skin will contain more tannin than the larger Pinot Noir because of the smaller ratio of pulp (sugar and acid) to skin (tannin and pigmentation).

Nowadays, winemakers can't afford the luxury of producing wines that take twenty years to mature. Economic considerations dictate that wines be table ready much sooner, so producers reduce the amount of tannin in their wines by destemming the grape bunches before fermentation and by using special techniques such as carbonic maceration (see page 45), which is used in producing Beaujolais Nouveau so that we can drink the wine when it is only six weeks old.

ACIDITY

Acid is the backbone of wine which gives it its structure and its ability to stay fresh without oxidizing. Acid by itself would make a wine taste sour, but in balance with sugar and alcohol it can be very refreshing. A wine lacking in acidity will taste soft and flabby and will have no length in the mouth.

There are several acids in wine. Here are the most important:
Tartaric: has a harsh taste
Malic: tastes of green apples
Citric: lemons
Lactic: milky
Succinic: a flavour enhancer
Acetic: vinegar

IN THE VINEYARD

*The French have a
saying:
"The vinestock is the
Mother.
The soil is the Father.
The climate is its
Destiny."*

In our quest to live forever we have a natural ally in wine. Wine is humanity's way of turning one of Nature's perishable gifts (grape juice) into something with pretensions to immortality. A few bottles of Rheingau Riesling exist in the cellars of Schloss Schönborn in Hattenheim which date back to 1735. These have been sampled in the last few years and declared still alive and drinkable. However, most of us are content if we are ever given the opportunity to taste the wine of our birth year. Mine is 1939, a disastrous vintage, so I say I was conceived in 1938, which was moderately better. (If you are touring a Bordeaux château or the caves of the Loire and the cellar master asks you the year you were born, lie! Look him straight in the eye and tell him 1928, 1945, 1947 or 1961 —

3

*People who get
headaches from
drinking red wine but
have no ill effects from
white are probably
reacting to tannin in
the wine. Tannin can
release histamines in
some people, and if you
are allergic to
histamines you will
react badly. The red
wine with the lowest
amount of tannin is
Beaujolais Nouveau.*

whichever you can get away with, even if you are still in your teens. They were all exceptional vintages and the wines are still magnificent.)

- Why is one year better than another?
- How important are vintage dates?
- And why does one wine last longer than another?

These are questions that will be answered in the course of this book but first we should establish why wines look, smell and taste the way they do and what makes one better than another. To understand the differences we have to consider the five basic factors that govern the character and flavour of all wines wherever they come from.

1 The grape variety or varieties from which the wine is made.
2 The soil in which these grapes are grown.
3 The amount of sunshine, rain, wind and fog the vines are subjected to.
4 The vineyard practices of the winegrower (planting, pruning, spraying, etc.).
5 The winemaking, blending and ageing techniques used by the producer.

The winegrower can choose the site of the vineyard and the variety of grape planted. The grower can determine the density of vine plants to commit to a given area of ground, the method of training used, how the vines are pruned and when they are sprayed against insects and diseases. What cannot be controlled is the weather — how much sunshine the vineyard enjoys and the amount of rainfall during critical growing periods. Rain at flowering or just prior to harvest is the winegrower's greatest fear: water can knock off the flowers and substantially reduce the crop; at harvest time the vine roots will absorb water, swelling the berries too much and diluting their sugars and acids. This dilution will result in weak, flabby wines that are light in colour and lack intensity of flavour.

THE FAMILY OF GRAPES

Basically, there are three classes of grape. Although the correct term would be species, there is a similarity of temperament and style to what has become recognized as the class system in our society. The social structure of grape society is illustrated on the opposite page.

Vitis vinifera The nobility, as it were, are the white and red *Vitis vinifera* varieties. *Vitis* is Latin for "vine" and *vinifera*

SOCIAL STRUCTURE OF GRAPE SOCIETY

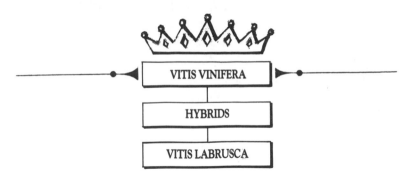

The Life of the Vine

A newly planted vine will produce a commercial crop of grapes after three years, but the grapes will not make good wine until the vine has matured. The fruit of young vines gives the wine a green, slightly astringent taste.

Château Lafite, one of the finest red Bordeaux, will not use the fruit of vines that are less than twelve years old in wine bearing its prestigious label. The immature wines are either blended into their second label, Carruades de Lafite, or sold off to other merchants.

The average life-span of a vine is thirty-five to forty years after which time it will be uprooted and replaced. Old vines, like human beings, lose their vigour with age and will not yield as much as younger ones. Vines, however, can live over 100 years. At Château Tahbilk in Victoria, Australia, there is an ancient Shiraz vineyard of pre-phylloxera vines growing in sandy soil. The wine produced is magnificent but minuscule in quantity.

means "wine-bearing." Generally, these are the European varieties such as Chardonnay, Sauvignon Blanc, Riesling, Gamay, Cabernet Sauvignon, and Pinot Noir. There are some fifty *V. vinifera* varieties used in winemaking, many of which are profiled on pages 10–16. These well-bred grapes are susceptible to all manner of diseases such as rot and mildew.

Hybrids   These are the middle-class grapes. Hybrids are the result of crossing two varieties — usually North American *labrusca* stock with *V. vinifera* — to develop characteristics such as being more disease resistant, an earlier ripener, a higher yielder or more winter hardy.

Some examples are

- Maréchal Foche — a cross between a *labrusca* variety and Gold Riesling
- Vidal — a cross between Ugni Blanc (the grape of Cognac) × Rayon d'Or (itself a hybrid)
- Villard Noir — a cross between two hybrids, Chancellor × Seibel 6095 (named after the man who made the crossing)

Wines made from hybrids are not as elegant or as long-lived as those produced from *V. vinifera* varieties.

Vitis labrusca   These are the native North American varieties, originally found growing wild along river banks on the northeast coast and subsequently domesticated. They are characterized by their sturdiness, winter hardiness and resistance to disease. *Labrusca* varieties make good grape juice, jams, jellies and food flavourings. Unfortunately, the wines they produce taste as if they have had a close encounter with an agitated fox. Some examples are Concord, Niagara, Delaware and Catawba.

While *V. labrusca* varieties have little stature in the wine world (Ontario has banned them from table wines, although a wine called Fragolino is an under-the-counter delicacy in the Friuli region of northern Italy), their close cousins *V. riparia*, *V. rupestris* and *V. berlandieri* are responsible for virtually all the fine wines we drink today.

The reason for this is a louse called phylloxera. This tiny insect feeds on the roots of vines, and in the late 1860s its ancestors were unwittingly transported from North America to Europe on *labrusca* vines destined to be planted in the Rhône Valley. The native North American vines were immune to the depredations of the phylloxera bug but not the noble *Vitis vinifera* of France, Italy, Spain and Portugal. For the next thirty years an army of insects ate its way through Europe's vineyards destroying millions of hectares of vine plants. The only ones spared were those in very sandy soils where the louse could not survive. Notable among them are the Colares region of Spain, the Naçional vineyard at Quinta do Noval in Portugal and a Bollinger Pinot Noir vineyard in Champagne.

The only remedy to halt the depredations of phylloxera was to replant the vineyards with the immune North American rootstock and graft on the noble European varieties. Today, virtually all vineyards around the world, except for those in Chile, are planted on North American rootstock.

THE SUN FACTOR

Grapes get their sugar from sunshine. Through photosynthesis the leaves of the vine convert solar energy into equal parts of glucose and fructose which the sap delivers for storage inside each berry.

The more sunshine, the higher the grape's sugar reading (and as we have already seen, the higher potential alcohol in the wine after fermentation). As a rule of thumb, the cooler the growing region the lower the alcoholic strength of the wines. Compare the Riesling wines grown in the Mosel region of northern Germany to Riesling grown in California and you will see the effect of sunshine on wine grapes. Mosel Riesling is very dry and acidic, low in alcohol, while the California model is fleshy and round with lots of fruit and low acidity.

If we look at a map of France we can see the effect of sunshine hours on one specific grape variety — Chardonnay.

In northerly growing areas, such as Champagne and Chablis, the site of the vineyard is crucial for quality. In order

THE WINE GRAPE ZONES

These bands north and south of the equator are the zones in which wine grapes will grow. Below 30 degrees latitude is too hot; above 50 degrees latitude is too cold to sustain the vine plant.

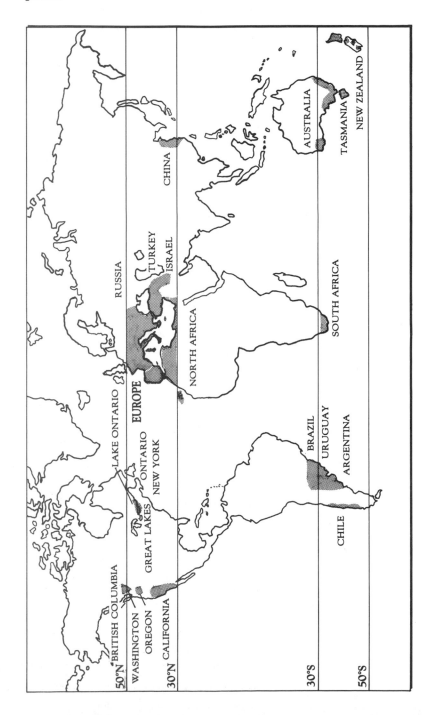

SUNSHINE HOURS AND LATITUDES OF THE GRAPE GROWING REGIONS IN FRANCE

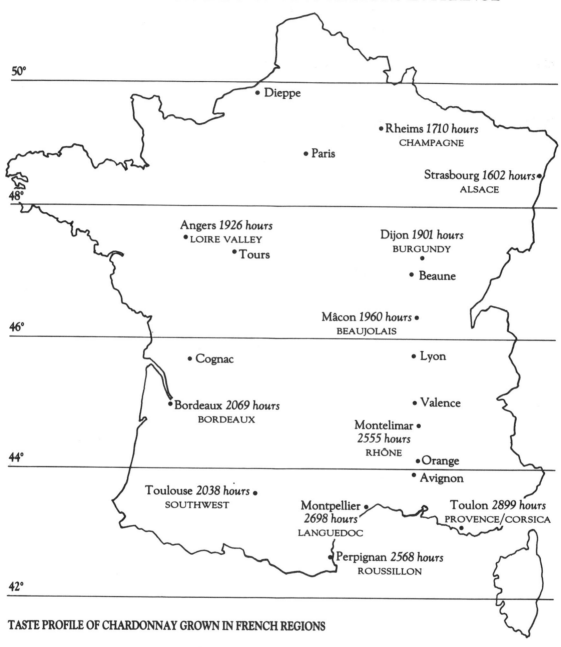

50°

• Dieppe

•Rheims *1710 hours*
CHAMPAGNE

• Paris

Strasbourg *1602 hours*•
ALSACE

48°

Angers *1926 hours*
•LOIRE VALLEY

Dijon *1901 hours*
BURGUNDY

•Tours

• Beaune

Mâcon *1960 hours* •
BEAUJOLAIS

46°

• Cognac

• Lyon

•Bordeaux *2069 hours*
BORDEAUX

• Valence

Montelimar •
2555 hours
RHÔNE

44°

•Orange
• Avignon

Toulouse *2038 hours* •
SOUTHWEST

Montpellier •
2698 hours
LANGUEDOC

Toulon *2899 hours* •
PROVENCE/CORSICA

•Perpignan *2568 hours*
ROUSSILLON

42°

TASTE PROFILE OF CHARDONNAY GROWN IN FRENCH REGIONS

Rheims *Blanc de blancs* champagne (from white grapes only).

Wine Style Very dry, light-bodied. Crisp acidity and green apple tartness.

Chablis The most northerly district of Burgundy.

Wine Style Very dry, good body, flinty, appley character.

Beaune	The classic home of the great white Burgundies (Meursault, Montrachet).
	Wine Style Elegant, buttery, nutty character; generally more fruit extract than Chablis.
Macon	Southerly part of Burgundy (Pouilly-Fuissé, St. Véran).
	Wine Style Full-bodied, pineapple and caramel flavours.
Rhône	Shippers such as Louis Latour have vineyard holdings in the Ardèche.
	Wine Style Powerful, high alcohol, toasty wines.

to get as much sunshine as possible the vineyards should face south or southeast and should be planted on slopes. The angle will ensure that the majority of vines receive direct sunlight from sunrise to sunset. A sloping vineyard also provides better drainage. If a vine plant's roots are sitting in water the grape juice will be thoroughly diluted.

RECOGNIZING WINE BY THE LABEL

All wines are named in one of four ways:

1 By varietal. The name of the grape appears on the label. Examples: Hugel Gewürztraminer, Dry Creek Sauvignon Blanc.
   For a blended wine: Hardy's Cabernet Sauvignon/Shiraz.
2 By geographical designation. Examples: Barolo, Mâcon-Villages (specified appellation of origin), Drouhin's Beaune Clos des Mouches (a single Burgundy vineyard).
3 By the name of the shipper. Examples: Calvet Reserve, Kressmann Selectionné.
4 By a fantasy name. Examples: Mastroberadino Lachryma Christi, San Pedro Gato Negro.

   There was a time when fantasy names suggested inexpensive blends with easily recognizable labels, invariably sold in screw-top, one-litre bottles. But now such fine and expensive wines as Mondavi-Rothschild Opus One, Alpha Bordeaux and Lungarotti San Giorgio have made nonsense of this rule of thumb.

THE GRAPE WHO'S WHO (synonyms in brackets)

VARIETY	ORIGIN	WINE STYLE
WHITE WINES		
Aligoté	French	Poor man's Burgundy. Pale, light, crisp wine. Not for ageing.
Bacchus	German	Silvaner × Riesling and Müller-Thurgau cross. Flowery, light Muscat bouquet, low acidity. Used mainly for blending.
Bual	Madeira	Sweet full-bodied fortified wine, burnt amber colour, fig-like bouquet.
Chardonnay	French	Ranges from crisp, apple-like flavours in cool climates to caramel, pineapple and tropical tones in warm areas. Buttery, toasty or clove-like finish. Ages well, usually in oak.
Chasselas	E. Europe	Light, crisp wine with delicate bouquet in Switzerland. Rather insipid elsewhere.
Chenin Blanc	French	Honeyed, high-acid wines in the Loire. Lots of fruit. Ages many years. California model is much softer and fruitier.
Colombard	French	(French Colombard) Originally a cognac grape, now grown in California for soft, flowery wines.
Emerald Riesling	California	High-yielding Muscadelle × Riesling cross. Aromatic, soft, fruity.
Fumé Blanc	California	Californian name for Sauvignon Blanc or Sauvignon/Sémillon blend. Fruitier and less grassy than Loire model.
Folle Blanche	French	Once a major grape in Cognac. High acid, not much character.
Furmint	Hungary	Principal grape of Tokay. Can be dry, off-dry or sweet. Apple or apricot and toffee bouquet, depending on style.

VARIETY	ORIGIN	WINE STYLE
Gewürztraminer	Italy	(Traminer) Spicy, exotic, rose petal and lychee bouquet. Can be dry (Alsace) or sweet (Germany, California).
Grüner Veltliner	Austria	Fresh, lively, fruity, dry wine for drinking young as in the "new" wine, Heurige.
Hárslevelü	Hungary	Spicy, full-bodied, aromatic. Good for sweet wines.
Jacquère	French	Light, very dry and brisk wine from Savoie.
Kerner	German	Red Trollinger × Riesling cross. Spicy, fruity wines with good acidity.
Malvasia	Greek	Produces lusciously sweet dessert wines in warm climates and crisp dry ones in northern areas. The grape of the sweet Madeira, Malmsey.
Marsanne	French	Deep-coloured, high-alcohol wines blended with the more delicate Roussanne in the Rhône.
Morio-Muscat	German	Silvaner × Pinot Blanc cross. Full-bodied, fruity with spicy bouquet.
Müller-Thurgau	German	Riesling × Silvaner cross (or two clones of Riesling). Less acidic than Riesling, soft and fruity. Lacks ageing potential.
Muscadelle	French	Perfumey grape used to add bouquet to some white Bordeaux (Sauvignon and Sémillon).
Muscadet	French	(Melon de Bourgogne) Light, pale, racy wines with lively acidity from the Loire.
Muscat	Greek	Perfumed, raisiny bouquet with a characteristic spiciness in dessert wines. Can also be made dry as in Alsace and Australia.
Palomino	Spanish	The grape of sherry. Neutral wine, low acidity.

VARIETY	ORIGIN	WINE STYLE
Picolit	Italian	Dessert wine grape of Friuli. Deep coloured, rich, slightly bitter.
Pinot Blanc	French	(Pinot Bianco/Weissburgunder) Relative of Chardonnay but with less character and ageing potential. Best from Alsace.
Pinot Gris	E. Europe	(Pinot Grigio/Tokay d'Alsace/ Rülander) Full-flavoured, elegant wines capable of ageing.
Riesling	German	(Johannisberg Riesling/Rhine or White Riesling) Finest German variety, capable of making a range of wines from steely dry to toffee-sweetness. Floral nose, keen acidity.
Rkatsiteli	E. Europe	All-purpose grape producing ordinary table wines, dessert wines and fortified wines.
Sacy	French	The name suggests it all. Frisky, tart wine from Chablis region.
Savagnin	French	Makes Sherry-style *vin jaune* in the Jura region.
Sauvignon Blanc	French	Makes grassy, gooseberry, smoky wines in the Loire and accompanies Sémillon in dry and sweet wines of Bordeaux. California model is rounder and fruitier and fig-like.
Scheurebe	German	Silvaner × Riesling cross. Aromatic, fruity with pronounced acidity. Best in dessert style.
Sémillon	French	Honey and apricot bouquet when affected by *Botrytis* (see page 22). Blended with Sauvignon Blanc for dry Bordeaux. Lacks acidity.
Sercial	Portugal	Produces the driest, lightest style of Madeira. Good acidity. Ages well.
Seyval Blanc	French	Hybrid. Makes dry wines with a grassy, green plum flavour. Does not age well.

VARIETY	ORIGIN	WINE STYLE
Silvaner	Austrian	Mild, neutral wine with good body. Useful for blending.
Trebbiano	Italian	(Ugni Blanc/St. Emilion) Pale colour, high acid, medium-body, shy bouquet.
Verdelho	Spain	Produces off-dry Madeira and soft, nutty table wines.
Verdicchio	Italian	Crisp, dry wines with a hint of bitterness.
Vernaccia	Italian	Very dry, slightly bitter wines of great character.
Vidal	French	Hybrid. Good fruit and acidity. Can range in styles from tart Sauvignon Blanc to Late Harvest and Icewine.
Viognier	French	Rich, elegant, full-bodied, floral-peachy wine especially in the Rhône. Capable of ageing.
Viura	Spanish	(Macabeo) Fruity aromatic wines with high acidity capable of wood ageing.
Welschriesling	French	(Riesling Italico/Laskiriesling/ Olaszriesling) Floral, zesty, versatile but not as elegant as Johannisberg (White or Rhine) Riesling.

RED WINES

VARIETY	ORIGIN	WINE STYLE
Aglianico	Greek	Tannic, tarry wines of great breed and lasting power from southern Italy.
Alicante	French	Hybrid. Undistinguished grape with highly coloured juice, *teinturier*.
Baco Noir	French	Hybrid. Full-bodied, deep colour, smoky blackberry flavour.
Barbera	Italian	Medium colour, high acid, dry quaffing wine.
Cabernet Franc	French	(Bouchet) Usually blended with Cabernet Sauvignon or Merlot. Medium-weight, herbaceous wines suggestive of violets and raspberries.

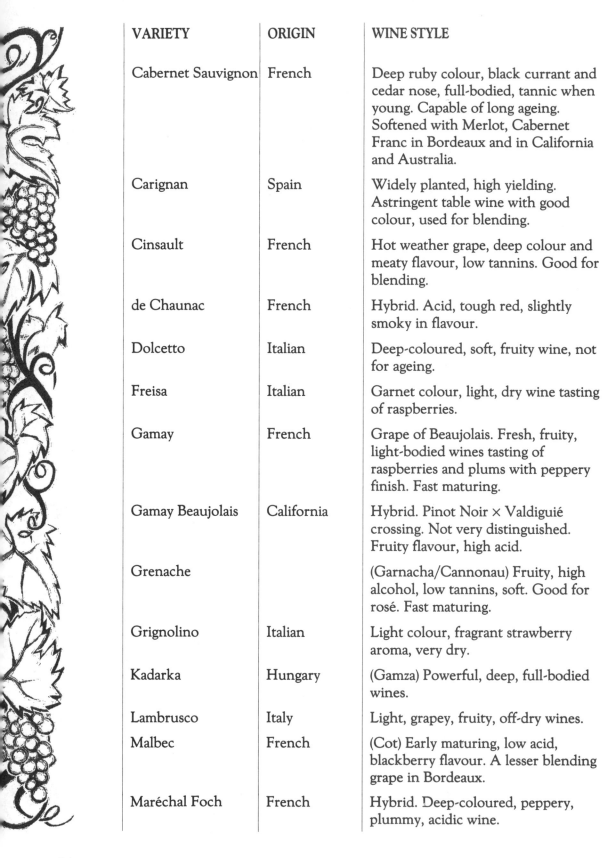

VARIETY	ORIGIN	WINE STYLE
Cabernet Sauvignon	French	Deep ruby colour, black currant and cedar nose, full-bodied, tannic when young. Capable of long ageing. Softened with Merlot, Cabernet Franc in Bordeaux and in California and Australia.
Carignan	Spain	Widely planted, high yielding. Astringent table wine with good colour, used for blending.
Cinsault	French	Hot weather grape, deep colour and meaty flavour, low tannins. Good for blending.
de Chaunac	French	Hybrid. Acid, tough red, slightly smoky in flavour.
Dolcetto	Italian	Deep-coloured, soft, fruity wine, not for ageing.
Freisa	Italian	Garnet colour, light, dry wine tasting of raspberries.
Gamay	French	Grape of Beaujolais. Fresh, fruity, light-bodied wines tasting of raspberries and plums with peppery finish. Fast maturing.
Gamay Beaujolais	California	Hybrid. Pinot Noir × Valdiguié crossing. Not very distinguished. Fruity flavour, high acid.
Grenache		(Garnacha/Cannonau) Fruity, high alcohol, low tannins, soft. Good for rosé. Fast maturing.
Grignolino	Italian	Light colour, fragrant strawberry aroma, very dry.
Kadarka	Hungary	(Gamza) Powerful, deep, full-bodied wines.
Lambrusco	Italy	Light, grapey, fruity, off-dry wines.
Malbec	French	(Cot) Early maturing, low acid, blackberry flavour. A lesser blending grape in Bordeaux.
Maréchal Foch	French	Hybrid. Deep-coloured, peppery, plummy, acidic wine.

VARIETY	ORIGIN	WINE STYLE
Merlot	French	Purple, full-bodied wines, blackberry flavour. Less tannic and earlier maturing than Cabernet Sauvignon. Ages very well.
Mourvèdre	Spanish	(Mataro) Deep-coloured, powerful wines with a spicy blackberry taste.
Nebbiolo	Italian	(Spanna/Chiavennasca) The noble grape of Piedmont producing long-lasting wines that take time to soften. Brick red, truffles and violets on the nose with an austere dry finish.
Petite Sirah	French	Californian name for the French Duriff. Full-bodied, deep-coloured wines with peppery flavour.
Pinot Noir	French	(Pinot Nero/Spätburgunder) One of the grapes of champagne and the grape of red burgundy. Difficult to cultivate. Garnet colour, barnyard bouquet, raspberry flavour, medium weight. Ages very well.
Pinot Meunier	French	Secondary grape of champagne. Fruity, acidic, low alcohol.
Pinotage	S. Africa	(Hermitage) Pinot Noir × Cinsault crossing. Robust, powerful red, inky nose. Fast maturing, ageing potential.
Primitivo	Italy	Massive black wines of high alcohol and intense fruit. Thought to be progenitor of the Californian Zinfandel.
Ruby Cabernet	California	Carignan × Cabernet Sauvignon crossing. Deep-coloured, fruity wines but lacking the finesse and breeding of Cabernet Sauvignon.
Sangiovese	Italian	A Chianti grape usually blended with Canaiolo. Earthy, truffle-scented wines with fine acidity and ample tannins. Capable of long ageing.
Syrah	Middle East	(Shiraz) Powerful black, aromatic wines tasting of blackberries and white pepper. Capable of long ageing.

VARIETY	ORIGIN	WINE STYLE
Tempranillo	Spanish	(Ull de Llebre) Pinot Noir-like character. Pale ruby colour, coconut and sandalwood bouquet. Dry strawberry flavour. Ages elegantly.
Touriga Naçional	Portugal	The best port grape. Intense dark wine with high tannin and a lovely berry nose. Other port grapes include Mourisco, Tinta Francisca, Tinta Amarela, Tinta Cao and Touriga Francesa.
Xynomavro	Greek	Black wines of high acidity and tannin that age well.
Zinfandel	California	Versatile grape that can produce powerhouse to medium-weight reds, rosés and blush wines. Characterized by a blackberry flavour and intense fruit. Also late harvest with port-like sweetness.

How
Wine
Is
Made

THE
WINEMAKING
PROCESS

A great wine can only be made from healthy, sugar-rich juice. Using modern technology, the wine-maker can rescue a poor vintage and produce a tolerable wine. Sugar can be added during fermentation to increase alcohol; lower acidity can be achieved by adding low-acid grapes or cutting the juice with a sugar and water solution. However, the great wines only come from the best grapes picked at the peak of ripeness.

In cool climates such as Germany and northern France, the problem is to achieve full ripeness and good sugars. In hot regions such as Corsica and California's Central Valley, the problem is retaining sufficient acidity in the grapes to balance the sugars.

Once harvested the grapes should not be crushed until they arrive at the press house, otherwise the juice will oxidize thereby introducing "off" flavours into the wine. The grapes are then destemmed (to prevent harsh tannins from getting into the juice), crushed and pressed.

Nowadays, most producers use temperature-controlled stainless steel tanks to ferment their white wines at temperatures of 10°C to 15°C (50°F to 59°F). The process is slow so that the aromas and fruit flavours do not escape with the carbonic gas. Many producers prefer to ferment Chardonnay in oak barrels to give the wine more complexity.

17

HOW WHITE WINE IS MADE

CRUSHER/
DESTEMMER

PRESSING

FERMENTATION

MATURATION
(*EITHER IN CASKS OR
VATS*) AND BOTTLING

HOW RED WINE IS MADE

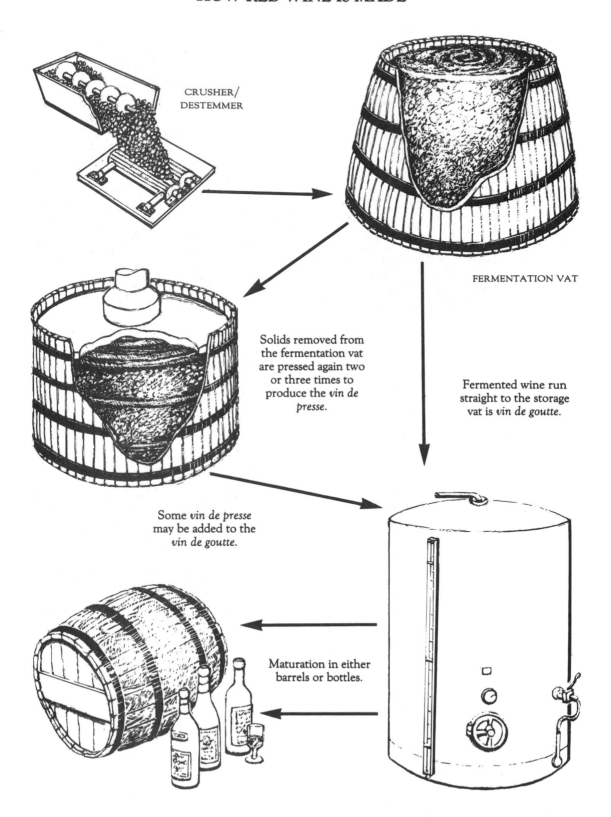

CRUSHER/
DESTEMMER

FERMENTATION VAT

Solids removed from
the fermentation vat
are pressed again two
or three times to
produce the *vin de
presse.*

Fermented wine run
straight to the storage
vat is *vin de goutte.*

Some *vin de presse*
may be added to the
vin de goutte.

Maturation in either
barrels or bottles.

*Following the alcoholic
fermentation, the
winemaker will in most
instances induce a
malolactic
fermentation which
converts the sour-apple
malic acid to the softer
lactic acid, reducing
the malic acid by half.
This process is useful
for cool climate whites
and reds, especially in
Burgundy, to rid the
young wine of its
greenness or hardness.*

Reds wines are fermented at warmer temperatures of 25°C to 30°C (77°F to 86°F) to extract colour from the skins. Grape skin and juice contact will vary from four days to several weeks depending on the grape variety and the winemaker's intention. The shorter the time spent in the fermentation vat, the fewer the tannins are extracted and the sooner the wine can be consumed.

Following fermentation the wine is racked (siphoned or pumped) off its lees (the dead yeast cells and solid particles) and left to age either in stainless steel tanks (for many white wines and simple reds) or in oak casks for reds and the better whites.

White wines generally receive three to six months of wood ageing before bottling; reds require from six months to two years. The length of time is contingent on the variety and the quality of the harvest.

Prior to bottling, the wine is fined (clarified) with such substances as eggs whites, isinglass (fish glue), bentonite (diatomaceous earth) or dried ox blood. It is then filtered to ensure that the wine is bright and clean in the bottle and there are no micro-organisms in it to start a delayed fermentation.

BARREL SIZES

Every wine growing region has developed its own traditional barrel size and shape. The name may be the same but the capacities may differ.

WINE/REGION	BARREL NAME	LITRES
Alsace	Foudre	not standardized
Beaujolais	Pièce	216
Bordeaux/Rhône	Barrique	225
Burgundy	Pièce	228
Chablis	Feuillette	132
Champagne	Pièce	205
Anjou/Layon/ Saumur	Pièce	220
Vouvray	Pièce	225
Mâconnais	Pièce	215
Mosel	Fuder	1,000
Rhine	Stück	1,200
Port	Pipe	522.5
Sherry	Butt	490.7
Madeira	Pipe	418
Tokay	Gönci	136
Cognac	Hogshead	545.2
Armagnac	Hogshead	272.6

SWEET WINES

Think back to the very first wine you ever enjoyed. It was probably sweet. As your palate became more sophisticated you began to "dry out," appreciating drier wines. And now you may look back on those "stepping-stone" products that brought you into the wine world with disdain. Once you have developed a taste for dry wines you have to re-acquire a palate for dessert wines, and this means searching for the best — those that have a good balance of sweetness and acidity so that they don't lay heavy and cloying on the palate. The best sweet wines will have an extraordinarily high level of acid which would be mouth-puckering in a dry wine.

Sugar is like make-up. It can mask a lot of deficiencies. But when a sweet wine is well made, like a château-bottled Sauternes or a Late Harvest Riesling or an Icewine, it can be an absolute joy — in small amounts. A glass at the end of a meal is quite sufficient.

In ancient times the Greeks used to add honey to their wines to sweeten them. Today there are laws prohibiting producers from adding sugar or any sweetening agent to finished wines. In certain regions they can add sugar to the juice at the time of fermentation but only to raise the alcoholic strength by a degree or two in poor vintages.

Icewine

Icewine, or Eiswein as the Germans call it, is the product of frozen grapes. A small portion of the vineyard is left unpicked during the harvest and the bunches are allowed to hang on the vine until the mercury drops to at least −7°C. At this frigid temperature the sugar-rich juice begins to freeze. If the grapes are picked in their frozen state and pressed while they are frozen as hard as marbles, the small amount of juice recovered will be intensely sweet and high in acidity.

Like most gastronomic breakthroughs the discovery of Icewine was accidental. Producers in Franconia in 1794 made virtue of necessity by pressing juice from frozen grapes. They were amazed by the abnormally high concentration of sugars and acids which hitherto they had achieved only by allowing the grapes to desiccate on straw mats before pressing or by the effects of Botrytis cinerea.

It was not until the middle of the last century in the Rheingau that German winegrowers made conscious efforts to produce Icewine on a consistent basis. They found they could not make it every year since the sub-zero cold spell has to last for several days to ensure that the berries remain frozen solid during picking and the lengthy pressing process which can take up to three days or longer. Grapes are eighty percent water and when this water is frozen and driven off under pressure as shards of ice the resulting juice will be miraculously sweet. If there is a sudden thaw, the ice will melt diluting the sugar in each berry.

In Ontario, the climate allows winemakers to produce Icewine every year from Riesling and Vidal grapes.

Unlike noble rot wines, Icewine will have very high acidity which gives it a freshness on the palate. It is very expensive, but will keep for many years.

There are several ways to make a sweet wine.

1 The vintner can stop the fermentation process by killing off the yeast or filtering it out. This will leave unfermented sugar in the wine; or the yeast can die before all the sugar has been converted into alcohol.

2 The vintner can ferment a wine to dryness and then blend back an amount of unfermented grape juice or concentrate of the same variety to the finished wine (this technique is extensively used in Germany and is called *Süssreserve*, meaning sweet reserve).

3 The fermentation can be stopped prematurely by the addition of grape brandy. Port is made in this manner.

4 The vintner can leave the grapes on the vine until they reach super-maturation (the late harvest effect).

5 In certain climates the vineyards will be attacked by a fungus called *Botrytis cinerea* which further concentrates the grape sugars (see below).

6 The picked grape bunches can be left for several weeks to dry out before fermentation so that their water evaporates thus concentrating the sugar. The Italians call this *passito* and they use it to make such wines as Recioto della Valpolicella. The French call it *vin de paille* (the grapes are dried on mats of straw).

7 The grapes can be left on the vine until the first frost, then picked and pressed while frozen solid. The result is an intensely sweet and acidic Icewine.

8 The fresh grape juice is stopped from fermenting by the addition of grape brandy as in the Cognac region aperitif, Pineau des Charentes.

Noble Rot

Nothing looks more disgusting than a bunch of grapes afflicted with Botrytis cinerea, what the French call pourriture noble, *the Germans* Edelfäule *and the Italians* Muffa Nobile. *This benign disease causes certain grape varieties to shrivel, rot and turn brown in the late fall. But the wine made from such grapes can taste like the nectar of the gods. In damp, humid climates such as Sauternes, the Rhine Valley and Hungary, a mushroomlike fungus will attack the ripe berries, piercing their skins and allowing the juice to evaporate. This effect concentrates the sugars and acids but produces very low quantities of juice. The wine made from this sugar-rich juice is intensely sweet with a honeyed tropical fruit character overlaid with apricots and barley sugar. The nose will have a distinctive petrol and lime bouquet.*

Sémillon, Sauvignon Blanc, Riesling, Gewürztraminer, Pinot Gris and the hybrid Vidal are highly susceptible to Botrytis. Given the small amount made and the labour-intensive nature of its production, noble rot wines will always be expensive. They are usually sold in half bottles and will cellar well for many years because of the high sugar content.

Sweet wines are generally served either by themselves as an aperitif or with dessert. They should be well chilled and served at a lower temperature than you would offer white wines. Chilling brings down the perception of sweetness and heightens the presence of acidity.

Classics	The classic dessert wines are as follows:
France	**Bordeaux** Sauteurnes, Barsac, Cérons, Loupiac, Ste-Croix-du-Mont (made from Sémillon and Sauvignon Blanc grapes)
	Loire Anjou, Vouvray, Coteaux du Layon, Quarts de Chaume, Bonnezeaux (Chenin Blanc grapes)
	Alsace Vendange Tardive (Late Harvest) wines of Riesling, Gewürztraminer, Tokay-Pinot Gris
	Southwest France Jurançon (Petit Marseng), Monbazillac (Sémillon, Sauvignon Blanc, Muscadelle)
	Jura Vin de Paille (Savagnin)
	Rhône Muscat Beaumes-de-Venise
	Roussillon Rivesaltes, Frontignon (Muscat)
Italy	**Veneto** Recioto di Soave (Gargenega), Recioto della Valpolicella (Corvina, Rondinella, Molinara)
	Tuscany/Umbria Vin Santo (Malvasia, Grechetto, Trebbiano)
	Friuli-Venezia-Guilia Verduzzo, Picolit
	Piedmont Asti Spumante (sparkling Muscat)
Germany	Auslese, Beerenauslese, Trockenbeerenauslese and Eiswein of any designated grape varieties
Hungary	Tokaji Aszu (Furmint, Hárslevelü, Muskotalyi)
Greece	Samos (Muscat), Mavrodaphne (red)
Cyprus	Commandaria (sun-dried grapes)
United States	Late Harvest or Botrytis Affected (Johannisberg Riesling, Gewürztraminer, Sauvignon Blanc)
Canada	**Ontario** Icewine, Late Harvest, Botrytis Affected (Vidal, Riesling)

Australia	**South Australia** Late Harvest and Noble Rot (Semillon, Riesling), Liqueur Muscat
South Africa	Late Harvest, Special Late Harvest and Noble Rot (Steen, Riesling)

FORTIFIED WINES

A fortified wine is one to which grape brandy or a neutral spirit has been added such as sherry or port or vermouth. They have an alcoholic content ranging from fifteen percent by volume to twenty-five percent. Once a wine has been fortified it will no longer develop, but it will last longer in a bottle once it is opened because of the higher alcohol content.

Wines were originally fortified for practical reasons: they travelled better on long sea voyages to foreign markets, and the addition of brandy helped to mask some of the deficiencies in the quality of the product when winemaking was a craft rather than art and science.

Fortified wines can range from the very dry (fino sherry and sercial madeira) to the very sweet (cream sherry and marsala superiore). They are usually served chilled, except for port which is served just below room temperature.

Sherry

While the term sherry is loosely used in new world wine regions to describe a fortified white wine, its true meaning belongs to a region of southwest Spain, centred around the town of Jerez de la Frontera.

Sherry is fortified not to stop the fermentation but when the fermentation is complete, which means that in its natural state it is a dry wine. The various styles of sherry are achieved by blending and by ageing.

The production of sherry is an act of God as well as man. When the fermentation of Palomino grapes starts the vintner does not know whether the wine he makes will be a fino or an oloroso. Finos develop a blanket of yeast cells on the surface of the wine called *flor*. It looks rather like heavy cottage cheese which protects the young wine from air and dramatically reduces oxidation. Olorosos develop only partial flor or none at all and will develop differently.

Finos are fortified to about fifteen percent of alcohol (so as not to inhibit the growth of flor) and olorosos to eighteen percent (to kill the yeast). The cellar master then classifies the wine as either fino or oloroso with a chalk mark on the butts. Both are then sweetened with fresh wine or concentrate from

Pedro Ximenez (PX) grapes. From this point the two styles will develop very differently.

Manzanilla is a special kind of fino grown around the Atlantic coastal town of Sanlucar de Barrameda. The salt air is said to impart a saline quality to the wine.

The young wines are then introduced into their own solera systems where they are blended and aged. A solera — from the Latin meaning floor — is a scale of barrels usually four or five in height. One-quarter to one-third of the sherry is drawn off from the oldest butts for bottling and this butt is topped up from one that contains wines a year younger. The younger wine will quickly take on the character of the older wine. This process is repeated until the youngest butts are refreshed with the new vintage.

When finos age for several years they deepen in colour and turn into a style called amontillado. Because of the quirky nature of the flor growth an oloroso can take on the style of a fino, in which case it is called a palo cortado.

HOW SHERRY DEVELOPS

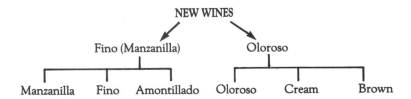

Manzanilla   The lightest, driest and most delicate of sherries (from Sanlucar de Barrameda). Hard to find. Example: Garvey La Lidia

Fino   As dry as manzanilla but usually fuller bodied. Deteriorates quickly. Very dry. An excellent aperitif. Best purchased in half bottles. Example: Tio Pepe

Amontillado   An aged fino. Deeper in colour with a nutty flavour. Dry. Example: Savory & James Amontillado Deluxe

Medium   An amontillado sweetened with PX. Example: Dry Sack

Palo Cortado   An oloroso displaying the finesse and character of an amontillado. Rare and tends to be more expensive. Example: Williams & Humbert Dos Cortados

Oloroso Full-bodied and raisiny. From dry to medium sweet. Example: Gonzales Byass Nutty Solera Oloroso

Cream Rich and sweet, usually very deep in colour. Example: Harvey's Bristol Cream. Can also be in pale style such as Croft Original.

Brown The sweetest sherry of all. Example: Harvey's Copper Beech

Since sherry is a blended product you will rarely find one that is vintage dated.

Sherry and Food

- Sherries, particularly chilled finos and manzanillas, make wonderful aperitifs to stimulate appetite before a meal. They also are elegant accompaniments for salted nuts and olives, smoked salmon and shellfish.
- Amontillados go well with soups, cheese and fish salads.
- Olorosos complement sweet desserts, cakes, sweet biscuits, nuts and raisins.
- Creams/Browns go well with rich sweet desserts or blue cheeses.

Port

The home of port is the Douro Valley in the northern part of Portugal, though like sherry, other new world wine producers have co-opted the name for their fortified red wine. But port can be white and dry too.

The wine can be made from forty-eight different varieties but the major ones are Touriga Naçional, Touriga Francesca, Tinta Cao, Roriz and Barroca. White port is made from white varieties, particularly Malvasia Fina and Malvasia Grosso.

The finest port is still made in the traditional way — crushing the grapes by foot. The wine matures in large barrels called pipes which contain 534.2 litres. When the wine has reached the right alcoholic strength the fermentation is stopped by the addition of brandy — 100 litres for every 450 litres of wine.

In the spring following the vintage the young port is assessed for quality to determine its future. The best will be bottled after two years to become vintage port.

Only vintage port needs to be aged once you have bought it. Old port will throw a deposit which must be separated from the wine by decanting (see page 81). One of the great taste sensations is port and Stilton cheese.

PORT STYLES	AVERAGE AGE	DESCRIPTION
Ruby	3 years old	Basic port. Young, sweet, full-bodied.
Late Bottled Vintage (LBV)	4 – 6 years	Aged longer in wood. May carry a vintage date but will not improve in the bottle. Drink now.
Vintage Character	4 – 6 years	The same quality as LBV but a blend of different years.
Tawny	3 – 5 years	Ruby blended with white port. Usually drier than rubies.
Aged Tawny	5 – 10 years	Ruby long-aged in wood until it loses colour. Labels saying 10, 20, 30 years are a blend of old and young wines.
Single Quinta	vintage dated	Ports made from a single vineyard usually in vintage style, bearing a year.
Vintage	vintage dated	Superior Ruby bottled after two years and allowed to mature for a decade or more. Each house declares whether it considers its port good enough to be a vintage two years after it is produced.
White port	3 – 5 years	Can be dry or medium-dry. Serve as an aperitif, chilled or on the rocks.

Madeira

This mountainous Portuguese island in the Atlantic Ocean, 500 kilometres west of Casablanca, produces a remarkable fortified wine in almost as many styles as sherry. The best are named after the noble grape varieties from which they are made.

Sercial The driest style of Madeira, pale in colour. Grown in the highest vineyards, this wine resembles a dry sherry. Drink chilled.

Verdelho Medium-dry, deeper in colour. Rainwater is a name given to a very pale and light style, after an American wine lover named Rainwater Habisham who developed it. Good with soups or as aperitifs.

Bual Amber colour, sweet. Try with cake, sweet biscuits or blue cheese.

Malmsey Deep gold to brown and very sweet. Try as dessert wine or digestif.

The wine is first fermented in oak casks and then fortified with grape brandy at different times, according to the grape variety. The sweeter the style, the earlier the fortification to leave residual sugar in the wine. In January following the harvest the new wines are then "cooked" by the heat from hot water pipes for six months to one year. The best madeiras are allowed to oxidize naturally in the heat of the sun. They are placed in barrels at the top of the lodges and left there for five to eight years.

Madeira Classifications

Fine, Choice, Selected   Three years old. No grape variety named on the label. Probably made from lesser grapes such as Tinto Negra Mole.

Reserve   Youngest wine in the blend will be five years old. At least eighty-five percent of the noble varieties will be used, especially if one is named on the label.

Special Reserve   Youngest wine in the blend is ten years old with eighty-five percent grape variety regulation.

Extra Reserve   Youngest wine in the blend is fifteen years old with eighty-five percent grape variety regulation.

Vintage   One hundred percent of a single named noble variety from one year aged in cask for a minimum of twenty years.

Solera   This wine will carry the year when the solera (see page 25) was established. Only ten percent is allowed to be drawn off from the oldest casks.

Madeira is one of the longest lasting wines. Bottles from the mid-eighteenth century are still drinkable. Unlike table wines, the bottles should be stored standing upright. Once opened the wine will remain fresh for a long time if securely stoppered.

Marsala

What sherry is to Spain, marsala is to Italy. This fortified wine which varies from seventeen to nineteen percent alcohol can occasionally be dry but is more normally sweet to very sweet. The wine is named after the a port city in Sicily where it was originally produced by English wine merchants in the latter half of the eighteenth century who were looking for cheaper versions of sherry and port. The wine is made from the Grillo, Catarratto and Inzolia grapes and in its natural state, like sherry, it is dry. Marsala Vergine is the most sought after.

Sweeter versions are made by grape must called *cotto* (concentrated by boiling down) or *sifone*, sweet wine with grape brandy. Four basic styles are designated under the DOC, Italy's wine law.

Marsala Fine   The lowest grade of around seventeen percent alcohol which contains more concentrated must than sweetened wine. It can also bear the older designation of Italy Particular (IP) or Italia.

Marsala Superiore   One degree more alcohol and at least two years of wood ageing. Ranging from dry to sweet, depending upon the producer. Initials on the label will indicate traditional descriptions: SOM — Superior Old Marsala, LP — London Particular, GD — Garibaldi Dolce.

Marsala Speciale   An extra degree of alcohol with flavouring additives such as coffee, cream, egg, banana and orange. Non-DOC.

Marsala Vergine   Dry to very dry without any sweetening agents added. Must be aged for at least five years in wood and may spend time in a solera (see page 25). Vergine Stravecchio is aged for ten years.

Wine
Tasting
at
Home

So you want to put on a wine tasting? Easy. All you need is a few bottles of wine, some interested friends, enough glasses, good light and a smoke- and perfume-free environment.

A communal tasting is a good way for you to discover what wine styles you prefer. Comparing the bouquets, flavours and "mouth-feel" of different wines will enable you to make your own judgements more satisfactorily. Keeping the memory of a taste in your mind while you compare it with what is in your glass is very difficult. But if you have a row of glasses in front of you it is a simple matter to go back and forth to make the comparisons.

Basically there are two different types of wine tasting events: structured tastings and table-top tastings.

THE STRUCTURED TASTING

Participants are seated at a table with a glass for each wine to be tasted in front of them. A white tablecloth or a white paper place-mat allows the taster to judge the true colour of the wines. Each person has a tasting sheet to make notes, a glass of water and a spittoon or small plastic container. The red wines are pre-poured so that they are all at the same temperature. The whites are served individually so that they remain chilled.

This format allows tasters to compare the wines one against another.

THE TABLE-TOP TASTING

This type of tasting is used for large groups. Wines to be tasted are opened and placed on tables. The whites are kept cool in ice trays or buckets. Participants move from table to table with their own glass and are served a two-ounce measure for tasting. Dump buckets should be available to throw away unwanted wine and jugs of water are needed to rinse out glasses between samples.

This format is generally the one that wine shows use. The drawback is that with a single glass there is no opportunity to compare the bouquets and taste the subtle differences between products. Also, standing while tasting and note-taking can be difficult and distracting, but a lot of people can be accommodated in this way.

GLASSES

Use only plain glass or crystal without colour in the bowl or stem. Try to ensure that tasting glasses are all the same size and shape. Believe it or not the same wine can smell and taste different when tasted from a variety of glass designs. Look for glasses with a tulip shape. The chimney effect helps to concentrate the wine's bouquet.

Make sure the glasses are spotlessly clean and free from detergent odours which could influence the smell and the taste of the wine.

THEMES

All tastings are either vertical or horizontal (which has nothing to do with your condition before or after the event). Vertical tastings are narrow in focus — usually several vintages of the same wine. Horizontal tastings are wide-ranging such as different wines of the same vintage, grape variety or region or price bracket.

Twelve Possible Wine Tasting Themes

1 White wines under $8
2 Chardonnays of the world
3 Rhône reds
4 The Crus of Beaujolais (Fleurie, Moulin-á-Vent, Regnié, etc.)
5 Château-bottled Bordeaux reds
6 Cabernet Sauvignon taste-off: Bordeaux vs. California vs. Australia

7 Sparkling wines
8 Chiantis
9 South American reds and whites
10 House wines
11 Dessert wines
12 Wines of the same vintage

TASTING SHEETS

Print up a tasting sheet for your guests which they can take home with them for future reference. List the wines with their vintage dates and prices. Allow sufficient room for their comments. If you want them to rank the wines and give them points, use a simple ten-point system, assigning values according to the three specific sensory responses: Appearance (0 – 2), Bouquet (0 – 3) and Taste (0 – 5).

Tips

1 Always pour identical amounts when tasting comparatively. (With red wines the more you have in the glass the deeper the colour looks.)
2 Ensure that all wines are at the proper — and the same — serving temperature. (If reds get too warm they taste flabby and alcoholic. Whites taste sweeter when not chilled.)
3 Have a white background against which to assess colour such as a white tablecloth or white tasting sheets.
4 To ensure your guests do not mix up the glasses, number each foot with a grease pencil or sticker or, better still, provide a sheet with numbered circles on which to position the glasses.
5 The first wine should be poured into the left-hand glass.
6 Serve young wines before older; light wines before those with high alcohol.
7 Ensure there are no flowers in the room, cooking odours or smoky fires.
8 Make sure you have an adequate supply of pencils. (It's amazing the number of people who arrive without a writing instrument.)
9 A lighted candle is ideal for judging the clarity of a wine but don't blow it out before the end of the tasting. The smell of wax lingers in the nostrils.
10 Dip your little finger into red wines and touch it against the corresponding name on your tasting sheet notes. When each spot dries you will have a permanent record of the colour intensity.

TASTING SHEET

NAME OF EVENT _____   DATE _____

VENUE _____   TASTER'S NAME _____

WINES*	SIGHT	BOUQUET	TASTE	SCORE/RANKING
1				
2				
3				
4				
5				
6				

*Name of wine, vintage, shipper, region, price, etc.

BLIND TASTING

Even for beginners this can be fun. Ask them what country the wine comes from? You can go the whole hog and give no information at all. Your guests have to speculate on what is in their glass from the look, smell and taste of the wine. This is double-blind tasting where even the bottle shape and colour is hidden in a bag or under tin foil. The tricky host will decant the wines and make sure the corks are not in view.

You could also give minimal information, such as "The wines are all from the same country/grape variety/vintage," or "Name the communes from which these red Bordeaux come," or "These are all red DOCG Italian wines from the 1985 vintage."

Tips for Blind Tasting

1 Never second guess yourself. Your first instincts are usually correct.
2 Good wines change in the glass. Go back and check the bouquets.
3 You can tell a lot about the age of a wine from its colour and condition. Try to establish the age of the wine from its colour and state of maturity. (Young reds are purplish and tannic. Older reds lose their colour and take on brick and orange tones at the rim. The bouquet of older wines is more intense. Whites start life with very little colour and go more golden with age.)
4 Smell all the wines before you taste the first one. This should give you an indication as to the theme. (Are they all the same grape variety or different wines from the same vintage?)
5 Isolate the predominant grape type and determine whether the character of the wine suggests a hot or cool growing region. (Dense, deep colour and rich, jammy fruit extract with low acidity suggests a hot region.)
6 Determine the quality of the wine. Is it average house wine quality, a good wine or a great wine? (The bouquet and taste, especially the length of the aftertaste, will tell you this.)
7 Determine whether the wine has been in new oak barrels or not (from the vanilla smell and spicy clove-like flavour).

FOOD AT TASTINGS

Experts do not eat while they are tasting, not even dry bread or biscuits. They clean their palates with bottled water. But you should always have something in your stomach before you imbibe beverage alcohol. If you are tasting wines do not eat spicy or hot food before the event. Avoid greasy or oily foods and sweet desserts. Fried or fatty foods can coat the tongue and sugar will lower your sensitivity.

After the tasting serve foods that complement the wines you have chosen. (See the Food and Wine Affinity Chart on page 54).

Finally, true wine tasters always travel with a corkscrew. Have you ever heard of a hockey player turning up to a game without a stick?

The
Art
of
Wine
Tasting

THE GLASS

When it comes to assessing a wine the choice of glass is as important to the process as the product you intend to pour into it. An all-purpose tasting glass should be completely plain, without any colour or etching which can distort the wine's colour or refract the light. It should have a stem long enough so that you can hold it without your hand having to touch the bowl (you want to see the colour of the wine and not warm it up with body heat). The circumference of the bowl should be larger than the aperture so that you get a chimney effect which concentrates the bouquet of the wine. And finally, the glass itself should be thin. You should not be aware of it touching your lips.

USING YOUR
SENSES

Wine tasting is rather like choosing a spouse: you start with a negative attitude. What's wrong with it? Is the colour murky or dull? Does it smell like a locker-room after a heavy work-out? Does it taste like salad dressing? Once you have established that there are no negatives then you can begin to analyze the wine for its good qualities.

Wine appeals to all five of our senses: sight, smell, taste, touch and even hearing. We are enchanted by the sound of a popping cork and the bursting of sparkling wine bubbles. Next comes sight, the way the wine looks in the glass, its

THE WINE GLASS

The ISO Glass
(the ideal glass)

Unsuitable Glasses
(coloured or
engraved)

colour and transparency or opaqueness. Then comes the smell as we lift the glass to our lips. Finally, the taste of the wine and the feel of its body or weight on our palates. For assessment purposes we are really looking at sight, smell and taste, in that order.

Sight

Hold the glass up to the light. (Natural daylight is best. Neon can give a bluish tint and coloured walls can alter the shade.) What we are looking for is clarity and colour. All wines should be bright and clean, free of particles or sediment. Mark down hazy or cloudy wines.

White wines have a range of colours from water white to deep golden depending on sugar content and maturity. Red wines range from dense purple to pale cherry depending on grape variety and age. (Incidentally, white wines gain colour with age as opposed to reds which lose colour and fade.)

Older reds will exhibit gradations of colour from the "eye" of the wine to the rim. Against a white background, tilt the glass slightly and see how the wine changes colour. The wine may be deep ruby at its centre but where its rim touches the glass it may be brick, orange, mahogany or even water white. Diminishing density of hue is a sign of age. A red wine that

37

holds its colour to the edge is a young wine. A browning edge may suggest that the wine is too old or oxidized.

Now swirl the wine in the glass and let it settle. Hold the glass up to the light and look for the transparent wetness left on the sides of the glass. This will fall back to the surface in "tears" or "legs" (the Germans call them "church windows"). This effect can tell you the alcoholic strength of the wine. The thicker the "legs" and the slower moving down the glass, the higher the alcohol.

Smell

Your nose will tell you seventy-five percent of what you want to know about a wine. Our noses are much more sensitive than our palates. We can smell as little as 400 molecules of a substance but we can taste it only if we have at least 25,000 molecules.

A healthy person can distinguish among some 5,000 smells but our palates only register four taste sensations: sweet, salt, sour and bitter. These basic tastes are fanned out into thousands of nuances at the top of the nose so if we have a cold we will find it difficult to smell and taste. In terms of wine, sweet = grape sugar, sour = acidity, salt = saltiness (rare) and bitter = tannin.

Recognizing Wine's Components

Your nose will help you detect the main components of wine.

Acidity: A fresh, citrus-like smell suggests high acid. If you find yourself salivating after smelling a wine's bouquet you are reacting to the presence of acid.

Fruit: A sweet berry or fruit smell. The warmer the growing region the more tropical the fruit will be in character. For whites: pineapple, mango, melon and fig. The more northerly are apples, pears, quince and gooseberry. For reds from warm climates: black currant, blackberry, plum; from cool growing regions: cherry, pomegranate, raspberry, strawberry.

Alcohol: The presence of alcohol heightens our perception of sugar. While we cannot actually smell alcohol we are aware of its presence as a "hot" sensation in the nose (and as it goes down the throat).

Tannin: This naturally occurring compound is experienced as an astringent taste and feel on the back of the palate and cheeks. You can perceive tannin in the bouquet of a red wine when it is young and particularly heavy. It will come across as a bitter, woody, inky smell.

Oak: Wines that have been barrel-aged will extract flavours and tannins from the oak. New French oak imparts a discernible vanilla quality to the wine. American oak, favoured in Rioja, gives the wine a coconut quality. Oak will also add a spicy character to the wine reminiscent of cloves or cinnamon.

To get the most concentrated smell of the wine first swirl the wine in the glass. This action creates friction and causes the wine's esters to evaporate. The esters carry the wine's aromas. Sniff the glass in short, sharp little in-takes of air. First look for faults. Are there any off odours (the smell of musty barrels or the vinegary scent of oxidation, for example)?

Once you have established that the bouquet is clean, assess its quality. Is it concentrated or light? Does it smell of fresh fruit or berries, dried fruit, flowers, nuts, spices, herbs, vegetation? Does it have an overlying vanilla or cedar scent from oak barrels? Does it show age and maturity with a smell of leather, coffee beans, truffles or chocolate?

Store the memory of the smell so that you can identify it when you experience it again. Remember, the nose is like a muscle: the more you use it, the more refined it will become. We tend to take our sense of smell for granted. Odours are either pleasant or unpleasant. We don't tend to break them down and analyze them. Most people find it difficult to describe what they smell in a wine, but when they hear a description that approximates their own experience they will agree.

Using an accurate term to describe the bouquet of a wine will help you to remember it the next time you are served it. Enologist Ann Noble of the University of California at Davis has created a tool to help wine lovers identify and describe a whole range of smells found in wines, both good and bad. It's called the UC Davis Aroma Wheel, and it consists of three concentric circles. The smallest contains the most general terms to describe a wine's bouquet. The second circle becomes more specific, qualifying the first. The outer circle refines the perception down to a specific aroma description.

When you first sniff the wine ask yourself which descriptive term in the innermost circle best describes what you smell. Once you have established the category, sniff again and decide which smell it resembles in the quadrant fanning out from the original term. Then zero in on a specific description from the outermost circle. Wines with complex bouquets, such as aged Cabernet Sauvignon, Pinot Noir or Late Harvest Riesling, will have more than one aroma. First isolate the predominate smell (oak? berries? *Botrytis*?) and then identify the others.

THE AROMA WHEEL

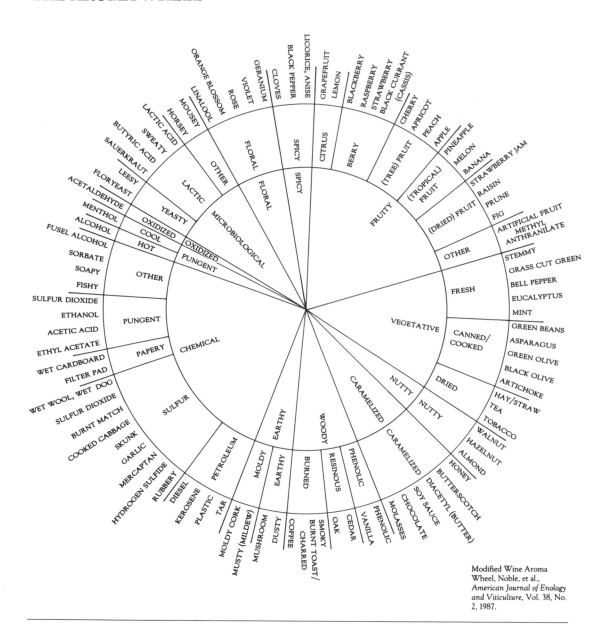

Modified Wine Aroma Wheel, Noble, et al., *American Journal of Enology and Viticulture*, Vol. 38, No. 2, 1987.

Taste

There is not one taste but three: the initial taste as the wine hits your palate, the secondary taste when the wine warms up in the mouth and the aftertaste once you have swallowed it. Let the wine wash over the entire palate. The first impression will be of the sweetness in the wine because of the position of the sugar-sensing taste buds. The sensation of sweetness is short and intense. Acidity is slower to reveal itself, but lasts much longer.

THE TASTING AREAS OF THE TONGUE

The Tongue

Different areas of the tongue are more sensitive to one taste sensation than another. The sensation of sweetness, for instance, is experienced at the tip of the tongue. A sugar lump placed at the back of the tongue will take a comparatively long time to register as sweet.
Sugar: *the tip of the tongue*
Salt: *the tip and upper front sides*
Acidity: *the middle sides and underside (and cheeks)*
Bitterness: *back of the tongue (and cheeks)*

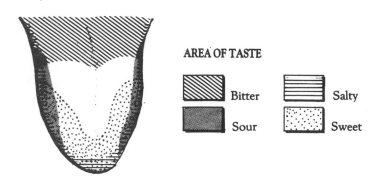

AREA OF TASTE

Bitter   Salty
Sour   Sweet

Note the presence of fruit, acidity, alcohol and tannin (in red wines, that dry aftertaste on the sides of the cheeks and back of the mouth). The longer the aftertaste lingers, the better the wine.

Check the harmony of the wine; all the elements should be in balance. A wine is made up of fruit (sugar), acid, alcohol and tannin or oak. Think of these as legs of a chair. If one of the legs is shorter than the others, the chair will be unbalanced. If one element, say, the acidity or the smell of oak, predominates then the wine is not harmonious.

WRITING WINE NOTES

It is a good idea to take notes on wines so that you can remember what you thought of them. This will give you a reference point when you want to choose wines to lay down in your cellar.

As you sample the wine, describe what you experience with your three senses, sight, smell and taste. Then give your opinion on the wine. Let's take a red and a white wine as examples.

Duboeuf Moulin-à-Vent 1989

Sight   Purple-ruby colour. Bright and lively.

Bouquet   Intense, spicy black cherry and plums.

Taste   Rich black cherry fruit. Peppery finish. Hot aftertaste suggesting high alcohol.

Comments   Very concentrated flavour. Lots of fruit. Could do with another year or two in bottle.

Dopff-au-Moulin Riesling Reserve 1988

Sight   Pale straw with green highlights.

Bouquet   Lemon and petrol, zesty.

Taste   Peachy floral character, round in the mouth. Great length.

Comments   Drinking beautifully now but will hold for several years.

There is a short-hand way to keep notes which does not involve any literary skill. It merely requires the circling of certain descriptive terms and making your comment. Here is a form you can photocopy and use each time you taste a wine. Keep them in a ring binder for easy access.

SCORING WINES

There are many systems used to score wines. You can rate them on the five-star principle or give them a numerical value based on a total assessment. Some professionals mark out of 20 points and some out of 100, but the consistent factor is the ratio of points for the different elements in a wine.

Your marks should reflect the relative importance of the components. The way a wine looks is not necessarily as significant as the way it smells. Your response to the bouquet will be qualified by how the wine tastes in the mouth. Therefore in any scoring system you decide to use give the most weight to taste, followed by bouquet.

If you want to use a 10-point system (you can always go to decimals if you want), award 0 – 2 for sight, 0 – 3 for smell and 0 – 5 for taste and overall impression.

The Psychology of Wine Tasting

The taste of a wine is altered by your mood, your state of health and the conditions under which you consume it.

Wine always seems to taste best when sampled in the cellars of its maker. You are in a more receptive frame of mind. You are a guest and it's boorish to criticize a man under his own roof. After all, you wouldn't say anything about his sense of humour, the way he drives or his wife's taste in furnishings. And winemakers by nature are outgoing, sharing, generous people who love to show you what they have done.

The same is true of the village where the wines are grown. A simple vins de pays that the patron buys by the barrel from his friend up the road will taste wonderful as you lunch under the trees, pouring it from a ceramic jug into glasses that look like tooth mugs. But if you buy a couple of bottles to try to recreate the holiday experience back home in the depths of winter you'll wonder what you ever saw in that mouthwash.

Even the most expensive wines of the highest pedigree can let you down. Imagine you are invited to lunch by your bank manager. He orders a Château Mouton-Rothschild 1961 and just as you are about to raise it to your lips he informs you that he is going to foreclose on your mortgage. That wine will taste like vinegar. Not only that, but every time you have it subsequently it will taste like vinegar.

By the same token, a simple bottle of Beaujolais, chilled in a stream will taste like nectar if you share it with someone you love.

SPEED CHECK TASTING NOTES

WINE _____ VINTAGE _____
PRODUCER _____ PRICE _____
COUNTRY _____ APPELLATION _____

APPEARANCE

- ☐ HAZY
- ☐ BRIGHT
- ☐ LIGHT

- ☐ SUSPENSION
- ☐ BRILLIANT
- ☐ MEDIUM

- ☐ DULL
- ☐ WATERY
- ☐ DARK

- ☐ CLEAR
- ☐ PALE
- ☐ DENSE

WHITE

☐ WATER WHITE ☐ PALE STRAW ☐ STRAW/GREEN ☐ YELLOW ☐ GOLD ☐ BROWN-GOLD

RED

☐ PURPLE ☐ PURPLE-RUBY ☐ RUBY ☐ CHERRY ☐ GARNET ☐ MAHOGANY

PINK

☐ PINK ☐ GREY-PINK ☐ ORANGE-PINK ☐ BLUE-PINK ☐ SALMON ☐ PALE RED

COMMENT

☐ UNACCEPTABLE ☐ POOR ☐ AVERAGE ☐ GOOD ☐ TERRIFIC

BOUQUET
FRUIT AROMA

☐ NEUTRAL ☐ SHY ☐ CLEAN ☐ IDENTIFIABLE ☐ CONCENTRATED ☐ OVERPOWERING

DESCRIPTORS

☐ FRUITY ☐ FLOWERY ☐ VEGETAL ☐ OAKY ☐ EARTHY ☐ SPICY ☐ HERBAL

COMMENT

☐ UNACCEPTABLE ☐ POOR ☐ AVERAGE ☐ GOOD ☐ TERRIFIC

TASTE
STYLE

☐ BONE-DRY ☐ DRY ☐ OFF-DRY ☐ MEDIUM-DRY ☐ MEDIUM-SWEET ☐ VERY SWEET

BODY

☐ LIGHT ☐ MEDIUM ☐ FULL ☐ HEAVY

ACID

☐ FLAT ☐ FRESH ☐ BALANCED ☐ EVIDENT ☐ EXCESSIVE

LENGTH

☐ SHORT ☐ MODERATE ☐ EXTENDED ☐ LINGERING

COMMENT

☐ UNACCEPTABLE ☐ POOR ☐ AVERAGE ☐ GOOD ☐ TERRIFIC

GLOSSARY OF WINE TERMS

One of the hardest jobs a wine instructor has is to communicate the sensory experience of wine in terms that other people will understand and identify with. What might smell like gooseberries to me may smell like newly cut grass to you. It really does not matter how you identify a particular bouquet or aroma as long as it is pleasant to you.

There is, however, a general vocabulary shared by most wine enthusiasts which allows you to describe the flavour or condition of a wine with a degree of accuracy that will communicate to someone else whether they will like the wine or not, whether to drink it now, cellar it or avoid it altogether.

Acetic: A flaw. The smell and taste of balsamic vinegar, from leaving wine exposed to air.

Acetone: If overly apparent, a flaw. The nail polish smell suggesting volatility. Prevalent in older reds.

Acidic: Too much acid will make a wine taste sharp. The right balance gives it freshness and length.

Aftertaste: The taste left on the palate once you have swallowed the wine. A mark of quality is the length of time it stays with you. Also referred to as the finish.

Alcoholic: The hot, heavy taste of too much alcohol, usually in wines from very warm growing regions.

Aroma: The scent of the fresh grapes in the wine, as opposed to bouquet which is the perfume of the fermented wine.

Aromatic: Grape varieties with a distinctive spicy character — Gewürztraminer, Muscat.

Astringent: The rasping, dry taste of young tannin in red wines.

Austere: A closed-in young red wine showing obvious tannin and acidity masking the fruit.

Backward: A wine that should be more developed than it is for its age.

Baked: A perceptible roasted quality in grapes grown in hot climates.

Barnyard: A positive term for the rotting straw and sweaty horse smell of a fine red or white Burgundy.

Barrique: The French name for a Bordeaux-style barrel of 225 litres.

Bitter: An aftertaste. Signifies the fruit of immature vines or excessive tannin.

Black currant: The predominant aroma in Cabernet grapes.

Body: The mouth-feel of the wine. The weight in the mouth. Light, medium or full depending on the amount of extract and alcohol.

Botrytis: A rot that affects grapes, concentrating the sugars and acids (see page 22).

Bottle-age: The quality that comes from ageing the wine in bottle rather than in barrel.

Bottle-sickness: A temporary condition of the wine closing up following bottling. With rest the wine comes into balance once more.

Bottle-stink: The smell of escaping air from the top of an old bottle when the cork is pulled. It soon dissipates and does not affect the wine's taste.

Bouquet: The perfume of the fermented wine.

Buttery: A smell, especially in oak-aged Chardonnay, not a tactile sensation.

Caramel: A burnt-sugar smell and taste in oak-aged Chardonnay from a hot year.

Carbon dioxide: The gas in champagne and sparkling wines. A prickling on the tongue denotes the presence of residual CO_2 in still wines.

Carbonic maceration: Fermentation for light red wines (especially Beaujolais) that takes place inside the skins of uncrushed berries in the absence of air.

Cat's pee: A self-explanatory expression for the smell of over-ripe Sauvignon Blanc.

Cedarwood: An element in the bouquet of Cabernet Sauvignon.

Chaptalized: The addition of sugar at fermentation to raise the alcohol level. Can give wine a candied nose.

Character: The distinctive personality of the wine that makes it instantly recognizable.

Chocolate: Detectable on the nose and finish of some full-bodied red wines.

Cigar box: A classic description of Médoc Cabernet Sauvignon, as in Château Mouton-Rothschild.

Citric: The smell of lemon, grapefruit or lime in the bouquet and as an aftertaste.

Claret: British word for red Bordeaux.

Clean: A wine free from "off" odours or tastes. The description can be pejorative if that is all there is to recommend the wine.

Closed: A young wine whose bouquet and flavour are locked in.

Cloying: A dessert wine with insufficient acidity to balance the sugar. Sits heavily on the palate like honey.

Complex: Offers a variety of perfumes and taste sensations.

Corked: An "off" bottle due to air spoilage or improper cellaring.

Corky: The smell of a rotten cork that infects the wine.

Creamy: The texture of champagne. Or the vanillan smell that new oak imparts to wine.

Crémant: A champagne with half the pressure, literally, a creaming wine.

Crisp: A green-apple freshness in white wines denoting lively acidity.

Depth: A multi-dimensional wine offering subtly changing flavours.

Disgorged: Removing the sediment from champagne after secondary fermentation in bottle.

Dry: A wine in which the sugars have been almost totally fermented.

Drying out: Denotes fading fruit in old red wines. Acid, tannin and oak begin to predominate over fruit flavours.

Dumb: A closed in wine which refuses to offer up its bouquet and flavour.

Earthy: Smelling of rich earth, minerally, as in Barolo. A positive comment.

Eiswein: The rare sweet German wine made from frozen grapes.

Elegant: A well-balanced wine showing finesse in all departments.

Eucalyptus: A characteristic in the bouquet of Cabernet Sauvignon grown in warm climates.

Flabby: A wine that lacks acidity, overly fleshy. Falls apart in the mouth lacking the definition acidity gives.

Fleshy: Lots of extract, particularly in reds, denoting concentrated flavour with limited tannin.

Flinty: The smell of struck flint in Pouilly-Fumé, Chablis and some Italian reds.

Floral/Flowery: A fragrant spring flower scent of aromatic whites, particularly Mosel and Rheingau Riesling.

Forward: A precocious wine mature before its time. The rocking motion of transatlantic travel has this effect on European wines.

Foxy: The characteristic smell of *labrusca* grapes. Evident in Concord grape juice.

Fresh: Acidity which suggests youth and liveliness on the palate.

Fruity: A wine with good extract from fully ripened grapes.

Full-bodied: High alcohol, concentrated fruit extract.

Geranium: A flaw. The smell of geraniums denotes a winemaking fault.

Glycerol: An alcohol formed during fermentation which adds sweetness and roundness to a wine.

Gooseberry: The quintessential scent in French Sauvignon Blanc. In warmer growing climates, the bouquet is of fresh figs.

Grapey: A strong impression of the fresh grape in wine. Example: Muscat in Asti Spumante.

Green: Unripe grapes, young vines produce a highly acidic taste in wine.

Hard: The mouth-puckering effect of unyielding youthful tannins and acidity which mask the fruit.

Harmonious: *See* Well balanced.

Harsh: Displaying excessive tannin.

Herbaceous: Having a grassy, vegetal bouquet and flavour. Example: Sauvignon Blanc.

Hock: Indiscriminate British term for all German wines from the Rhine Valley.

Hollow: A wine whose flavour drops out in the middle before the onset of acidity. *See* Short.

Honeyed: A term used to describe the unctuous sweetnesss of mature Sauternes or Late Harvest Riesling.

Hot: An expression of high alcohol. You feel it in the throat as an aftertaste.

Icewine: *See* Eiswein.

Inky: A metallic flavour in red wines.

Lanolin: A creamy smell associated with Chenin Blanc and Sémillon wines.

Lean: A spare wine with evident acidity. Example: Mosel Riesling QbA.

Lees: Dead yeast cells and small grape particles which settle at the bottom of the tank or barrel.

Legs: The wet residue left on the side of the glass after swirling which falls back to the surface as tears or "legs." The thicker the legs and the more slow-moving they are signals high alcohol content.

Length: The duration of flavour on the palate. The longer it stays with you the finer the wine.

Light: Refers to body (as in a Mosel white) or to flavour.

Lively: Denotes perceptible acidity.

Luscious: The unctuous quality of a classic Sauternes or other Noble Rot wine.

Maderized: In white wines, oxidation which turns the wine brownish and flat.

Meaty: For red wines, a full-bodied, chewy wine which can even offer a nose of raw meat.

Medium-dry: Contains residual sugar. Examples: Vouvray or Riesling Spätlese.

Mercaptan: A fault. An unpleasant rubbery smell due to the breakdown of sulphur used to preserve the wine.

Minty: A smell that Cabernet Sauvignon wines can have in warm growing climates.

Must: Grape juice, pulp and skins prior to fermentation.

Musty: An "off" odour caused by dirty barrels or rotten grapes in the fermenting tank.

Nervous: A wine that has an abundance of alcohol and acidity in balance.

Noble Rot: A benign disease afflicting certain grapes in the fall, producing naturally sweet wines (see page 22).

Nose: The bouquet of the wine, also yours.

Nouveau: New wine fermented and bottled within weeks of the harvest for immediate consumption. The correct French term is *primeur*.

Nutty: The bouquet of certain fine barrel-fermented Chardonnays. Examples: Meursault, Corton-Charlemagne. Also amontillado and oloroso sherry.

Oaky: The toasted vanilla, coconut or sandalwood smell imparted by new oak to a wine.

Oxidized: A wine exposed to too much air which turns it to acetic acid. The colour browns, the taste flattens and turns vinegary.

Pétillant: Lightly sparkling, crackling.

Petrol: An agreeable oily-lime smell associated with maturing Riesling and Australian Semillon.

pH: A measure of the intensity of acid a wine contains. The lower the pH the more acidic the wine will be. Wines with a pH of 3.8 will be flat and very soft. Lemon juice has a pH of 2.3. Most dry wines have a pH between 3.3 and 3.0, similar to the pH of our stomach acids.

Racy: A light wine of quality with lively acidity. Example: Mosel.

Rancio: Spanish term for the bouquet of old sherries. Sweet, nutty, nail polish smell that comes from long wood ageing in contact with air.

Residual sugar: Sugar that remains in the wine when the fermentation has stopped or is then added as grape must.

Rubbery: A fault. The smell of old tires or rubber gloves experienced in old whites where the sulphur has broken down.

Schaumwein: German term for sparkling wine.

Sekt: German term for sparkling wine.

Sharp: The sensation of excessive acidity.

Short: A wine with little aftertaste.

Sinewy: A wine with good alcohol and acidity but less fruit extract.

Smoky: A smell associated with Loire Sauvignon Blanc, certain oak-fermented Chardonnays, Rhône reds and Baco Noir.

Soft: Mellow, well-rounded, mature tannins and little evidence of acidity.

Spätburgunder: German name for Pinot Noir.

Spicy: As in the bouquet of Gewürztraminer and Muscat.

Spritzig: German for a faint sparkle in the wine. Prickles the tongue.

Spumante: Italian term for sparkling wine.

Stalky: A green taste of young vines, under-ripe grapes or excessive maceration time.

Sulphur: Its presence is detectable as a burnt-match smell. Virtually all winemakers use sulphur products to some degree as an anti-oxidant and anti-bacterial agent.

Supple: Soft textured, round on the palate, fully mature tannins.

Sur Lie: As in Muscadet-sur-lie. The wine is left resting on the inactive yeast cells and grape particles (lees) in the barrel for several months before bottling.

Sweaty saddle: A fanciful description for the not unpleasant smell of old red wines, a leathery bouquet.

Sweet: The presence of unfermented sugar in the wine or back-blended sweet reserve juice. Sweetness is only a virtue if it is balanced with acidity to stop it from cloying.

Tafelwein: German term for table wine.

Tannin: A dry, astringent taste and mouth-feel from the compound extracted from the skins, stalks and pits of black grapes during fermentation. Helps preserve wine and will soften up over the years precipitating out as sediment. There are also tannins in oak barrels.

Tart: Sharp, green, overly acidic.

Tartaric acid: The main acid in wine.

Toasty: The barrel smell and taste imparted to oak-fermented white wines and barrel-aged white Burgundy.

Tonne: A measure of grapes which will produce about 1,000 bottles.

Unbalanced: Excess of one or more elements in wine: fruit, alcohol, acid, tannin or oak.

Ullage: The empty space between the surface of the wine and the end of the cork. When this slips to shoulder level you could have oxidation problems.

Vanilla: The smell of new oak.

Varietal: A single grape variety the name of which will be featured prominently on the label.

Vin de paille: Sweet wine from grapes first dried on straw mats.

Vin doux naturel: French sweet wine fortified with brandy to seventeen percent alcohol by volume.

Vin gris: Literally "grey wine," refers to pale rosé.

Vinous: The winey quality, good fruit extract.

Volatile acidity: When too apparent, a flaw. Acetone smell of nail polish or balsamic vinegar.

Well balanced: Perfect harmony among the wine's elements — fruit, acid, alcohol, oak (if used) and, in red wines, tannin. The ultimate compliment.

Woody: The sensation of old wood in a wine. From overly long ageing in cask. Not to be confused with oaky which is a virtue if it is not overdone.

Yeasty: The bready smell of yeast most evident in champagnes which spend three years in bottle resting on their lees.

Matching Food and Wine

FOOD AND WINE PRINCIPLES

The old adage of "white wine with fish and white meat, red wine with red meat" is fine as far as it goes, but it limits you in your range of options. This rule of thumb was developed because certain oily fish such as salmon, sardines and anchovies will make robust tannic reds taste tinny; and, aesthetically, red wines look better with meat than white. If you do not drink red wines for any reason, it's no crime to have a glass of Chardonnay or champagne with your steak. Dionysus won't suddenly appear at your table and set about you with a vine stalk.

There are no rules for marrying food and wine, only certain principles which will help you in your choice. Always match the wine to the strongest flavour on the plate. Consider pairing a dish with a bottle of wine as you would two sparring partners. They have to be the same weight and strength otherwise one will easily overpower the other. The weight and power of a wine depends upon its alcohol content and fruit character. A wine weighing in at 12.5 percent alcohol by volume or over (look at the bottom of the label) will be full-bodied whether it's white, red or rosé. Wines from hot growing regions such as the Rhône, California and Australia will generally be high in alcohol and will exhibit lots of fruit character.

By contrast, the wines of northern Europe, especially the dry German whites, will be light and delicate and high in acidity. Acid is another component of wine that makes it marry well with certain foods. Wines that you may find too dry for your taste when consumed as an aperitif will marry well with salty dishes. (Try Muscadet with anchovies or fino sherry with olives, for example.)

To give you a sense of the gradation of food and wine from rich and heavy to light and delicate examine the Food and Wine Affinity Chart. It starts with game, the heaviest and most highly flavoured of meats, and works its way down through the red meats to the white. In the fish/seafood section the richest flavours are salmon, lobster and crab working down through white fish and more delicate shellfish to oysters and mussels which demand the driest of white wines.

Each category lists the generic style of wine that would best accompany the dish and suggests certain wine regions or grape varieties. However, what complicates the equation is the manner in which you prepare the dish in question. For instance, a plain grilled steak calls for a medium- to full-bodied red wine. But if you were to prepare it as a pepper steak or steak tartare with Worcestershire sauce, onions and pepper, the additional condiments would require something a little more powerful to match up. So you would move up the ladder a notch and choose something from the heavy reds section.

A simple steamed sole calls for a crisp, light white (as in a Soave or a dry Riesling), but if you add a cream sauce to the dish the added sweetness of the cream will suggest a white wine one step up with more body and fruit (Californian or Australian Chardonnay, a white Beaune or a Riesling Spätlese).

These food categories and the complementing wine styles are only offered as a rough guide.

1   If you like your hamburger heavily spiced with garlic and pepper, move up a step to a heavier wine style. The spicier the dish, the more powerfully flavoured the wine has to be to stand up to it.

2   If you are using a tomato-based sauce choose a wine with more acidity. Tomatoes are very acidic. Go for a northern Italian red (Barbarbesco, Chianti, Valpolicella) rather than a

FOOD AND WINE AFFINITY CHART

	REDS				WHITES			
DISH:	GAME	BEEF LAMB DUCK	HAM PORK HAMBURGER	CHICKEN VEAL	SALMON LOBSTER CRAB	WHITE FISH	SHRIMPS SCALLOPS	OYSTERS MUSSELS
WINE STYLE:	Rich, full-bodied reds	Full-bodied to medium-bodied reds	Medium-bodied to light-bodied reds	Light-bodied reds	Full-bodied, oak-aged whites	Medium-bodied whites	Medium to light-bodied whites	Light crisp wines
	Châteauneuf-du-Pape	Château-bottled Bordeaux	Young Bordeaux	Alsatian/German Pinot Noir	White Burgundy	Chablis	Entre-Deux-Mers	Muscadet
	Côte Rôtie	Red Burgundy	Loire Reds	Beaujolais	Château-bottled Graves	Pinot Blanc	Sauvignon Blanc	Loire Sauvignon
	Hermitage	Cabernet Sauvignon	Valpolicella	Corbières	Pouilly-Fumé	Dry Vouvray	Dry Riesling	Petit Chablis
	Petite Sirah	Pinot Noir	Beaujolais Crus	Minervois	Sancerre	Riesling Kabinett	Aligoté	Coteaux Champenois
	Shiraz	Barolo	Fronsac	Savoie	White Rhône	Orvieto	Auxerrois	Frascati
	Amarone	Barbaresco	Grignolino	Bardolino	Condrieu	Soave	Grüner Veltliner	Galestro
	Brunello	Chianti Classico	Valais	Dolcetto	Pinot Gris/Grigio	Verdicchio	Tocai Friulano	Mosel Riesling
	Zinfandel	Vino Nobile	Chelois	Santa Magdalener	Old Rioja (W)	Rioja/Penedes Whites	Seyval Blanc	Vinho Verde
	Baco Noir	Rioja		Dry Rosé				Fendant
		Dão/Bairrada						
		Maréchal Foch						

French red (Bordeaux or Burgundy) or a New World Cabernet Sauvignon.

3 If you use a lot of butter or cream in the dish you are introducing sweetness to it. This means you will require a wine with lots of fruit. If the choice had been a white Burgundy switch to a Chardonnay from California or Australia.

4 The chicken and veal section is a cross-over category between red and white. Your choice will depend on how you prepare the dish and what colour you want your sauce to be. If you're cooking Coq au vin, the traditional recipe calls for a bottle of red Burgundy. It would be sensible to have that wine on the table. But in Alsace they prepare the dish with Riesling.

THE MARRIAGE COUNSELLOR'S GUIDE TO FOOD AND WINE

1 Salty foods require wines with high acidity. High-acid red and white wines come from northerly growing areas such as Germany, Alsace, Loire, Ontario and New York State.

2 Fried or greasy foods need wines with good acidity and/or effervescence to clean off the palate.

3 Sweet wines with good acidity, such as Vouvray and Riesling, go well with sweet and sour dishes.

4 Any dish prepared in a tomato sauce will require a wine with good acidity to match the acid in the tomatoes (Chianti, Valpolicella, Loire and Alsatian reds, Ontario reds).

5 Duck and goose will taste less fatty if consumed with young red wines with evident tannin (young red Bordeaux, red Burgundy, Barbaresco, Maréchal Foch).

6 If you like your meat rare choose a red wine with good tannin (young Bordeaux, Burgundy, etc.). If you like your meat well done without a trace of blood opt for a fruity red with as little tannin as possible (Beaujolais or any red made by carbonic maceration, mature Spanish Rioja).

7 When matching a sweet wine to a dessert make sure that the wine is sweeter than the dish otherwise the food will bring out the wine's acidity.

8 The best all-round wine for Chinese food is a dry Vouvray from the Loire. (Try a lightly chilled Beaujolais-Villages with Peking Duck!)

9 The best wine with Indian food is beer. If you must have a wine choose a rosé from the Rhône or a German Riesling Spätlese.

10 The most versatile wine for food is champagne. It's even good with breakfast.

11 When in doubt choose a sharper, more acidic wine for food. Bitter is better. Wines you may find tough to drink by themselves (too acidic, too full-bodied, too tannic) go well with the particular food group in the Food and Wine Affinity Chart.

12 If you are serving more than one wine with the meal, choose the main course wine first. Serve lighter before heavier wines, younger before older. (Immature wines suffer by comparison to older bottles.)

13 Keep in mind the time of day and the season. Save your heavy wines for dinner and the cold weather. Don't serve your great wines outdoors at barbecues; you're competing with smoke and garden smells. And remember, wine always tastes better out of thin crystal glasses with stems long enough that you don't have to touch the bowl and warm up the wine.

14 Don't serve white wines too cold. When the wine starts to frost the glass you're losing flavour. When red wines get too warm the alcohol starts evaporating and they begin to taste flat and flabby. Five minutes in an ice bucket will refresh them.

SOME CLASSIC DISHES AND A WINE TO MATCH

There is, of course, no one white wine that is perfect for a dish to the exclusion of all others. However, as a guide to a felicitous match-up, here are some suggestions for pairing up well-known recipes — up and down the scale — with an appropriate wine style. The recommendations are by way of grape variety and/or region.

Chicken

Cacciatore — Chianti

Kiev — white Burgundy

Tandoori — Australian Shiraz

Coq au vin — red Burgundy

Curried — Gewürztraminer

Duck

à l'Orange — Riesling Auslese

Duck Pâté — Alsace Muscat

Peking Duck — Beaujolais Crus

Turkey

Dark meat — St. Julien (Bordeaux)

White meat — Californian Chardonnay

Seafood/Fish	Coquilles St. Jacques — Pouilly-Fumé
	Fish & Chips — Soave
	Fritto Misto Mare (deep-fried seafood) — dry Vouvray
	Frog's Legs — Sauvignon Blanc
	Gefilte Fish — Pinot Blanc (Alsace)
	Gravadlax — white Rhône
	Lobster Newburg — Californian Chardonnay
	Moules Marinières — Muscadet
	Oysters — Brut Champagne/Chablis
	Prawn Cocktail — white Graves
	Quenelles — Chardonnay
	Smoked Salmon — dry Gewürztraminer
	Sardines — Vinho Verde
	Smoked Trout — Sancerre
Beef	Goulash — red Zinfandel
	Wellington — Côte de Beaune
	Boeuf Bourguignon — red Burgundy
	Chili con Carne — Amarone
	Escalope of Veal — Chablis
	Calves' Liver — red Mâcon
	Pepper Steak — Barolo
	Roast Beef — Médoc
	Shepherd's Pie — Beaujolais
	Spaghetti Bolognaise — Barbaresco
	Steak Tartare — Brunello di Montalcino
	Veal Cordon Bleu — Puligny-Montrachet
Lamb	Couscous — Crozes-Hermitage
	Irish Stew — Entre-Deux-Mers
	Leg of Lamb — red Rioja
	Rack of Lamb — red Bordeaux
	Shish Kebab — red Zinfandel

Pork	
	Bacon and Eggs — Beaujolais
	BBQ Spare Ribs — Barbera
	Frankfurters and Beans — Shiraz
	Ham Omelette — Cabernet d'Anjou
	Hot Dog — Beaujolais
	Prosciutto and Melon — LBV port
	Roast Pork and Apple — Vouvray
	Salami — Barbaresco

Desserts	
	Apple Pie — Late Harvest Riesling
	Baked Alaska — sweet sparkling
	Cake — Madeira (Malmsey)
	Cheesecake — sweet Vouvray
	Chocolate — LBV port
	Christmas Pudding — off-dry sparkling
	Crème Brûlée — Sauternes
	Pumpkin Pie — Cream sherry
	Strawberries and Cream — Champagne Extra Dry

Cheeses	
	Asiago — Barolo/Barbaresco
	Bel Paese — Valpolicella/Barbera
	Bleu de Bresse — Beaujolais crus
	Boursin — dry rosé/Beaujolais
	Brick — Cabernet Sauvignon/Sancerre
	Brie — red Bordeaux/Cabernet Sauvignon
	Caerphilly — Mosel dry Riesling/Manzanilla sherry
	Camembert — red Bordeaux/Burgundy
	Cheddar — red Rhône/Barolo
	Chèvre — Sancerre/Rioja red
	Colby — red Médoc/Barbaresco
	Cottage Cheese — Soave/sparkling Vouvray
	Cream Cheese — Verdicchio
	Danish Blue — red Burgundy/sweet white (Barsac)

Edam — Rhine Riesling/Dolcetto

Emmenthal — light Chardonnay/Rheinpfalz Riesling

Feta — Retsina/Chablis

Gorgonzola — red Rhône/red Zinfandel

Gouda — Beaujolais/Bourgueil

Gruyère — Pinot Noir/Australian Chardonnay

Havarti — Soave/Silvaner

Lancashire — tawny port/dry sherry

Liederkranz — Rioja red/Australian Cabernet

Limburger — red Rhône/Traminer

Livarot — red Burgundy/Bordeaux

Mascarpone — Monbazillac/Müller-Thurgau

Monterey Jack — Cabernet/Petite Syrah

Mozzarella — Chianti/Valpolicella

Muenster — Gewüztraminer/dry Muscat

Oka — white Rhône/Verdicchio

Parmesan — Chianti/Bonardo

Pecorino — red Zinfandel/red Rhône

Pont l'Evêque — red Bordeaux/Burgundy

Port-Salut — Chardonnay/red St. Julien

Provolone — Gigondas/Pouilly-Fumé

Reblochon — Gamay/red Rioja

Romano — Chianti Classico/Barbaresco

Roquefort — Sauternes/red Zinfandel

Saint André — Pouilly-Fuissé/Orvieto

Saint Paulin — red Bordeaux/white Burgundy

Stilton — port/Sauternes

Tilsit — Silvaner/Beaujolais

Vacherin — Cabernet d'Anjou/Sancerre

Wensleydale — red Rhône/white Burgundy

Nuts

Almonds — Chianti Classico Riserva/Orvieto Aboccato

Brazil — Pineau des Charentes/old Barolo

Cashews — Alsatian Silvaner/German Müller-Thurgau

Chestnuts — roasted: Recioto della Valpolicella Amarone/ Late Harvest Zinfandel; pureed: Sauternes/sweet Champagne

Hazelnuts — white Burgundy/vintage port or cider

Macadamia — Tokaji Aszu/Setubal

Mixed Nuts — Amontillado sherry/Bual

Nuts and Raisins — Amarone/dry Muscat

Pecans — Madeira/port/Pineau des Charentes/sparkling Vouvray

Pistachio — Asti Spumante/Piccolit

Smoked Nuts — Traminer/red Rhône

Walnuts — chilled Beaujolais Nouveau/port/sweet sherry/ Malmsey

Wine
in
Restaurants

*Y*ou only have to walk into a restaurant to know if the proprietor is serious about wine service in his establishment. Here are thirteen ways to know if a restaurant cares little about its wines.

1 The bottles are stored in open racks around the room, happily oxidizing in the heat.
2 The waiter asks you to order from the wine list by number.
3 The bottle is brought to your table already opened.
4 Wines on the list are misspelled, the most common: Gewurtztraminer instead of Gewürztraminer.
5 You see no-one else dining in the restaurant with wine on their table.
6 The waiter suggests you try the Riesling, only he pronounces it "Rise-ling."
7 When you ask the name of the house wine, the waiter replies, "It comes from Italy."
8 The Beaujolais Nouveau is presented in a wicker wine cradle.
9 The waiter argues with you if you suggest the wine is off.
10 The waiter puts the bottle between his knees to extract a stubborn cork.
11 Two vintages are printed when only one is available. Example: Chablis 86/87.
12 The list gives the name of the wine but without the vintage, the name of the producer or the shipper.
13 The waiter fills your glass to the top.

THE HOUSE WINE SYNDROME

Eighty percent of wines sold in restaurants are house wines. They are, of course, the cheapest wines on the list, but that is not necessarily the primary reason why they are purchased in such quantities.

The majority of house wine is bought because of the "Embarrassment Factor." An employee hosting his boss or a person out on a date for the first time doesn't want to appear ignorant by not knowing his way around a wine list, or worse by tripping over a difficult French or German name. So the novice avoids the minefield altogether by asking for the house wine, red or white.

Now this makes communication easy for the waiter who probably knows little more than the customer about wine, but he too can understand and pronounce house wine. If you were to ask him for an Östricher Lenchen Riesling Spätlese Trocken 1986 he might have a problem.

House wines used to be cheap. The idea was that the restaurant owner went to a vineyard in his region and bought a red and a white wine he liked by the barrel and had them bottled under his own label. His clientele could rely on his judgement. His choice of wine set the tone for his restaurant.

Today, the concept of house wine is very different. It means the least expensive screw-top litre that can be found in the wine store, sold at prices between the extortionate and the unconscionable. Immediately as a cheaper wine comes onto the market the switch is made.

Because house wines are the largest selling item on the list the proprietor makes his profits here. The mark-up on this wine is in most cases higher than it would be on a wine with some provenance.

You are far better off to pay a couple of dollars more for a bottle of wine that has a recognizable grape variety than some anonymous blend with a fantasy name.

House wines are also bland since they have to do double duty as an aperitif and a wine to be consumed with the meal. As a result, they are chosen to appeal to as wide a segment of the dining public as possible and will have no discernible personality. They will also have some residual sugar since most people do not enjoy a fully dry wine.

Corkmanship

A rough guide to the quality of a wine is the length of its cork. Cork is an expensive product. It can range in price from twenty-five cents to seventy-five cents or more per piece. The longer the cork the more costly it is. If there were an entry in the Guinness Book of Records the prize would go to Angelo Gaja, the Barbaresco producer in Piedmont, whose corks for his single vineyard products measure sixty-one millimetres in length. His Barbarescos are acknowledged to be not only the finest, but the most expensive.

HOW TO SPEED READ A RESTAURANT WINE LIST

Just because a wine list is long does not necessarily mean it is good. What is important is how easy it is for you, the diner, to access the information, especially in dim light, and find a wine to match your choice of food. Most restaurant wine lists are set out in one of six ways.

The Conventional

White and red on separate sheets, listed by country and region (invariably beginning with France unless it is an Italian restaurant). This is the most common method and usually directs you to the wines you are most familiar with.

The Varietal

Wines listed by grape variety. (Example: under Cabernet Sauvignon a list from various identified growing regions.) This method allows you to experiment with grape varieties you enjoy. If you like Chardonnay you may enjoy a change from white Burgundy and try an Italian or a Chilean instead.

The Trendy

Wines listed by style. (Example: Full-bodied Dry Reds, Dry Whites With Character.) This method allows you to match the food with the wine more easily. If your dish is light you'll head for a light wine.

The Old-Fashioned

Wines listed by labels. This is usually found only in more upmarket restaurants. This presentation shows you exactly what you are getting though it is time-consuming because you have to turn many pages.

The No-Nonsense

The wines are simply listed under two headings: Red and White in ascending order of price with the country or region stated in brackets.

The Marketing-Minded

Wine and Food Lists. The marriage of wine and food is becoming of greater interest and restaurants see profits from extra wine sales by suggesting two or three wines with each dish or a glass of wine with each course. This has the benefit of overcoming the Embarrassment Factor — the choice is made for you.

HAVE WE GOT A WINE FOR YOU!

Many wine lists will give descriptions of the wine, telling you in hyperbolic terms that each wine is fit for an emperor's table. Beware of such hucksterism. Especially if the descriptions are as vague and contradictory as an astrologer's predictions. Expressions such as "Crisply dry, packed with sweet black currant flavour, round and mellow on the palate, elegant finish" are meaningless unless you have experienced the wine before. What you want to know about the wine is:

1   Does it go with the food?
2   What is the grape variety or blend?
3   Is it full-bodied, medium or light?
4   Is it dry, off-dry or perceptibly sweet?
5   Where does it come from and who made it?
6   Is it ready for drinking?
7   Is it being served to me at the right temperature?
8   Am I going to have to take out a second mortgage to afford a bottle of it?

TIPS FOR SELECTING WINE

- Avoid the house wine. It usually comes in screw-top litres. It could be oxidized. If you do go with the house wine, remember it is more economical to buy a half-litre carafe than two glasses.
- Choose your food first, then select a wine style to complement it (see the Food and Wine Affinity Chart on page 54).
- If you want to try an unfamiliar wine, order it by the glass if possible to see if you like it.
- Ask what half bottles are available.
- Establish what you are prepared to pay for a bottle before you make your decision. You may find better value under lesser known regions, such as Chile, Spain or Portugal.
- In an Italian restaurant stick to Italian wines. They grew up with the cuisine. The proprietor probably did too, so he will be more familiar with them than the wines of other countries. The same principle holds for German, Spanish, Portuguese, Greek restaurants, etc.
- If a red wine is too warm or you prefer your Beaujolais lightly chilled asked for an ice bucket to refresh it.
- If the names on wine lists confuse you, zero in on a grape variety you enjoy — Chardonnay, Sauvignon Blanc, Riesling, for example in whites; Cabernet Sauvignon, Pinot Noir, Gamay in reds.
- Remember the producer's name of the last bottle you enjoyed and see if that house is represented on the list.
- Avoid fine red wines that are too young to drink. They will be an expensive disappointment (for example, Château-bottled red Bordeaux of the classified growths less than seven years old).
- When in doubt ask if the restaurant has a wine steward to advise you.

SENDING WINE BACK

Most people are too embarrassed to complain about wine. They will send food back if it is cold, over-cooked, under-cooked or crawling with cockroaches. But they will suffer through a white wine that tastes of swamp water because they are not sure if that's the way it's meant to taste.

Wines are sent back in restaurants for three reasons:

1   The wine is patently off. It smells like a sewer, is suffering from terminal flotsam and jetsam and is deep brown in colour.
2   The wine tastes differently from what the customer expected and he doesn't like it. An expedition into new territory that went awry.
3   The wine is fine. He's trying to impress his girl-friend.

In all cases the smart restaurateur will take the wine away and offer another bottle even if the wine is sound. (It can always be sold by the glass at the bar and a dispute would interfere with the dining pleasure of those at neighbouring tables.)

The waiter should give you ample opportunity to ensure that the wine you ordered is in fact the wine you ordered and comes in good condition.

THE RESTAURANT RITUAL

Let's say that you have ordered a bottle of Mondavi Chardonnay Reserve 1987. The waiter brings the bottle to your table and shows you the label to confirm that this is, in fact, what you have ordered.

If the wine he brings is a 1988 vintage, it is not the wine you asked for. If it is a Mondavi Chardonnay (but not the Reserve — which means specially selected grapes given extra oak ageing), again, it is not the wine you ordered.

Wine Diamonds

You have grounds to send a wine back if there is any foreign matter in the bottle other than sediment. However, you may come across certain white wines — and some reds — containing tiny crystals in the bottom of the bottle and adhering to the inside of the cork. They may look like shards of glass but they are potassium bitartrate crystals and are, in fact, a mark of quality. The trade calls them "wine diamonds."

They only exist in wines that have not been cold-stabilized to remove them before bottling. If you subject a fine white wine to a dramatic drop in temperature it will precipitate these crystals. They are colourless and odourless and will not alter the taste of the wine. In a word, they are completely harmless and merely unsightly. Their presence is a sign of a fine wine because this circumstance will never occur in a wine that has been pasteurized and rapidly chilled before bottling.

Rather than sending the bottle back ask the waiter to decant the wine.

*Ironically, you have to
uncork the bottle before
you can tell if you have
a corked wine. This
condition has nothing
to do with bits of cork
floating on the surface.
A corked wine is one
which smells off —
either musty or
vinegary.*

*Cork is the bark of a
tree and is susceptible
to the ravages of
insects. A cork weevil
can leave tracks that
act as a channel for air
into the wine. Over
time the air will oxidize
the product and turn it
brown and smelly.*

*Old corks lose their
elasticity and dry out
with age which is why
vintage port producers
put a wax seal over the
top to protect them. The
top Bordeaux châteaux
will recork their fine
old wines every twenty-
five years.*

As a white wine, it should come to you chilled ready for drinking. Touch the bottle and see if it is cold enough.

Once you have accepted the bottle, the waiter will draw the cork and present it to you. He expects you to feel the cork and smell it.

The cork has been in contact with the wine during its life in the bottle. It will pick up the smell of the wine and the condition of the cork will tell you a lot about the condition of the wine. An experienced waiter will take a discreet sniff of the cork himself as soon as he pulls it from the bottle to ensure that the wine is healthy.

- If the cork smells musty you may have a problem with the wine.
- If the cork is overly spongy and wet this means that air may have gotten into the wine and oxidized it.
- If you see a red wine stain covering the outside of the cork, it will mean the hermetic seal with the bottleneck has been broken; air has entered the wine and it will be off.
- If a cork is rock hard it has dried out. Again, you will have a problem with air getting into the wine.

The waiter will pour you an ounce or two to sample the wine. This tradition goes back before the eighteenth century when wine was transported in barrels that were sealed with wooden bungs. The bungs were wrapped in burlap and dipped in olive oil. Naturally, the oil and bits of burlap would drop into the wine. The cask would be broached and the wine drawn off in jugs for service at the table. Once poured into jugs, the surface of the wine would be skimmed in the kitchen. When the wine was brought to the table the host would be offered the first glass in case there were any bits still floating around on the top. When glass bottles were introduced the practice was maintained, only then it became a test of the quality of the wine. (Incidentally, the term "butler" orginally referred to the man in charge of the cellar, the bottler.)

As with wine tasting, you assess the sample in front of you for faults. Is the colour clear and brilliant? Are there any off odours in the bouquet? Does it taste clean and typical of the single or predominating grape variety?

When you order a second bottle, even of the same wine, insist that the waiter bring you a clean glass to taste it from. He could be pouring a corked wine into your guests' glasses.

Once you have established that the wine is sound, what about the temperature?

WINE SERVING TEMPERATURES

A white wine, still or sparkling, is served too cold if it frosts the glass. Chilling a wine lowers our perception of sugar and heightens the freshness of the product, but if it is too cold we cannot taste it.

Sparkling wine served too cold has an explosive effect on a warm stomach. Not only will you feel uncomfortable, it may also embarrass you.

Twenty minutes in an ice bucket half filled with water and ice cubes is sufficient time to bring dry white wines down to their optimum serving temperatures.

Sweet wines should be served colder than dry whites to allow the acidity to express itself more fully.

Red wines should be served a few degrees below room temperature. We keep our homes and restaurants at a warmer ambiance than the traditional room temperature of a Bordeaux château or an English country house. The alcohol in red wines begins to evaporate more quickly when warm and the wine will taste flabby, losing its structure. The change is quite dramatic and is worth experiencing. Take a bottle of Valpolicella and pour a glass. Cover it with plastic wrap and put it in the refrigerator for fifteen minutes. Pour another glass and cover it and set it near a heat source for fifteen minutes. Now taste the two wines. The chilled Valpolicella will be fresh and lively. The warmed glass will be flat, dull and perceptibly sweeter.

Certain red wines, especially those grown in northern climates, such as Beaujolais, Loire reds, Alsatian Pinot Noir, Valpolicella, Bardolino, Grignolino and German reds, improve in taste if served slightly chilled.

Warning

Do not serve white wines below 4°C (40°F) or you will not be able to see their colour (frosting on the glass), smell their bouquet or taste their flavour adequately.

Do not serve red wines at temperature above 20°C (68°F) or you will destroy the balance and render them into something like warm grape soup.

Wine
at
Home

*I*t is much cheaper to explore the world of wine at home since you are paying the retail price only. If you are buying good bottles try to let them rest for a few weeks before you open them. This is particularly true for wines you have bought abroad and carried home. Wine, that most human of beverages, can get travel sick and requires complete rest after the exigencies of modern travel.

CELLARING   Store your wine in a cool, dark place, free from light sources, heating pipes, vibrating machinery (such as power tools or spin driers) and strong odours (paints, solvents, etc.). Next to storing them upright, dramatic fluctuation of temperature is the worst thing you can subject your wines to.

The cork must remain wet at all times to ensure a perfect seal. Sudden changes in temperature will age your wines prematurely. Vibration and heat will massage and bake them into oxidation. Strong smells will permeate the corks over time and taint the wine. Bright light will cause the wines to oxidize.

The optimum cellar temperature to allow wines to mature slowly is 12°C (55°F) with minimal fluctuation either way. In today's homes this is not possible unless you install an air conditioning unit in an insulated room or buy a wine storage cabinet. However, your wines will not suffer unduly if they are kept at temperatures no higher than 18°C (65°F) as long as this is a constant reading.

Places NOT to Cellar Your Wine

In the kitchen, especially above the refrigerator (temperature fluctuation, vibration)

In the wall of the den (heat)

Under the front stairs in an uninsulated shed (cold and heat)

Against a south-facing wall (heat)

Near a radiator or heat source (drying effect on cork)

Under spot lights (light will oxidize wine)

In an old refrigerator in the basement (too cold, vibrations)

Places to Cellar Your Wine

A dark corner of the basement where the temperature is relatively constant

The floor of a bedroom closet

An insulated cupboard with good air circulation

An old root cellar

A wine storage unit built for that specific purpose

What to Avoid in Wine Stores

1 Avoid bottles that have been left standing upright on display. Their corks may have dried out.
2 Avoid wines that have been placed in shop windows. The light and heat have probably destroyed them.
3 Avoid bottles that have been stored under bright lights for the above reasons.
4 Check the fill of the bottle. If it is more than an inch below the cork find another one. A low fill suggests too much air in the bottle which could oxidize the wine.
5 Avoid wines in which the
corks are not flush with the lip of the bottle. A protruding cork is a sign that the wine has be stored too hot.
6 Avoid older vintages of white wines unless you are specifically looking for an aged wine. Most whites are made to be consumed within a year or two of their vintage date.
7 Avoid wines that look murky. Natural sediment would have settled and will only cloud the wine when shaken up. A turbid wine is a faulty wine.
8 Avoid wines with leaking
capsules. If the wine can get out, air can get in and oxidize the bottle.
9 If the ambient temperature of the store is too warm, shop somewhere else for your wines. It may be fine for the serving staff, but the wines will suffer.
10 Avoid bottles with soiled labels. It may be an indication as to how the wine has been handled.
11 Do not be put off by the presence of tiny crystals in some white wines. These are wine diamonds and can be a sign of quality! (See page 65.)

BOTTLE SHAPES

The standard size bottle nowadays is 750 mL (26 oz) which will provide eight reasonably sized servings (four from a half bottle).

For wines that require ageing the bottles will be dark or dead-leaf green or brown (occasionally blue or black) to block out ultra-violet rays that can prematurely age the wine. Clear glass is used to show off the colour of whites and rosés and for sweet dessert wines.

Many wine regions around the world have established a traditional bottle for their wines, and in the case of Burgundy and Bordeaux these shapes are now more or less universally accepted for these wine styles.

The Burgundy bottle is a slope-shouldered shape with dead-leaf to dark green colour. It is used for red and white wines. It has become the standard shape for Chardonnay and Pinot Noir wines around the world. Italian Barolo uses this style in brown.

The Bordeaux bottle is round shouldered with a punt and dark to pale green in colour. This is the standard shape for Cabernet Sauvignon and Sauvignon Blanc (Fumé Blanc) around the world. Many Italian wines such as Chianti, Brunello di Montalcino and Vino Nobile di Montepulciano come in this format in either green or brown bottles.

The Alsace flute is reminiscent of a German bottle though it comes only in green. It is taller than the Burgundy or Bordeaux bottle. In Germany, the green bottle is reserved for wines of the Mosel and brown for the Rhine. Vinho Verde also uses the green Alsace bottle.

The Boxbeutel, said to have been modelled after a goat's scrotum, is associated with wines from the German regions of Franconia and Baden. This shape is also used in South Africa and Chile and for the popular Mateus rosé from Portugal.

The Champagne bottle is thicker and heavier than ordinary wine bottles because it must withstand pressures up to ninety pounds per square inch.

STARTING A CELLAR

When buying wine it is best to purchase at least two bottles of the same product. If you buy only a single bottle and you really like it, you will kick yourself for the lost opportunity. This purchasing pattern will also give you the chance to see how the wine develops with a year's bottle age in your cellar. You may find the wine is too young when you open it, and

THE PARTS OF A BOTTLE

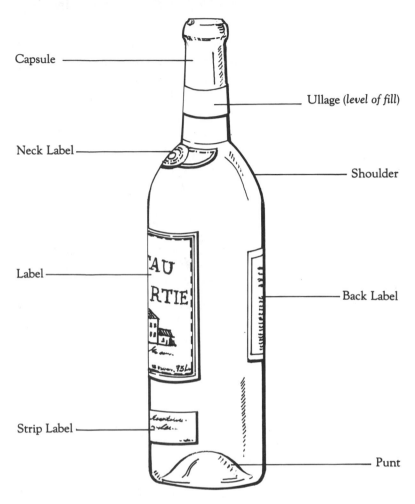

Capsule

Ullage (*level of fill*)

Neck Label

Shoulder

Label

Back Label

Strip Label

Punt

BOTTLE SHAPES

BORDEAUX   CHAMPAGNE   BURGUNDY   BOXBEUTEL   ALSACE

you can look forward to the experience of tasting a wine you have aged yourself in the future.

There are other good reasons for starting a cellar:

1   Time — you won't waste time looking around for the wine style you need for an impromptu dinner.
2   Money — wine prices are going up all the time. If you age the wine yourself you will be drinking much cheaper in future.
3   Availability — a given vintage or winery product may be sold out when you go to look for it.
4   Satisfaction — a stock of carefully chosen wines can only improve with age.

The Cellar: An All-purpose Starter Cellar (Sixty Bottles)

4 red Bordeaux (château-bottled third to fifth growths or Cru Bourgeois)

4 red Burgundies (Volnay, Beaune, Pommard, Gevrey-Chambertin)

2 Beaujolais (named villages, for example, Fleurie, Morgon, Moulin-à-Vent)

2 Rhône (Châteauneuf-du-Pape, Gigondas, Crozes Hermitage)

4 Italian reds (Chianti Riserva, Barolo, Barbaresco, Valpolicella)

2 Spanish reds (Rioja, Penedes)

2 Portuguese reds (Garrafeiras — Dão, Bairrada)

2 Californian reds (Cabernet Sauvignon)

2 Oregon reds (Pinot Noir)

2 Australian Cabernets (Coonawarra)

2 Chilean Cabernet Sauvignon (Maipo Valley)

2 Rosés (Rhône, Provence)

4 white Burgundy (Pouilly-Fuissé, Chablis, Puligny-Montrachet)

4 white Loire (Muscadet, Sancerre, Vouvray)

2 white Bordeaux (château-bottled Graves, Entre-Deux-Mers)

2 white Alsace (Gewürztraminer, Tokay-Pinot Gris)

2 Rhine (Riesling Spätlese, Auslese)

2 Mosel (Riesling Kabinett)

2 white Italian (Soave, Orvieto, Verdicchio)

2 Californian Chardonnay (Sonoma, Napa)

2 Australian Chardonnay (Hunter Valley, South Australia)

2 Dessert wines (Sauternes, Late Harvest Riesling)

2 Ontario Chardonnay

2 Sparkling wines (Champagne, Spanish Cava)

The easy way to build up a cellar is to replace immediately each bottle you consume with two bottles of the same or similar wine.

WINES TO LAY DOWN FOR YOUR GRANDCHILDREN

Wine lovers enjoy the idea of laying wines away for a long time. The thought of pulling out a dusty bottle thick with cobwebs that has slumbered for twenty years in a dark corner of the cellar is very appealing. But too often the moment of truth turns out to be a monumental disappointment when the stuff tastes awful.

Very few wines will last twenty years because of the way they are produced. If they were made for long ageing they could be destroyed by bad cellaring.

If you want to stash a few bottles away for little Johnny's twenty-first birthday or a future wedding anniversary, tuck them away in the coolest, most remote corner of your cellar (nearest the floor). Keep in mind that the larger the format the longer the wine will live. Magnums are the best size container for allowing the product to mature slowly.

In the longevity stakes, the following wines from the best vintage years have an established track record for surviving two decades.

Fortified

1 Vintage port
2 Vintage or Solera Madeira (especially Malmsey and Terrantez)
3 Australian liqueur Muscat

Red

1 Château-bottled red Bordeaux (classified growths)
2 Single domaine Grand Crus Burgundies
3 Hermitage, Côte Rôtie (Rhône)
4 Recioto della Valpolicella
5 Barolo Riserva
6 Certain Rioja Gran Reserva reds (Marques de Murrieta, Muga, Lopez de Heredia)
7 Some Portuguese garrafeiras
8 Château Musar (Lebanon)

	9 Vega Sicilia (Spain)
	10 Barca Velha (Portugal)
	11 Grange Hermitage (Australia)

White

1 Tokay Essencia (Hungary)
2 Château-bottled Sauternes
3 Top white single domaine Burgundies
4 Single vineyard Vouvray
5 Riesling Beerenauslese, Trockenbeerenauslese
6 Riesling Eiswein
7 Marques de Murrieta Ygay Blanco (Rioja)
8 Jura vin de paille
9 Vin Jaune (Château-Châlon)

Wines NOT to Lay Down for the Long Haul

1 Champagne and sparkling wine
2 Sherry
3 Spirits (they only improve in the wood)
4 Most dry white wines
5 Beaujolais, Valpolicella and other simple reds
6 Fantasy blends
7 Rosé wines
8 Most half bottles (they mature much faster than 750 mL bottles)
9 Wines without a vintage date

It should be noted that wines do not necessarily age at the same rate, especially when they get older. Even if you have a case of the same wine you may find a difference in maturity after several years of cellaring. A good analogy would be picking a bunch of roses and placing them in a vase. They will not all open up at the same rate and when in full bloom some will hold their petals longer than others.

Wine
Service

*W*hile bringing the temperature of a wine down quickly by sticking it in the freezer for fifteen minutes does not impair the flavour, the same cannot be said of a cool red that is brought to room temperature by placing it near a heat source. The ideal way to bring a red wine to the proper temperature is to stand it upright in the dining room in the morning before the evening you wish to consume it. This will allow any sediment to settle which you can later decant (see page 81).

If you forget to take the wine out of your cellar and you want to bring its temperature up quickly, the best way is to warm a decanter with hot water, empty it, shake out the excess drops and pour in the chilly wine. The combination of the warm decanter and the ambient air temperature will raise the wine's heat within the hour.

Tips for Maintaining a Wine's Temperature at the Table

White Wines   Ice buckets are too cold (unless it's a sweet dessert wine). Wrap the bottle in a wet napkin and place in an empty ice bucket or buy a simple transparent plastic wine cooler that will maintain the temperature for the duration of the meal or wine tasting.

Red Wines   Have an ice bucket handy and give the bottle a five-minute dip to refresh it if the wine begins to taste "soupy," or, again, use a plastic wine cooler.

WINE SERVING TEMPERATURES

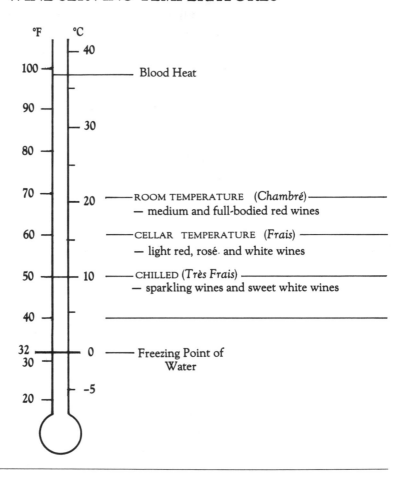

CORKSCREWS

Corkscrews come in many different sizes and shapes, but they are all designed to draw the cork from the bottle. Some models are easier to use than others.

Lever

This is the most universally used model in restaurants. It has a small blade for cutting off capsule tops. This is the least expensive and most practical tool for everyday use. Degree of skill required to operate: medium-low.

Ah-So

The Ah-So consists of two steel blades, one longer than the other, that are worked down the side of the cork in a rocking motion. When fully inserted a twisting pull will draw the cork. This type is used for old corks that might crumble. You can also replace corks by reversing the process. Degree of skill: expert.

Screwpull	The most user-friendly of all corkscrews, it has a long teflon-coated helix (spiral) and very sharp point. The helix is guided into the centre of the cork by a plastic "clothes peg" that sits over the neck. You screw down in the same direction until the cork rides up the shaft. It is very effective, but costs around $20. The plastic peg will break eventually and the helix can be pulled out of shape. Degree of skill: minimal.
Butterfly	This consists of two wings that rise as you insert the helix into the cork. When fully engaged you press down with both hands on the wings and the cork rises. It is labour intensive and apt to become difficult as the ratchets wear. Degree of skill: medium.
Simple T-bar	This is the original corkscrew. It takes a lot of strength to operate and looks ungainly in operation. The helix on these

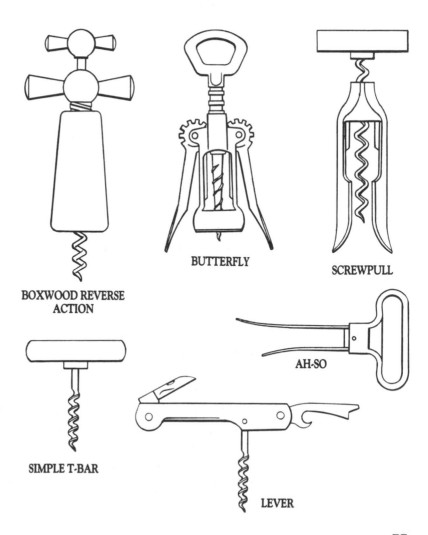

BUTTERFLY

SCREWPULL

BOXWOOD REVERSE
ACTION

AH-SO

SIMPLE T-BAR

LEVER

models is generally too short to pierce longer corks far enough. Inexpensive. Degree of skill: medium.

Boxwood Reverse Action

The long wooden shaft of this corkscrew contains the metal helix attached to a wooden screw. Once the helix is driven into the cork (clockwise) you turn the wooden screw (counter-clockwise) to raise it into the shaft. The disadvantage is you cannot see the cork during the operation. Degree of skill: minimal.

Corkscrews to Avoid

- Any opening device that involves pumping air into the bottle. A faulty bottle could explode.
- Plastic corkscrews (they can't take the pressure).
- Corkscrews with a central core (they will force the cork apart).
- Corkscrews in which the helix has a sharp edge (they will shred the cork).

How to Open a Wine Bottle Using a Lever Corkscrew

1 Cut around the lead capsule, foil or plastic below the lip of the bottle. When you actually pour the wine it must not come in contact with the capsule in case bits fall into the glass.
2 Clean any cellar mould that has accumulated on the top of the cork. (This will not affect the wine so long as it does not come in contact during pouring.)
3 Insert the point of the corkscrew into the centre of the cork. (Ensure that the point is sharp. A blunt helix will make it difficult for you.)
4 Twist the corkscrew down, making sure it enters the cork at ninety degrees. An off angle could result in breaking through the side of the cork which would create debris on the surface of the wine. Penetrate as deeply into the cork as you can without breaking through.
5 Clamp the lever against the bottle lip with your forefinger so that it will not slip during the levering process.
6 Lever gently upward. As your elbow begins to rise, switch your grip to the underside of the corkscrew and finish drawing the cork.
7 Wipe the aperture of the bottle clean.
8 Remove cork from corkscrew and sniff the end that has been in contact with the wine to check its health.

GLASS SHAPES

Glasses have been designed for individual wines such as Rhine and Mosel, sherry and champagne, Anjou and Bourgueil, but you won't want to end up with a cupboard full of glassware you hardly ever use. The I.S.O. glass (International

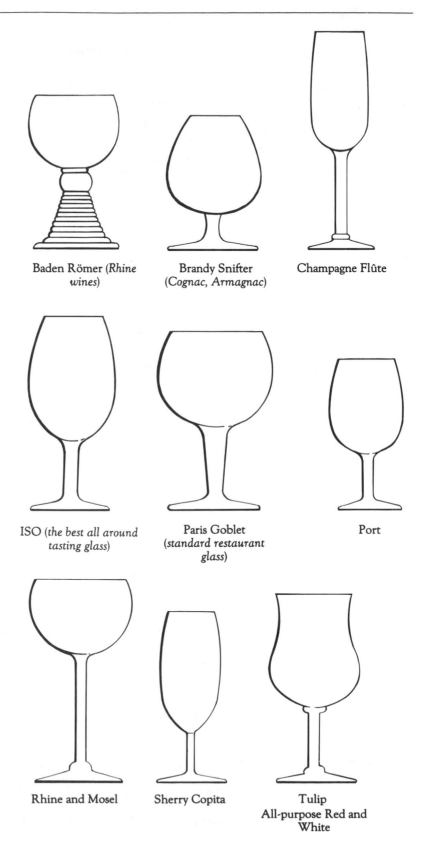

Baden Römer (*Rhine wines*)

Brandy Snifter (*Cognac, Armagnac*)

Champagne Flûte

ISO (*the best all around tasting glass*)

Paris Goblet (*standard restaurant glass*)

Port

Rhine and Mosel

Sherry Copita

Tulip
All-purpose Red and White

Standards Organization) is recognized as the one shape from which you can successfully taste all wines, including sparkling. While you may want to have two or three different glass styles for use at your dining-room table — and a plainer one to be used when eating in the kitchen — those you select should embody the principles of the I.S.O. glass.

The I.S.O glass has a smaller diameter of the aperture than that of the bowl. This has the effect of concentrating the bouquet as it rises in the glass. A glass with a mouth larger than the surface area it contains will dissipate the wine's aromas (so avoid V-shaped wine glasses). The stem is long enough that it can be held without allowing fingers to come in contact with the bowl. It is thick enough to be dishwasher-safe. The glass is plain, untinted, unengraved and thin enough so as to be unobtrusive to the mouth.

Glass is a means to an end, not an end in itself. If the glass is more beautiful than the wine, change your wine.

Red wines show their best in glasses that permit a large surface area to be exposed to the air (narrowing to the mouth). This allows the wine to deliver up its aromas more quickly. The brandy snifter is an exaggerated (and stunted) form of the ideal red wine glass.

White wines will warm up too quickly in such glasses and require a slim tulip shape with sufficient roundness to the bowl to give you an ample pour.

Function Planning Guide

Estimating the quantity of wine you will need for a party depends upon the nature of the event, its duration and whether people are standing or seated at table. Guests tend to drink more when standing because their glass is always in their hand. At stand-up cocktail receptions calculate a half-bottle per person. Buy two bottles of white for each one of red. If there is a champagne toast to be drunk estimate a four ounce serving per person. That means you will get just over six glasses per bottle. When buying champagne for large groups, purchase it in magnums because they keep better than single bottles. You will also not waste as much wine by leaving an inch in the bottom of the bottle.

Lunch: Calculate two to three glasses per head (eight to ten ounces).

Pre-dinner aperitif table wine: One bottle for every four people.

Dinner: Calculate three to four glasses per head (ten to fifteen ounces).

Dessert wine: Two and one-half ounce servings (ten people per twenty-six ounce bottle).

Wedding receptions: Half a bottle per person, still or sparkling wine.

Beer and wine parties: Estimate two beers per guest and one-third of a bottle of wine.

BYOB parties: Start the bar with a magnum of red and white and let your guests fill in the rest.

Wine and cheese parties: Estimate half a bottle of red per person.

Wine punch: One gallon will serve fifteen guests.

Sparkling wines need tall, slender glasses to prolong the activity of the gas, to show the upward passage of the bubbles and to ensure that the wine remains chilled as long as possible.

BREATHING

How long should a wine breathe? Should it breathe at all? These are two of the most asked questions in the wine world.

As with human beings, the moment a wine starts to breathe its days are numbered. Oxygen can bring out the best in wine but it can ultimately kill it.

As soon as you pull the cork the wine in the bottle is exposed to air. Very little of the wine is exposed — just that tiny surface disc in the neck of a bottle. You would have to leave it for many hours to get the same amount of aeration achieved by pouring the wine into the glass. You only give a wine air when you pour it into the glass or decanter. The tumbling effect is what aerates the wine.

Oak-aged reds require more air to express their true character than reds matured in stainless steel. This is especially true of young tannic reds such as red Bordeaux, Burgundy, Rhône, the Nebbiolo wines of Italy (including Barolo, Barbaresco), Sangioveses (Chianti, Brunello, Vino Nobile), Rioja reds and Portuguese Dão and Bairrada.

I have found that two hours for French reds and up to six hours in a decanter for Nebbiolo and Sangiovese wines does wonders for the bouquet and flavour.

New World Cabernets and Pinot Noirs tend to be much softer and less tannic and require little aeration to show their paces.

Simple reds (that is, inexpensive blends) are greatly improved by the introduction of air. Whites, because they are served chilled, need not be given breathing time. The act of pouring them into the glass is sufficient to release their bouquets.

DECANTING

There are basically two reasons to decant a wine:

1   to give it air, and
2   to separate it from its sediment.

You can give your guests more visual enjoyment of a quite simple red wine by decanting it at the table. If you want to put on the dog with a flagrantly ordinary bottle you can dress it up by emptying it into a decanter before they arrive. The air will probably improve its flavour.

Sediment is a dusty deposit thrown by some old reds usually after several years in the bottle. The substance is a combination of precipitated tannin and colouring matter from the grape skins. It does not affect the smell, only the look of the wine. Once stirred up it will make the wine muddy, which is not a pretty sight at the dinner table. It will also taste astringent.

To check for sediment hold the bottle up to the light and examine the sides. If there is a dark stripe down the inside where the tannin has stuck to the glass or there is a visible deposit in the bottom you'll know you have to decant it.

To decant the wine you will need a clean, dry vessel (preferably glass so that you can admire the colour of the wine at table). Make sure it is large enough to hold the quantity of wine in the bottle because once you start the operation there is no turning back! You will also need a candle or a bright light source.

Decanting Steps

1 Stand the bottle upright for several hours to allow the sediment to settle at the base.
2 Carefully cut the entire lead capsule away from the bottle neck.
3 Gently clean the neck of the bottle with a damp cloth.

The Best of the Biggest Producers

Small is beautiful in the wine world. The finest wines come from small vineyards with favoured microclimates and exposures. These wines are expensive and not always easy to come by. Most of the wines that are generally available on a worldwide basis come from large co-operatives or medium to large size companies or corporations. Such enterprises may own extensive vineyards, but they also will buy grapes from other growers to augment their needs. Because they produce in large volumes their wines are by definition commercial products which have to establish a niche in the international marketplace and maintain a consistent quality from year to year.

Within the portfolio of most large companies are wines worth buying, but only a few have established a reputation for quality across the board. I recommend the following producers:

France: Hugel (Alsace)
Duboeuf (Beaujolais)
B & G (Bordeaux,
Loire)
Bouchard Père & Fils (Burgundy)
Moët & Chandon (Champagne)
Jaboulet (Rhône)
Italy: Frescobaldi (Tuscany) Antinori (Tuscany, Umbria)
Germany: Deinhard, Sichel
Portugal: Fonseca
Spain: Torres
Austria: Lenz Moser
California: Mondavi, Wente Bros., Fetzer
Chile: Concho Y Toro
Australia: Hardy, Lindemans

4 With as little movement as possible, uncork the bottle and clean the neck.
5 Light the candle.
6 Hold the bottle by the label with one hand and hold the decanter with the other. Position yourself directly over the candle flame so that when you look down the neck of the bottle is illuminated.
7 Begin to pour the wine slowly into the decanter. Don't let it tumble and don't stop pouring. Any movement of the bottle at this point will stir up the sediment.
8 Keep pouring until you see the first dregs begin to run into the neck then tilt the bottle upright immediately. You should be left with two inches of wine or less in the bottle. (If it's very expensive wine, use a coffee filter in a glass for those last few ounces and drink it yourself in the kitchen.)

Hit Parade of Wines that may Require Decanting

Most red wines made these days won't throw a sediment by the time they are consumed. However, some traditional producers do not like to filter their wines before they bottle them. These wines will show sediment after a decade or so.

1 Vintage Port
2 Red Burgundy
3 Château-bottled red Bordeaux
4 Côte Rôtie, Hermitage, Châteauneuf-du-Pape
5 Barolo, Barbaresco
6 Chianti Classico Riserva
7 Brunello di Montalcino
8 Spanish Reservas
9 Portuguese garrafeiras
10 Some Oregon Pinot Noir
11 Unfiltered wines (will say so on the label)

Wine Find

*I*f the name of a wine is unfamiliar to you, this section will help you to determine its style, the region where it is grown, its ability to age and whether it is considered a quality wine or not. It will also give you the grape(s) from which the wine is produced.

WINE NAME	STYLE	REGION	GRAPE VARIETY
Abymes	dry white†	Savoie	Jacquère
Aglianico del Vulture	dry red	Basilicata	Aglianico
Ahn	dry white	Luxembourg	Traminer
Ahrweiler	dry red†	Ahr	Pinot Noir
Aigle	dry white†	Swiss	Chasselas
Ajaccio	dry rosé/**red**	Corisca	Sciaccarello
Albana di Romagna	dry/sweet white/ sparkling	Emilia-Romangna	Albana di Romagna
Aleatico	sweet white/red	Cen./S. Italy	Muscat clone
Alicante	red	Spain	Monastrell
Aligoté	dry white	Burgundy	Aligoté
Aloxe Corton*	dry red dry white	Burgundy	Pinot Noir Chardonnay
Amarante	dry white†	Portugal	Alvarhino, Loureiro
Amarone*	dry red	Veneto	Corvina, Rondinella, Molinara
Amigne	dry white†	Swiss	Amigne
Anjou	off-dry white rosé/dry red	Loire	Chenin Blanc *Cabernet Franc*, Cabernet Sauvignon, Gamay
Anghelu Ruju*	sweet red	Sardinia	Cannonau (Grenache)
Apremont	dry white†	Savoie	Jacquère, Chardonnay, Aligoté

KEY TO SYMBOLS   Bold indicates wines that need ageing. * indicates quality wines. † indicates light wines. Italic indicates predominate grape variety in blend. + indicates additional grape varieties.

WINE NAME	STYLE	REGION	GRAPE VARIETY
Arbois	dry white†	Jura	Savignin, Chardonnay, Pinot Blanc
	dry red/rosé		Poulsard, Trousseau, Pinot Noir
Arneis*	dry white	Piedmont	Arneis
Assmannshausen	dry red†	Rheingau	Pinot Noir
Asti Spumante	sparkling off-dry/ sweet	Piedmont	Muscat
Auxey Duresses*	dry red	Burgundy	Pinot Noir
Baco Noir	dry red	New York/ Ontario	Baco Noir
Bairrada	dry red	N. Portugal	Baga+
Bandol	dry red/rosé	Provence	*Mourvèdre*, Grenache, Cinsault+
Banyuls	sweet red	Roussillon	*Grenache Noir*, Maccabéo, Tourbat, Muscats
Barbaresco*	dry red	Piedmont	Nebbiolo
Barbera	dry red	Piedmont	Barbera
Barca Velha*	dry red	Portugal	Tinta Roriz, Tourega Francesca, Tinta Barocca
Bardolino	dry red†	Veneto	*Corvina*, Molinara, Rondinella
Barolo*	dry red	Piedmont	Nebbiolo
Barsac*	sweet white	Bordeaux	*Sémillon*, Sauvignon, Muscadelle
Bâtard-Montrachet*	dry white	Burgundy	Chardonnay
Béarn	dry red†	SW. France	*Tannat*, Cabernets, Fer, Manseng+
Beaujolais	dry red	Burgundy	Gamay
Beaumes-de-Venise	sweet white	S. Rhône	Muscat

KEY TO SYMBOLS Bold indicates wines that need ageing. * indicates quality wines. † indicates light wines. Italic indicates predominate grape variety in blend. + indicates additional grape varieties.

WINE NAME	STYLE	REGION	GRAPE VARIETY
Beaune*	dry white dry red	Burgundy	Chardonnay Pinot Noir
Bellet	dry red	Provence	Braquet, Cinsault, Folle Noir+
Bergerac	**dry red**	Dordogne	Cabernet Sauvignon, Cabernet Franc, Merlot
	dry/sweet white		Sémillon, Sauvignon, Muscadelle.
Bernkastel	dry-sweet	Mosel	Riesling
Bianco di Custoza	dry white	Veneto	Garganega, Trebbiano, Tocai Friulano, Cortese
Bienvenue- Bâtard- Montrachet*	dry white	Burgundy	Chardonnay
Blagny*	dry white dry red	Burgundy	Chardonnay Pinot Noir
Blanquette de Limoux	sparkling	Languedoc	*Mauzac*, Chardonnay, Chenin Blanc
Blaye (Côte de, Blayais)	dry white	Bordeaux	Sauvignon, Sémillon, Muscatelle
	dry red		Cabernet Sauvignon, Cabernet Franc, Merlot, Malbec
Bonnes Mares*	dry red	Burgundy	Pinot Noir
Bonnezeaux*	sweet white	Loire	Chenin Blanc
Bordeaux*	dry/sweet white	Bordeaux	Sémillon, Sauvignon, Muscadelle
	dry red*		Merlot, Cabernet Sauvignon, Cabernet Franc, Malbec

KEY TO SYMBOLS Bold indicates wines that need ageing. * indicates quality wines. † indicates light wines. Italic indicates predominate grape variety in blend. + indicates additional grape varieties.

WINE NAME	STYLE	REGION	GRAPE VARIETY
Bourg (Côte de, Bourgeais)	dry/sweet white	Bordeaux	Sémillon, Sauvignon, Muscadelle
	dry red		Cabernet Sauvignon, Cabernet Franc, Merlot
Bourgogne	dry white dry red	Burgundy	Chardonnay · Pinot Noir
Bourgogne Passe-tout-grains	dry red	Burgundy	*Gamay*, Pinot Noir
Bourgueil	dry red†	Loire	*Cabernet Franc*, Cabernet Sauvignon
Bouzy Rouge	dry red†	Champagne (still)	Pinot Noir
Brouilly*	dry red	Beaujolais	Gamay
Brunello di Montalcino*	dry red	Tuscany	*Sangiovese*, Canaiolo, Trebbiano, Malvasia
Bucellas*	dry white	Portugal	Arinto
Bugey	dry white	Savoie	Chardonnay, Altesse, Aligoté+
	dry red		Gamay, Pinot Noir, Mondeuse+
Bull's Blood (see Egri Bikavér)			
Buzet (Côtes de)	dry/sweet white	SW. France	Sémillon, Sauvignon, Muscadelle
	dry red/rosé		*Merlot*, Cabernet Sauvignon, Cabernet Franc, Malbec
Cadillac*	sweet white	Bordeaux	Sémillon, Sauvignon, Muscadelle
Cahors	dry red	SW. France	Malbec, Jurançon, Merlot, Tannat, Malbec

KEY TO SYMBOLS Bold indicates wines that need ageing. * indicates quality wines. † indicates light wines. Italic indicates predominate grape variety in blend. + indicates additional grape varieties.

WINE NAME	STYLE	REGION	GRAPE VARIETY
Canon Fronsac	dry red	Bordeaux	Cabernet Sauvignon, Cabernet Franc, Merlot, Malbec
Carema*	dry red	Piedmont	Nebbiolo
Carmignano*	dry red	Chianti	*Sangiovese*, Canaiolo, Cabernet Sauvignon.
Cassis	dry white	Provence	Ugni Blanc, Sauvignon, Grenache Blanc+
	dry red/rosé		Grenache, Carignan, Mourvèdre+
Castel del Monte	dry white	Apulia	Pampanuto, Trebbiano, Bombino
	dry rosé/**dry red***		Montepulciano, Nero di Troia, Bombino Nero
Castelli Romani	dry white	Latium	Malvasia, Trebbiano
Cerons	sweet white	Bordeaux	*Sémillon*, Sauvignon, Muscadelle
Chablis (Grand, Premier Crus*)	dry white	Burgundy	Chardonnay
Chagny*	dry white	Burgundy	Chardonnay
Chambertin*	dry red	Burgundy	Pinot Noir
Chambolle-Musigny*	dry red	Burgundy	Pinot Noir
Champagne*	sparkling dry off-dry/rosé	Champagne	Chardonnay, Pinot Noir, Pinot Meunier
Chapelle-Chambertin*	dry red	Burgundy	Pinot Noir
Charmes-Chambertin*	dry red	Burgundy	Pinot Noir
Chassagne-Montrachet*	dry white	Burgundy	Chardonnay

KEY TO SYMBOLS Bold indicates wines that need ageing. * indicates quality wines. † indicates light wines. Italic indicates predominate grape variety in blend. + indicates additional grape varieties.

WINE NAME	STYLE	REGION	GRAPE VARIETY
Château-Chalon*	dry white	Jura	Savagnin
Château Grillet*	dry white	N. Rhône	Viognier
Châteauneuf-du-Pape*	dry red	S. Rhône	*Grenache*, Syrah, Mourvèdre, Picpoul+
	dry white	S. Rhône	*Roussanne*, Clairette, Bourboulenc+
Chénas*	dry red	Beaujolais	Gamay
Chevalier-Montrachet*	dry white	Burgundy	Chardonnay
Cheverney	dry white	Loire	Chenin Blanc, Arbois, Chardonnay+
	dry red/rosé†		Gamay, Cabernet Sauvignon, Pinot Noir+
Chianti (Riserva*)	dry red	Tuscany	*Sangiovese*, Canaiolo
Chinon	dry red†	Loire	*Cabernet Franc*, Cabernet Sauvignon
Chiroubles*	dry red	Beaujolais	Gamay
Chorey-lès-Beaune*	dry red	Burgundy	Pinot Noir
Ciro	dry red	Calabria	Gaglioppo
Clairette de Die	sparkling/dry white	N. Rhône	*Clairette*, Muscat
Clos de la Roche*	dry red	Burgundy	Pinot Noir
Clos de Tart*	dry red	Burgundy	Pinot Noir
Clos des Lambrays*	dry red	Burgundy	Pinot Noir
Clos St. Denis*	dry red	Burgundy	Pinot Noir
Colares	dry red	Portugal	Ramisco
Colli Albani	dry white	Latium	Malvasia, Trebbiano
Colli Berici	dry red	Veneto	Cabernet, Merlot, Tocai Rosso
Collioure	dry red	Roussillon	*Grenache*, Syrah, Cinsault, Carignan+

KEY TO SYMBOLS Bold indicates wines that need ageing. * indicates quality wines. † indicates light wines. Italic indicates predominate grape variety in blend. + indicates additional grape varieties.

WINE NAME	STYLE	REGION	GRAPE VARIETY
Condrieu*	dry white	N. Rhône	Viognier
Commandaria	sweet white	Cyprus	Muscat
Constantia*	sweet white	S. Africa	Muscadelle
Corbières	dry red	Languedoc	*Carignan*, Cinsault, Syrah+
Cornas*	dry red	N. Rhône	Syrah
Cortese	dry white	Piedmont	Cortese
Corton*	dry red	Burgundy	Pinot Noir
Corton-Charlemagne*	dry white	Burgundy	Chardonnay
Corvo	dry white	Sicily	Inzolia+
Costières du Gard	dry red	Languedoc	*Carignan*, Grenache, Cinsault+
Côte de Beaune (-Villages)	dry white	Burgundy	Chardonnay
	dry red		Pinot Noir
Côte de Brouilly*	dry red	Beaujolais	Gamay
Côte de Castillon	dry red	Bordeaux	*Merlot*, Cabernets, Malbec
Côte de Nuits (-Villages)	dry red	Burgundy	Pinot Noir
	dry white		Chardonnay
Côte Roannaise	dry red/rosé†	Auvergne	Gamay
Côte Rôtie*	dry red	N. Rhône	*Syrah*, Viognier
Côteaux Champenois	dry white†/red	Champagne (still)	Chardonnay/Pinot Noir, Pinot Meunier
Côteaux d'Aix	dry red/rosé	Provence	Cabernet Sauvignon, Carignan, Cinsault+
Côteaux d'Ancenis	off-dry white	Loire	Pineau de la Loire, Chenin Blanc, Malvoisie
	dry red		Gamay, Cabernet Franc
Côteaux du Layon*	sweet white	Loire	Chenin Blanc
Côteaux du Tricastin	dry red	S. Rhône	Grenache, Syrah, Cinsault, Mourvèdre

KEY TO SYMBOLS   Bold indicates wines that need ageing. * indicates quality wines. † indicates light wines. Italic indicates predominate grape variety in blend. + indicates additional grape varieties.

WINE NAME	STYLE	REGION	GRAPE VARIETY
Côtes de Duras	dry white	SW. France	*Sauvignon*, Sémillon, Muscadelle+
	dry red		Cabernet Franc, Cabernet Sauvignon, Merlot, Malbec
Côtes du Frontonnais	dry red	SW. France	*Negrette*, Cabernet, Malbec+
Côtes du Luberon	**dry red**/rosé	S. Rhône	Carignan, Grenache, Syrah, Mourvèdre, Cinsault+
Côtes du Rhône (-Villages)	dry rosé/**red**	S. Rhône	*Grenache*, Syrah, Mourvèdre, Picpoul, Cinsault, Carignan
Côtes du Roussillon (-Villages)	dry red	Roussillon	*Carignan*, Cinsault, Grenache, Syrah+
Côtes du Ventoux	**dry red**	S. Rhône	*Grenache*, Syrah, Mourvèdre, Picpoul, Cinsault, Carignan
	dry white		Clairette, Bourboulenc+
Coulée de Serrant*	sweet white	Loire	Chenin Blanc
Crémant d'Alsace	white/rosé sparkling	Alsace	Riesling, Pinot Blanc, Gris, Noir.
Crémant de Bourgogne	red/white sparkling	Burgundy	Pinot Noir/Blanc, Gris, Chardonnay
Crémant de Loire	white/rosé sparkling	Loire	Chenin Blanc, Cabernet Franc, Pinot Noir, Chardonnay
Crépy	dry white†	Savoie	Chasselas
Criots-Bâtard-Montrachet*	dry white	Burgundy	Chardonnay

KEY TO SYMBOLS Bold indicates wines that need ageing. * indicates quality wines. † indicates light wines. Italic indicates predominate grape variety in blend. + indicates additional grape varieties.

91

WINE NAME	STYLE	REGION	GRAPE VARIETY
Crozes-Hermitage	dry red* dry white	N. Rhône	Syrah *Marsanne*, Roussanne
Dão (garrafeira*)	dry red	Portugal	Tourigo, Tinta Pinheira, Tinta Carvalha, Alvarelhao, Bastardo
	dry white		Arinto, Dona Branca, Barcelo, Cerceal
Dolcetto	dry red†	Piedmont	Dolcetto
Debröi Hárslevelü	dry white	Hungary	Hárslevelü
Dôle	dry red†	Swiss	Gamay, Pinot Noir
Échezeaux (Grands)*	dry red	Burgundy	Pinot Noir
Edelzwicker	dry white	Alsace	Pinot Blanc, Silvaner, Gewürztraminer, Riesling+
Egri Bikavér	dry red	Hungary	Kékfrankos, Kadarka, Cabernet, Merlot
Entre-Deux-Mers	dry white	Bordeaux	Sémillon, Sauvignon, Muscadelle
Erbaluce	dry white	Piedmont	Erbaluce
Est!Est!Est!	dry white†	Latium	Trebbiano
Étoile*	dry white	Jura	Chardonnay, Poulsard, Savagnin
Falerno	dry red	Latium	Barbera, Aglianico
Faugères	dry red	Languedoc	Carignan, Grenache, Syrah, Mourvèdre+
Fendant	dry white†	Swiss	Chasselas
Fiano di Avellino*	dry white†	Campania	Fiano di Avellino

KEY TO SYMBOLS Bold indicates wines that need ageing. * indicates quality wines. † indicates light wines. Italic indicates predominate grape variety in blend. + indicates additional grape varieties.

WINE NAME	STYLE	REGION	GRAPE VARIETY
Fitou	dry red	Languedoc	Carignan, Grenache+
Fixin*	dry red	Burgundy	Pinot Noir
Fleurie*	dry red	Beaujolais	Gamay
Frascati	dry white†	Latium	*Malvasia*, Trebbiano
Franciacorto Rosso*	dry red	Lombardy	*Cabernet Franc*, Barbera, Nebbiolo, Merlot
Freisa	dry red†	Piedmont	Freisa
Fronsac	dry red	Bordeaux	Merlot, Cabernet Franc, Cabernet Sauvignon, Malbec
Frontignan (Muscat de)	sweet white	Languedoc	Muscat
Gaillac	dry-sweet white/ sparkling	SW. France	Len de L'El, Mauzac, Muscadelle, Sauvignon+
	rosé/red		Duras, Fer, Gamay, Syrah+
Gambellara	dry white	Veneto	Garganega, Trebbiano
Gamza	dry red	Bulgaria	Kadarka
Gattinara*	dry red	Piedmont	Nebbiolo
Gavi*	dry white	Piedmont	Cortese
Galestro	dry white†	Tuscany	Trebbiano, Malvasia
Gevrey-Chambertin*	dry red	Burgundy	Pinot Noir
Ghemme*	dry red	Piedmont	Nebbiolo
Gigondas*	dry red	S. Rhône	*Grenache*, Syrah, Mourvèdre, Cinsault
Givry*	dry red	Burgundy	Pinot Noir
	dry white		Chardonnay
Granjo	sweet white	Portugal	Malvasia Fina, Malvasia Rei+

KEY TO SYMBOLS   Bold indicates wines that need ageing. * indicates quality wines. † indicates light wines. Italic indicates predominate grape variety in blend. + indicates additional grape varieties.

WINE NAME	STYLE	REGION	GRAPE VARIETY
Graves (G. de Vayres)	dry red	Bordeaux	Cabernet Sauvignon, Merlot, Cabernet Franc, Malbec, Petit Verdot
	dry white		Sémillon, Sauvignon, Muscadelle
Greco di Tufo*	dry white	Campania	Greco di Tufo
Grignolino	dry red†	Piedmont	Grignolino
Griotte-Chambertin*	dry red	Burgundy	Pinot Noir
Grumello	dry red	Lombardy	Nebbiolo
Haut-Médoc	dry red	Bordeaux	*Cabernet Sauvignon*, Cabernet Franc, Merlot, Malbec, Petit Verdot
Haut-Poitou	dry white	Loire	*Sauvignon*, Chardonnay, Pinot Blanc, Chenin Blanc
	dry rosé/red		*Gamay*, Pinot Noir, Merlot, Cabernet Franc
Hermitage*	dry red	N. Rhône	*Syrah*, Marsanne, Roussanne
	dry white		Roussanne, Marsanne
Heurige (new wine)	dry white	Austria	Grüner Veltliner
Inferno	dry red	Lombardy	Nebbiolo
Irancy	dry rosé/red	N. Burgundy	*Pinot Noir*, César, Tressot
Irouléguy	dry red	SW. France	Cabernet Sauvignon, Cabernet Franc, Tannat
	dry white		Courbu, Marseng

KEY TO SYMBOLS Bold indicates wines that need ageing. * indicates quality wines. † indicates light wines. Italic indicates predominate grape variety in blend. + indicates additional grape varieties.

WINE NAME	STYLE	REGION	GRAPE VARIETY
Jasnières*	dry/off-dry white	Loire	Chenin Blanc
Juliénas*	dry red	Beaujolais	Gamay
Jura (Côtes du)	dry red	E. Cen. France	Pinot Noir, Pinot Gris, Poulsard, Trousseau
	dry white		Chardonnay, Savignin
Jurançon	dry/sweet white*	SW. France	Manseng, Courbu+
La Clape	dry white	Languedoc	*Bourboulenc*, Clairette, Grenache blanc+
Lacyrma Christi	dry white	Campania	Coda di Volpe
Ladoix*	dry red	Burgundy	Pinot Noir
Lalande-de-Pomerol	dry red	Bordeaux	*Merlot*, Cabernet Franc, Cabernet Sauvignon, Malbec
Lambrusco	dry red†	Emilia-Romagna	Lambrusco
Languedoc (Coteaux du)	dry red	Midi	Carignan, Cinsault, Mourvèdre, Syrah, Grenache+
Latricières-Chambertin*	dry red	Burgundy	Pinot Noir
Lessona	dry red	Piedmont	Nebbiolo
Liebfraumilch	off-dry white	Rhine	Silvaner, Müller-Thurgau, Riesling
Lirac	dry rosé/red	S. Rhône	*Grenache*, Cinsault, Mourvèdre, Syrah
Listrac	dry red	Bordeaux	*Cabernet Sauvignon*, Merlot, Cabernet Franc, Malbec, Petit Verdot
Locorotondo	dry white	Apulia	Verdeca, Bianco d'Alessano
Loupiac	sweet white	Bordeaux	*Sémillon*, Sauvignon, Muscadelle

KEY TO SYMBOLS   Bold indicates wines that need ageing. * indicates quality wines. † indicates light wines. Italic indicates predominate grape variety in blend. + indicates additional grape varieties.

WINE NAME	STYLE	REGION	GRAPE VARIETY
Lussac-St-Émilion	dry red	Bordeaux	*Merlot*, Cabernets, Malbec
Mâcon	dry white **dry red**	Burgundy	Chardonnay Pinot Noir
Madiran	dry red	SW. France	*Tannat*, Cabernet Sauvignon, Cabernet Franc+
Malaga	sweet white	Spain	Pedro Ximenez, Lairen, Moscatel+
Maréchal Foch	dry red	Ontario/ New York	Maréchal Foch
Margaux*	dry red	Bordeaux	*Cabernet Sauvignon*, Merlot, Cabernet Franc, Malbec, Petit Verdot
Marsannay	dry rosé*/**red**	Burgundy	Pinot Noir
Maury	sweet red	Midi	Grenache, Muscats, Maccabéo+
Mavrodaphne	sweet red	Greece	Mavrodaphne
Mavroud	dry red	Bulgaria	Mavroud
Mazis-Chambertin*	dry red	Burgundy	Pinot Noir
Médoc	dry red	Bordeaux	Cabernet Sauvignon, Merlot, Malbec, Petit Verdot
Ménétou-Salon	dry white dry red	Loire	Sauvignon Pinot Noir
Mercurey*	dry white dry red	Burgundy	Chardonnay Pinot Noir
Meursault*	dry white dry red	Burgundy	Chardonnay Pinot Noir
Minervois	dry red	Languedoc	*Carignan*, Grenache, Syrah, Cinsault, Mourvèdre

KEY TO SYMBOLS Bold indicates wines that need ageing. * indicates quality wines. † indicates light wines. Italic indicates predominate grape variety in blend. + indicates additional grape varieties.

WINE NAME	STYLE	REGION	GRAPE VARIETY
Monbazillac	sweet white	Bergerac	*Sémillon*, Sauvignon, Muscadelle
Mondeuse	dry rosé/red	Savoie	Mondeuse
Montagny	dry white	Burgundy	Chardonnay
Montefalco Rosso	dry red	Umbria	*Sangiovese*, Trebbiano, Malvasia
Montepulciano di Abruzzo	dry red	Abruzzi	Montepulciano di Abruzzo
Monthélie*	dry white / dry red	Burgundy	Chardonnay / Pinot Noir
Montlouis	dry white/ sparkling	Loire	Chenin Blanc
Montrachet*	dry white	Burgundy	Chardonnay
Montravel	dry/off-dry white	Bergerac	Sémillon, Sauvignon, Muscadelle
Morellino di Scansano	dry red	Tuscany	Sangiovese
Morey St-Denis*	dry red	Burgundy	Pinot Noir
Morgon*	dry red	Beaujolais	Gamay
Moscatel de Setubal	sweet white	Portugal	Muscatel
Moulin-à-Vent*	dry red	Beaujolais	Gamay
Moulis	dry red	Bordeaux	*Cabernet Sauvignon*, Merlot, Cabernet Franc, Malbec, Petit Verdot
Musar (Château)*	dry red	Lebanon	*Cabernet Sauvignon*, Syrah, Cinsault
Muscadet	dry white	Loire	Muscadet
Muscat of Samos	sweet white	Greece	Muscat of Samos
Musigny*	dry red	Burgundy	Pinot Noir
Naoussa*	dry red	Greece	Xynomavro
Nebbiolo	dry red	NW. Italy	Nebbiolo
Nemea*	dry red	Greece	Agriorgitiko

KEY TO SYMBOLS Bold indicates wines that need ageing. * indicates quality wines. † indicates light wines. Italic indicates predominate grape variety in blend. + indicates additional grape varieties.

WINE NAME	STYLE	REGION	GRAPE VARIETY
Nuits (Côte de)	dry red	Burgundy	Pinot Noir
Nuits St-Georges*	dry red	Burgundy	Pinot Noir
Orvieto	dry/off-dry white	Cen. Italy	Trebbiano, Malvasia, Grechetto
Pacherenc du Vic Bilh	dry white	SW. France	Arrufiac, Courbu, Marsengs+
Palette	dry white†	Provence	Clairette, Ugni Blanc, Grenache Blanc, Muscats+
	dry rosé/red		Mourvèdre, Grenache, Cinsault+
Patrimonio	dry rosé/**red**	Corsica	Niellucio, Sciacarello, Grenache, Vermentino, Ugni Blanc
Pauillac*	dry red	Bordeaux	*Cabernet Sauvignon*, Merlot, Cabernet Franc, Malbec, Petit Verdot
Pécharmant	dry red	Bergerac	Cabernet Sauvignon, Cabernet Franc, Merlot, Malbec
Periquita	dry red	Portugal	Periquita
Pernand-Vergelesses*	dry white	Burgundy	Chardonnay
	dry red		Pinot Noir
Petit Chablis	dry white	Burgundy	Chardonnay
Picolit	sweet white	Friuli-Venezia-Giulia	Picolit

KEY TO SYMBOLS Bold indicates wines that need ageing. * indicates quality wines. † indicates light wines. Italic indicates predominate grape variety in blend. + indicates additional grape varieties.

WINE NAME	STYLE	REGION	GRAPE VARIETY
Pierrevert (Coteaux de)	dry white	S. Rhône	Clairette, Marsanne, Roussanne, Ugni Blanc
	dry red		Carignan, Cinsault, Grenache, Mourvèdre, Syrah
Piesporter	off-dry white	Mosel	Riesling
Pomerol*	dry red	Bordeaux	*Merlot*, Cabernet Sauvignon, Cabernet Franc, Malbec
Pomino*	dry red	Tuscany	Sangiovese, Cabernet, Pinot Noir
	dry white		Chardonnay, Pinot Bianco, Pinot Grigio
Pommard*	dry red	Burgundy	Pinot Noir
Pouilly-Fuissé* (**-Lorché,** **-Vinzelles**)	dry white	Burgundy	Chardonnay
Pouilly-Fumé*	dry white	Loire	Sauvignon
Pouilly-sur-Loire	dry white	Loire	*Chasselas*, Sauvignon
Primitivo di Manduria	dry red	Apulia	Primitivo di Manduria
Prosecco	dry/off-dry sparkling	Veneto	Prosecco
Provence (Côtes de)	**dry red**	Provence	Carignan, Syrah, Cabernet Sauvignon, Mourvèdre+
	dry white		Clairette, Sémillon, Ugni Blanc+
Puligny-Montrachet*	dry white	Burgundy	Chardonnay
Quarts de Chaume*	sweet white	Loire	Chenin Blanc (or Pineau de la Loire)

KEY TO SYMBOLS Bold indicates wines that need ageing. * indicates quality wines. † indicates light wines. Italic indicates predominate grape variety in blend. + indicates additional grape varieties.

WINE NAME	STYLE	REGION	GRAPE VARIETY
Quincy	dry white†	Loire	Sauvignon
Rasteau	sweet red	S. Rhône	Grenache Noir, Gris, Blanc
Ravat (Vignoles)	off-dry/sweet white	NE. United States	Ravat (Vignoles)
Recioto di Soave*	sweet white	Veneto	Garganega, Trebbiano
Recioto della Valpolicella*	sweet red	Veneto	Corvino, Rondinella, Molinara+
Refosco	dry red	Friuli-Venezia-Giulia	Refosco
Regaliali	dry white	Sicily	Catarratto, Inzolia, Sauvignon
	dry red*		Perricone, Nero d'Avola
Retsina	dry white/rosé	Greece	Savatiano/Rhoditis
Reuilly	dry white	Loire	Sauvignon
	dry rosé/red		Pinot Noir, Pinot Gris
Riceys (Rosé de)	dry rosé	Champagne (still)	Pinot Noir
Richebourg*	dry red	Burgundy	Pinot Noir
Rioja*	dry red	NE. Spain	*Tempranillo*, Garnacho, Graziano, Mazuelo+
	dry white		Viura, Malvasia
Rivesaltes (Muscat de)	sweet white/red	S. Rhône	Muscats+/ Grenache
Roero	dry red	Piedmont	Nebbiolo
Romanée, La*	dry red	Burgundy	Pinot Noir
Romanée-Conti (-St-Vivant)*	dry red	Burgundy	Pinot Noir
Rosé d'Anjou	dry rosé	Loire	Cabernets, Pineau d'Aunis, Gamay+
Roussette	dry white	Savoie	Roussette
Rosso Conero	dry red	Marches	*Montepulciano*, Sangiovese

KEY TO SYMBOLS Bold indicates wines that need ageing. * indicates quality wines. † indicates light wines. Italic indicates predominate grape variety in blend. + indicates additional grape varieties.

WINE NAME	STYLE	REGION	GRAPE VARIETY
Rosso di Montalcino	dry red	Tuscany	Sangiovese Grosso
Rosso di Montepulciano	dry red	Tuscany	Sangiovese Grosso
Rubesco*	dry red	Umbria	*Sangiovese*, Canaiolo
Ruchottes-Chambertin*	dry red	Burgundy	Pinot Noir
Rully	dry white	Burgundy	Chardonnay
	dry red	Burgundy	Pinot Noir
Ruster Ausbruch	sweet white	Austria	Welschriesling, Muscat-Ottonel
Sagrantino	dry red/off-dry	Umbria	Sagrantino
Saint-Amour	dry red	Beaujolais	Gamay
St-Aubin	dry white	Burgundy	Chardonnay
	dry red	Burgundy	Pinot Noir
St-Chinian	dry red	Midi	Carignan, Grenache, Lledoner, Mourvèdre, Syrah
Saint-Émilion*	dry red	Bordeaux	*Merlot*, Cabernets, Malbec
St-Estèphe*	dry red	Bordeaux	*Cabernet Sauvignon*, Merlot, Cabernet Franc, Malbec, Petit Verdot
St-Joseph*	dry red	N. Rhône	Syrah
St-Julien*	dry red	Bordeaux	*Cabernet Sauvignon*, Merlot, Cabernet Franc, Malbec, Petit Verdot
St-Péray	dry white/ sparkling	N. Rhône	Roussanne, Marsanne
St-Pourçain	dry red	Auvergne	*Gamay*, Pinot Noir
	dry white		*Tressalier*, Chardonnay, Sauvignon, Aligoté+

KEY TO SYMBOLS Bold indicates wines that need ageing. * indicates quality wines. † indicates light wines. Italic indicates predominate grape variety in blend. + indicates additional grape varieties.

WINE NAME	STYLE	REGION	GRAPE VARIETY
St-Romain	dry white dry red	Burgundy	Chardonnay Pinot Noir
St-Véran	dry white	Burgundy	Chardonnay
Ste-Croix-du-Mont	sweet white	Bordeaux	Sémillon, Sauvignon, Muscadelle
Ste-Foy	dry/off-dry white	Bordeaux	Sémillon, Sauvignon, Muscadelle
	dry red		Cabernets, Merlot, Malbec, Petit Verdot
Saké	dry/sweet white	Japan	rice wine
Sancerre	dry white dry red	Loire	Sauvignon Pinot Noir
Santa Magdalener	dry red	Trentino-Alto Adige	Schiava, Lagrein, Pinot Noir
Santenay*	dry red	Burgundy	Pinot Noir
Santorini	dry/sweet white	Greece	Asyrtiko
Sarmento	dry red†	Tuscany	Sangiovese
Sassella	dry red	Lombardy	Nebbiolo
Sassicaia*	dry red	Tuscany	*Cabernet Sauvignon*, Cabernet Franc
Saumur	dry white	Loire	Chenin Blanc, Chardonnay, Sauvignon
	sparkling white/ rosé		*Chenin Blanc*, Chardonnay, Sauvignon/ Cabernets, Pinot Noir, Gamay+
	dry red		Cabernets, Pineau d'Aunis
Sauternes*	sweet white	Bordeaux	*Sémillon*, Sauvignon, Muscadelle
Savennières*	dry white	Loire	Chenin Blanc or Pineau de la Loire

KEY TO SYMBOLS   Bold indicates wines that need ageing. * indicates quality wines. † indicates light wines. Italic indicates predominate grape variety in blend. + indicates additional grape varieties.

WINE NAME	STYLE	REGION	GRAPE VARIETY
Savigny-lès-Beaune*	dry red	Burgundy	Pinot Noir
	dry white		Chardonnay
Schloss Johanissberg*	dry white	Rheingau	Riesling
Seyssel	dry white†	Savoie	Roussette
	sparkling		Roussette, Chasselas, Molette
Seyval Blanc	dry white	Ontario/ New York	Seyval Blanc
Sfurzàt	dry red	Lombardy	Chiavennasca (Nebbiolo)
Sizzano	dry red	Piedmont	Nebbiolo
Soave	dry white	Veneto	*Garganega*, Trebbiano
Spanna	dry red	Piedmont	Nebbiolo
Szekszárdi	dry red	Hungary	Kadarka
Tâche, La*	dry red	Burgundy	Pinot Noir
Taurasi*	dry red	Campania	Aglianico
Tavel	dry rosé	S. Rhône	*Grenache*, Cinsault, Carignan, Syrah, Mourvèdre
Teroldego Rotaliano	dry red	Trentino-Alto Adige	Teroldego Rotaliano
Tignanello*	dry red	Tuscany	*Sangiovese*, Cabernet Sauvignon
Tocai Friulano	dry white	Friuli-Venezia-Giulia	Tocai Friulano
Tokay d'Alsace*	dry white	Alsace	Pinot Gris
Tokay (Tokaji)*	dry-sweet white	Hungary	Furmint, Harslevelü
Torgiano	dry white	Umbria	Trebbiano, Grechetto
Torbato di Alghero	dry white	Sardinia	Torbato
	dry red		Sangiovese, Canaiolo, Trebbiano

KEY TO SYMBOLS Bold indicates wines that need ageing. * indicates quality wines. † indicates light wines. Italic indicates predominate grape variety in blend. + indicates additional grape varieties.

WINE NAME	STYLE	REGION	GRAPE VARIETY
Toul (Côtes de)	dry red/rosé†	NE. France	Pinot Meunier, Pinot Noir, Gamay
	dry white†		Aligoté, Aubin, Auxerrois
Touraine	dry white	Loire	Chenin Blanc, Arbois, Chardonnay
	dry red/rosé		Cabernets, Malbec, Gamay, Pinot Noir+
Tricastin (Coteaux du)	**dry red**/rosé	S. Rhône	Grenache, Syrah, Cinsault, Mourvèdre, Carignan+
	dry white		Clairette, Grenache Blanc, Bourboulenc, Ugni Blanc, Picpoul
Tudia Bianco	dry white	Sicily	Inzolia, Trebbiano
Tursan	**dry red**/rosé	SW. France	*Tannat*, Cabernets, Fer
Vacquéyras	dry red	S. Rhône	*Grenache*, Syrah, Mourvèdre, Cinsault, Carignan
Valdepeñas	dry red	La Mancha	*Airén*, Cencibel (Tempranillo), Garnacha
Valgella	dry red	Lombardy	Nebbiolo
Valpolicella	dry red	Veneto	Corvina, Rondinella, Molinara+
Valençay	dry red/rosé	Loire	Cabernets, Cot, Pinot Noir, Gamay+
	dry white		Sauvignon, Arbois, Chardonnay, Chenin Blanc+
Valtellina	dry red	Lombardy	Nebbiolo

KEY TO SYMBOLS   Bold indicates wines that need ageing. * indicates quality wines. † indicates light wines. Italic indicates predominate grape variety in blend. + indicates additional grape varieties.

WINE NAME	STYLE	REGION	GRAPE VARIETY
Vega Sicilia*	dry red	NW. Spain	Cabernet Sauvignon, Merlot, Malbec, Tinto Aragonés, Garnacha+
Verdicchio	dry white	Marches	Verdicchio, Trebbiano, Malvasia
Verduzzo	dry-sweet white	Veneto/Friuli	Verduzzo
Vermentino	dry white	Sardinia	Vermentino
Vernaccia di San Gimignano*	dry white	Tuscany	Vernaccia
Vespaiolo	dry white	Veneto	Vespaiolo
Vidal	dry-sweet white	Ontario/ New York	Vidal
Vinho Verde	dry white†	N. Portugal	Alvarhino, Loureiro
Vin Jaune*	dry white	Jura	Savagnin
Vino Nobile di Montipulciano*	dry red	Tuscany	*Sangiovese*, Canaiolo, Trebbiano, Malvasia
Vin Santo*	sweet white	Cen./N. Italy	Grechetto, Malvasia, Trebbiano, (Trentino) Nosiola
Vivarais (Côtes du)	dry red	S. Rhône	Grenache, Syrah, Mourvèdre, Cinsault, Carignan
Volnay*	dry red	Burgundy	Pinot Noir
Vosne-Romanée*	dry red	Burgundy	Pinot Noir
Vougeot (Clos de)*	dry red	Burgundy	Pinot Noir
Vouvray*	dry-sweet white	Loire	Chenin Blanc
Yquem (Château d')*	sweet white	Bordeaux	*Sémillon*, Sauvignon Blanc
Zinfandel	blush/rosé, **red***	California	Zinfandel

KEY TO SYMBOLS Bold indicates wines that need ageing. * indicates quality wines. † indicates light wines. Italic indicates predominate grape variety in blend. + indicates additional grape varieties.

Substituting Wines

WINE ALTERNATIVES

$\mathcal{T}$here are times when you cannot find the wine you like in your local store, or perhaps you're feeling adventuresome and would like to try something new, something in the same style and weight but from a region you've never explored before. Here are some alternatives to well-known wines within the same taste and weight range.

WHITES
Very Dry
Chablis
(Chardonnay Grape)

Muscadet (Loire)

Aligoté (Burgundy)

Cortese di Gavi (Italy)

Soave (Italy)

Northern Italian Chardonnay

Torgiano (Italy)

Verdicchio (Italy)

Grüner Veltliner (Austria)

White Rioja (Spain)

White Penedes (Spain)

Weissburgunder (Germany)

Fendant (Switzerland)

New York/Ontario Chardonnay

Dry, Medium-bodied *Mâcon-Villages* *(Chardonnay)*	Pinot Blanc (Alsace) Sancerre (Loire) Dry Vouvray (Loire) Pinot Grigio (Italy) Central European Chardonnay Oregon Chardonnay Washington Chardonnay White Côtes du Rhône Soave (Italy) Corvo (Sicily) Sauvignon Blanc (Chile) Apelia (Greece)
Dry, Full-bodied *Puligny-Montrachet* *(Chardonnay)*	Californian Chardonnay Californian Sauvignon Blanc (Fumé Blanc) Australian Chardonnay New Zealand Chardonnay New Zealand Sauvignon Blanc Tokay-Pinot Gris (Alsace) Pouilly-Fumé (Loire) Condrieu (Rhône)
Medium-dry, **Medium-bodied** *Liebfraumilch* *(Müller-Thurgau/* *Silvaner/Riesling)*	Riesling (Germany/Austria) Silvaner (Alsace) Muscat (Alsace) Müller-Thurgau (Germany) Scheurebe (Germany) Traminer (Northern Italy/Yugoslavia) Riesling (Australia) Riesling (California)

Chenin Blanc (Australia)

Malvasia (Italy)

Gewürztraminer (Washington)

French Colombard (California)

REDS
Dry, Light-bodied
Beaujolais
(Gamay)

Valpolicella (Italy)

Bardolino (Italy)

Grignolino (Italy)

Sarmento (Italy)

Chinon/Bourgueil (Loire)

Pinot Noir (Alsace)

Clairette (Languedoc)

German reds

Swiss reds

Savoie reds

Jura reds

Gamay Beaujolais (California/Ontario)

Dry, Medium-bodied
Red Bordeaux
(Cabernet
Sauvignon/Cabernet
Franc/Merlot)

Bergerac

Californian Cabernet Sauvignon and Meritage blends

Australian Cabernet Sauvignon

New Zealand Cabernet Sauvignon

South African Cabernet Sauvignon

New York/Ontario Cabernets

Chilean Cabernet Sauvignon

Argentinian Cabernet Sauvignon

Spanish Cabernet Sauvignon

Camarate, Periquita (Portugal)

Italian Merlot

Dry, Medium-bodied
Red Burgundy
(Pinot Noir)

Oregon Pinot Noir

Californian Pinot Noir

German Spätburgunder

Austrian Blauburgunder

Italian Pinot Nero

Hungarian Nagyburgundi

Chilean Pinot Noir

New Zealand Pinot Noir

South African Pinotage

Ontario Pinot Noir
Barbera (Italy/California)

Dry, Full-bodied
Red Rhône
(Syrah, Grenache)

Zinfandel (California)

Petite Syrah (California)

Primitivo (Italy)

Barolo (Italy)

Amarone (Italy)

Castel del Monte (Italy)

Brunello di Montalcino (Italy)

Vino Nobile di Montepulciano (Italy)

Sicilian reds

Australian Shiraz/Hermitage

South African Roodeberg

Bull's Blood (Hungary)

THE MOST
COMMON WINE
MISTAKES

1 *Confusing Pouilly-Fuissé with Pouilly-Fumé.* The first is a Burgundy made from Chardonnay grapes. The second is a Loire wine made from Sauvignon Blanc.

2 *The pronunciation of Riesling.* Rhyme it with "freezing" — Reez-ling.

3 *Red wine is more fattening than white.* The number of calories in wine relate directly to the alcohol content or the alcohol and residual sugar. A Beaujolais at 11 degrees of alcohol by volume will be less fattening than a Chardonnay at 13 degrees.

4 *Opening champagne by levering the cork out with the thumbnails.* Any sparkling wine should be opened by holding the cork firmly and twisting the bottle away from it. The cork does not move. This way you avoid the pop and the ensuing fountain.

5   *Calling all sparkling wine Champagne.* Only sparkling wine from the delimited region of Champagne in northeastern France made by the traditional method deserves the name.

6   *All rosés are sweet or medium-dry.* The best are dry. Try Tavel or Lirac rosé from the Rhône.

7   *The vintage date tells you when the wine was bottled.* The year on the label denotes the year the grapes were harvested and fermented.

8   *Burgundy is a style of wine.* Burgundy is not a style but a region which produces red, white, rosé and even some sparkling wines. Wines from other countries which call themselves Burgundy are invariably blends that have never seen the Chardonnay or the Pinot Noir grape.

9   *Alsace is a German wine region.* Alsatian wines come in tall, green bottles that look like Mosel wines, but they are distinctively and defiantly French. The region borders on Germany west of the Rhine.

10 *Holding the wine glass by the bowl.* The heat of the fingers will warm up white wines or cover up the beautiful colour of reds. Hold the glass by the stem or the base.

11 *Filling a glass to the brim.* This may be a sign of generous hospitality, but it does not allow the wine lover to swirl the glass and sniff the wine. Fill to a maximum of two-thirds of the glass.

12 *Placing sparkling wine glasses in the freezer or in the ice bucket.* An iced glass or a wet one will turn a sparkling wine flat in no time. Chilling the wine is sufficient to bring it down to the proper serving temperature.

13 *Dry wines are completely dry.* There is no such thing as a totally dry wine. There is always a measure of unfermented grape sugar which may be as low as three grams per litre. Most so-called dry wines will have up to five grams per litre. High acidity will enhance the perception of dryness. Dryness denotes the absence of sugar, not the tactile sensation of tannin in red wines which can leave the mouth with a dry sensation.

14 *Leaving unopened champagne or wine for weeks in the fridge.* Sparkling wine will lose its bubble and still wines will oxidize if left too long in the fridge. The agitation of the compressor will shake them into old age very quickly.

All
That
Sparkles

*I*n the best of all worlds champagne would come only from the Champagne region of France. But the French were slow to protect the name and now consumers from Boston to Bangkok call anything that sparkles champagne, which is a pity since the generic expression "champagne" for all wines with bubbles devalues the real thing.

There are three ways to make a wine sparkle:

1   Ferment a still wine a second time in a closed bottle by adding yeast and sugar (*méthode champenoise* — the Champagne method).
2   Re-ferment wine in bulk in a large, stainless steel tank, remove and bottle under pressure (the Cuve Close or Charmat process).
3   Inject carbon dioxide into wine before closing the bottle (the Pop Wine method).

The first method is expensive and labour intensive, but the results can be stunning. Examples: Mumm's Cordon Rouge, Moët & Chandon Brut Imperial.

Method number two is inexpensive, but the quality is ordinary. Examples: Kriter, Café de Paris.

Number three is cheap and if the bubbles last longer than your first sip, you're lucky. Examples: Baby Duck, Wine Coolers.

CHAMPAGNE

The French say that champagne is the wine a young man drinks on the evening of his first mistake. In France they take these things very seriously. When I asked one producer what was the right time to drink champagne, he replied: "Before, during and after."

Champagne is the drink of celebration for a very good reason. It's the beverage that puts you in the party mood the fastest. In any sparkling wine the alcohol is contained in the bubbles and these bubbles when consumed pass immediately through your lower intestine. The alcohol gets into the bloodstream and is carried to the brain in short order. The alcohol in still wines such as Beaujolais or Entre-Deux-Mers takes much longer to metabolize through your system.

So, beware champagne — especially on an empty stomach.

On the other hand, if you want to break the ice at the annual convention of Wallflowers Anonymous or any other difficult social gathering, pop a few corks. The sound alone is enough to bring a smile to the face. After the first glass strangers will be talking to each other like old friends (unless the champagne is fit only for launching enemy battleships in which case they'll be at one another's throats).

Champagne Memories

I recall being at a champagne reception thrown by Moët & Chandon in a Toronto hotel. That company's roving ambassador, Robert Gourdin, was demonstrating his party tricks for the Toronto media. His finale was a wine fountain; he created it by piling dozens of Baccarat crystal glasses on top of each other in ever-decreasing circles until he had a six-foot-high cone with a single glass at the top. Into this glass he poured bottle after bottle of Moët. The overflow cascaded down and filled all the glasses below. It was a wonderfully decadent sight. When all the glasses were full he would hand them out to the gathering.

That was the theory. On this occasion Gourdin opted first to show the TV cameras the art of sabering the champagne. This tradition dates back to the Napoleonic wars when Bonaparte's officers would return victorious from the field of battle and call for champagne to slake their thirst. Too impatient to go through the procedure outlined above, they simply knocked off the head of the bottle with their sabres by striking the neck with an upward blow just below the cork. If executed properly, a ring of glass containing the cork comes cleanly away from the bottle. (This is not a trick I would advise anyone to try at home. The results could be disastrous.)

Well, Robert Gourdin sabred a couple of bottles but on his third attempt a cameraman asked him for a better angle.

Unfortunately, he was facing the Baccarat crystal fountain and when he sabered off the cork it flew across the room like a bullet straight into the would-be fountain. The whole thing was reduced to rubble.

The cameraman, who had recently returned unscathed from covering the Lebanese civil war, sustained a cut across the nose from a piece of flying glass.

Another hazard of champagne is its hidden talent of being able to turn itself, without warning, into a howitzer. A champagne cork can become a lethal weapon under certain circumstances and worse, you can lose half the bottle if you don't open it properly.

If you look at a champagne bottle you will notice that it is bigger and heavier than the conventional wine bottle. It also has a punt in the bottom as if the glass has been pushed in. The reason is to enable the bottle to withstand the pressure inside. The carbonic gas in champagne can measure up to six atmospheres or ninety pounds per square inch in pressure — the equivalent force that a woman in high heels exerts on the floor.

The mushroom-shaped cork is wired down for a very good reason. When released, the pressure inside the bottle will shoot the cork out at a speed of forty miles per hour for the first ten feet.

As kids we used to shake up bottles of fizzy drinks and squirt each other with them. Victorious racing car drivers and football teams still do it, invariably with jeroboams of champagne that hold the equivalent of four bottles. The point is that if a bottle of champagne has been shaken up it will explode like a gusher when you uncork it. The same effect will happen if the bottle is warm (elementary physics — gas expands when heated). Make sure that the bottle is handled gently and is well chilled. Twenty minutes in an ice bucket is long enough but make sure the bucket is half filled with ice cubes and water so that the bottle is evenly cooled. It should sit in the frigid water just up to the neck so that your hand doesn't get wet when you reach for it. If you chill it in the refrigerator, leave it for at least one hour.

How to Open Champagne Without Losing a Drop or Dropping a Guest

You will need a clean, dry cloth and glasses near at hand.

1. Hold the bottle in the cloth and point it away from your body (and anyone in proximity) at an angle of forty-five degrees. Peel off the foil that covers the cork.
2. Place your thumb over the cork to ensure that it does not eject prematurely as you untwist the wire muzzle. Remove the muzzle and wrap the end of the cloth around the cork.
3. Grip the cloth-covered cork in one hand and hold it steady as you slowly twist the bottle away from the cork. During this operation the cork remains still at all times; only the bottle moves.
4. The cork should come away with the sound of a lover's sigh and no wine will be wasted.

Silence is golden for the true champagne lover. The only sound worth hearing is the bursting of its bubbles. Some restaurants encourage their waiters to pop their champagne corks to draw attention to the party who ordered it. This is gauche, one step up from throwing bread rolls.

However, if it's New Year's Eve and you want to be theatrical, let it rip but make sure that no one is in the line of fire. And don't forget, a cork can bounce off a ceiling and still do damage.

Serving Champagne

1 For serving champagne and sparkling wines use tall, long-stemmed glasses, either flute or tulip shape. The shallow, wide-mouthed ice cream coupe favoured by many restaurants and hotels is the worst possible receptacle for champagne. Its large surface area allows the wine to warm up quickly; it encourages the bubbles to dissipate; and you give your nose a bath when you try to smell the bouquet. The large circumference means you take in too much wine when you try to sip.

Legend has it that the coupe shape was originally moulded from Marie Antoinette's breast. There exists a piece of Sévres porcelain belonging to the Antique Company of New York which might substantiate this.

2 The quickest way to make champagne go flat is to serve it in a wet or dirty glass. A tell-tale sign is large bubbles that loiter on the sides of the glass and refuse to budge. To avoid the social stigma of LBS (Lazy Bubble Syndrome) polish the glasses with a clean, soft towel to remove any residual dishwasher film.

3 If you come across a cork that sticks and won't budge, do not under any circumstances cut off the mushroom top and apply a corkscrew to what is left. This is a good way to dislocate your shoulder. Take a nutcracker and secure the cork while you turn the bottle — and do it in the kitchen away from the guests.

4 The mark of a good champagne is the size of the bubbles. The best are those with tiny bubbles that rise persistently.

5 Champagnes should not be kept too long. The producers age them three years before releasing them. They should be consumed young and fresh unless you subscribe to the English habit of waiting until they are slightly maderized (oxidized).

The Champagne Method

You may see the term *méthode champenoise* on a wine which is not produced in France. It means that the wine has been made by the traditional method used in Champagne from the late seventeenth century when a blind monk, Dom Pérignon, perfected the technique for stoppering a sparkling wine.

The time-honoured blend for champagne is Chardonnay, Pinot Noir and Pinot Meunier grapes in varying proportions depending upon the house style. Chardonnay gives the wine its acidic spine, its delicacy and finesse. The two black grapes, Pinot Noir and Pinot Meunier, add body and flavour.

The still wine (which is much more acidic tasting than normal table wines) is blended and then bottled. Before it is stoppered a solution of yeast and sugar is added. A secondary fermentation occurs in the bottle creating carbonic gas which has nowhere to go and becomes dissolved in the wine as bubbles.

A sticky residue of yeast cells is left which has to be cleaned out by a process the French call *remuage* and the English riddling. The bottles are inserted by the neck into A-shaped frames. Cellar workers shake each bottle daily for a period of up to four months until the unwanted sediment is resting on the cork. An expert *remueur* can riddle up to 40,000 bottles a day. (Machines are gradually taking over this work, because they can work around the clock and don't belong to a union.)

The neck of the bottle is then dipped into a bath of brine and frozen. The cork or crown cap is then removed. The pressure inside the bottle ejects a plug of ice that contains the debris, leaving a crystal clear wine with a few ounces missing. At this point the winemaker determines how dry or sweet his product will be. The bottle is then topped up with sweetened wine to the desired style.

Champagne Classifications

You can tell how dry a champagne will be by the designation on the label.

Brut Zero, Brut Sauvage, Brut Non-dosage, Sans Sucre, Ultra Brut   No sweetening wine added. The driest champagne made.

Brut   Less than 15 grams per litre of residual sugar. Dry to very dry depending on the style of the champagne house.

Extra Sec   12 to 20 grams residual sugar. Dry to off-dry.

Sec   17 to 35 grams per litre. Off-dry to medium-sweet.

Demi-sec   35 to 50 grams per litre. Sweet.

Riche or Doux   Over 50 grams per litre. Very sweet.

Non-vintage   No year will appear on the bottle. This will be a blend of wines from several years to produce a champagne that tastes consistently the same from year to year. The vast majority of champagnes available are non-vintage.

Each house will have its own style which will be based on the ratio of white grapes to black and the amount of sweetening wine added.

Vintage   When a champagne bears a year on the label this means that the wines were produced exclusively from that particular year's harvest. Such champagnes will have the character of the vintage and will not taste like the champagne house's non-vintage products.

Vintage champagnes are only made in good years which means that they will have a longer life than non-vintage sparklers.

Blanc de Blancs   Champagne made only from Chardonnay grapes. The style will be pale in colour, light on the palate and very dry.

Blanc de Noirs   Champagne made from only the black Pinot Noir and Pinot Meunier grapes. The style will be be rounder, fruitier and more full-bodied than a blend of white and black grapes.

Rosé or Pink Champagne   These can be produced by a short maceration on the skins to produce the pink colour or by blending red and white wines to the requisite hue before the secondary fermentation.

Crémant   This means creamy, a *pétillant* style of champagne which has less carbonic gas. Most champagnes will have a pressure of five to six atmospheres in the bottle. *Crémant* will have three and a half atmospheres.

Prestige Cuvées   The champagne houses all have their top-of-the-line product made from the finest wines. Examples: Moët & Chandon's Dom Pérignon, Roederer's Cristal, Pol Roger's Cuvée Sir Winston Churchill and Taittinger's Comtes de Champagne.

Coteaux Champenois   The still wine of Champagne before it undergoes secondary fermentation in bottle. Given its northerly situation the region produces the driest wines in France. The red wine made from Pinot Noir grapes around the town of Bouzy and called Bouzy Rouge is interesting but not worth the price.

Ratafia Grape brandy is added to the fresh juice from champagne grapes to produce this local aperitif (in the same manner as Pineau des Charentes in Cognac country).

Producer Styles

Light-bodied Alfred Rothschild, Ayala, Besserat de Bellefon, Boizel, Bonnaire, Bricout, de Castellane, Dom Pérignon, Dom Ruinart, Deutz, Jacquesson, Lanson, Moët & Chandon, Mumm, Bruno Paillard, Perrier-Jouët, Piper Heidsieck, Taittinger.

Medium-bodied Billecart-Salmon, Canard Duchêne, Charles Heidsieck, Charbaut, Gosset, Heidsieck-Monopole, Henriot, Jacquart, Joseph Perrier, Laurent-Perrier, Philipponat, Pol Roger, Pommery & Greno, Salon, de Venoge.

Full-bodied Paul Bara, Barancourt, Bollinger, Alfred Gratien, Krug, Louis Roederer, Veuve Clicquot.

Champagne Bottles

Nip	187 mL
Half (Split)	375 mL
Bottle	750 mL
Magnum (2 bottles)	1.5 L
Jeroboam (4 bottles)	3 L
Rehoboam (6 bottles)	4.5 L
Methuselam (8 bottles)	6 L
Salamanazar (12 bottles)	9 L
Balthazar (16 bottles)	12 L
Nebuchadnezzar (20 bottles)	15 L

Champagne and Food

Champagne is one of the most versatile food wines. If well chosen, it can accompany even the most highly flavoured meat dishes.

Soups, Seafood and Salty Fish Dishes *Blanc de blancs* or light Brut styles.

White Meats and Fish Brut and Extra Sec medium style.

Meat Dishes Full-bodied *blanc de noirs* or wines with high Pinot Noir content such as Bollinger or Krug.

Dessert Sec or Demi-sec style.

FRANCE'S OTHER SPARKLING WINES

Champagne is not the only region of France that makes sparkling wines. Outside the region they can only be called *vin mousseux*, even when they are made by the champagne method.

While I contend that there is no substitute for champagne, there are less expensive alternatives to be had from such regions as:

Alsace   Wine: Crémant d'Alsace. Grape varieties: Riesling, Pinot Blanc, Pinot Gris, Pinot Noir.

Burgundy   Wine: Crémant de Bourgogne. Grape varieties: Pinot Blanc, Pinot Gris, Pinot Noir, Chardonnay.

Loire   Wine: sparkling Saumur and Vouvray. Grape varieties: Chenin Blanc, Sauvignon Blanc, Chardonnay and Cabernet Sauvignon/Franc for rosés.

Jura and Savoie   Wine: Seyssel. Grape varieties: Savagnin, Melon d'Arbois, Chardonnay, and reds from Poulsard, Trousseau and Gros Noirien.

Rhône Valley   Wine: Clairette de Die. Grape varieties: Clairette, Muscat à petits grains. Wine: St-Péray. Grape varieties: Roussette, Marsanne.

South-west France   Wine: Blanquette de Limoux. Grape variety: Mauzac.

SPARKLING WINES
Spain

The Spanish call their sparkling wines produced by the champagne method Cava. Virtually all of them are made in the Penedes region of Catalonia where the chalky soil is not unlike that of Champagne.

The grape varieties are Macabeo, Parellada and Xarel-lo which give the wines an earthy, lemony character. They are excellent value, especially when it comes to marrying off a daughter.

Recommended Producers   Castellblanch, Castillo de Perelada, Codorniu, Freixenet, Marques de Monistrol, Segura Viudas.

Italy

Spumante is the Italian word for sparkling and the immediate association is with the wine of Asti — Asti Spumante. This sparkler ranging from very sweet to dry is made from the Muscat grape.

In 1975, a few sparkling wine producers in the northern provinces got together to form the Instituto Spumante Italiano Metodo Champenois. The idea was to make wines in champagne style by the traditional champagne method using only Chardonnay and the three Pinot grapes — *blanco* (white), *grigio* (grey) and *nero* (black) grown in Trentino Alto Adige, Piedmont and Lombardy. They call this dry style *Classimo*. These wines can be as expensive as champagne.

Recommended Producers Contratto, Ferrari, Antinori, Ca Del Bosco, Carpenè Malvolti, Frescobaldi.

Germany

While *Schaumwein* is the generic term for German sparkling wine, *Sekt* is the product with the pedigree. The grape variety and the village name will appear on the label. The best are made from Riesling.

Recommended Producers Fürst von Metternich, Deinhard (especially Bernkasteler Doktor), Kupferberg.

California

Several French champagne and Spanish houses have bought property in California or are working with local houses to create sparkling wines there — Moët & Chandon, Piper-Heidsieck, Laurent-Perrier, Roederer, Codorniu and Freixenet. The best California houses are Schramsberg in Napa and Iron Horse in Sonoma, commanding champagne prices. Californian producers (unlike those in Oregon) call their sparkling wines champagne.

Australia

Australians also call their sparklers champagne. The best are made from Chardonnay, Semillon and Pinot Noir.

Recommended Producers Petaluma, Seppelt, Seaview, Wolf Blass, Yalumba.

New Zealand

An ideal climate for sparkling wine. New Zealand producers do not call their wine champagne.

Recommended Producers Cellier Le Brun, Cooks, Montana, Morton, Penfolds, Selaks.

Canada

Canadian producers call their sparkling wines champagnes too.

Recommended Producers Château des Charmes, Inniskillin, Hillebrand Estates, Podamer.

A
*World
Guide to
Classic
Varieties
of Grapes*

CHARDONNAY

Chardonnay is a grape type that is now planted in virtually every wine-growing region on this planet, thanks to its enthusiastic acceptance by consumers around the world. But the wines produced from this grape can vary in style more than other classic varieties such as Riesling, Sauvignon Blanc or Gewürztraminer. Depending on where the grape is grown and how it is vinified, Chardonnay can range from the tartly acidic taste of green apples (as in the still wines of Champagne or the Trentino-Alto Adige region of northern Italy) to the mouth-filling, ripe, tropical fruit flavours of some Californian, Australian and South African Chardonnays. For the range of styles in France alone see pages 8–9.

Because of its global popularity most wine regions will trumpet the name Chardonnay on the label — but not in France where Chardonnay was first planted and where, arguably, it reaches its highest expression of excellence as white Burgundy. A few large producers in this region, such as Louis Latour, Mommessin and Moreau, use the varietal name on their labels but these mass-market regional products have little in common with the single vineyard wines from the Côte d'Or or Mâcon. These regional wines may be called Bourgogne Blanc or Bourgogne with a proprietor's fantasy

120

name tacked on, such as Lafôret (shipped by Drouhin) or Vendageurs (Bouchard Aîné), and will come from less favoured vineyard sites, generally on flat land or from newly planted vineyards.

In France you will not find the name Chardonnay on wines that are named after a village (for example, Mercurey) or an individual vineyard site (Beaune Clos des Mouches). Under the broad heading of Burgundy you will find a range of taste differences (see pages 145–158).

Italy

Italy has two distinct styles of Chardonnay.

1 Inexpensive light Chardonnay vinified and aged in stainless steel for immediate consumption. Pale in colour, very crisp and dry, not much varietal character. Virtually indistinguishable from Pinot Bianco or Tocai.

Recommended Producers of Non-oaked Chardonnay
Tiefenbrunner, Alois Lageder, Pojer e Sandri, Isole e Olena, Capezzana.

2 Barrel-aged Chardonnay (usually expensive).

Recommended Producers   Avignonesi, Banfi, Gaja, Gravner, Jermann, Borgo Conventi, Gallo Stelio.

Spain

Chardonnay is grown in Catalonia — the Penedes and Costers del Segre regions. Some producers like Miguel Torres and Jean Leon charge Burgundian prices for their excellent single vineyard wines, but there are bargains in wine produced by Raimat and Mont Marcal.

Central Europe

Hungary, Bulgaria and Rumania are sources of inexpensive Chardonnay, but don't look for finesse. The wines spend a long time in wood and tend to lack freshness. They will be assertive and somewhat heavy in style.

California

Next to Burgundy, California is the growing region where wine lovers look for good Chardonnay. The style can range from powerful, oaky, tropical fruit salad to the smoky, nutty, oaky flavours more reminscent of Meursault and Montrachet from Burgundy. California Chardonnays tend to be less acidic and fruitier than French Chardonnays, more readily accessible, but they can by their sheer amiability overpower the palate, especially with food.

Recommended Producers   Arrowood, Buena Vista, Far Niente, Ferrari-Carano, Château Potelle, Jordan, Hess Collection, Kendall-Jackson, Robert Mondavi, Edna Valley, Dry Creek, Simi, Mayacamus, Kistler, Matanzas Creek, Chateau Montelena, Sonoma-Cutrer, J. Lohr, William Hill.

Oregon, Washington, New York

The cooler climate makes for good acidity with less density of fruit in the wines than those of California. There is a tendency to over-oak Chardonnay which imparts vanilla and clove flavours and masks the apple character of the fruit.

Recommended Producers *Oregon:* Adams, Adelsheim, Amity, Cameron, Eyrie, Ponzi, Rex Hill, Shafer, Tualatin. *Washington:* Arbour Crest, Chateau Ste. Michelle, Columbia, Hogue, Zillah Oakes.
New York: Bedell, Bridgehampton, Casa Larga, Glenora, Hargrave, Knapp, Millbrook, Pindar, Wagner, Weimer.

Australia

The Australian Chardonnay profile falls between the elegant Burgundian model and the robust Californian style. There is perceptible sweetness in the fruit and evident oak. Chardonnays from the Hunter Valley tend to be lighter and more graceful in style than those grown in Western Australia or other more southerly regions, except for Rosemount which is styled as the Montrachet of Australia.

Recommended Producers *Hunter Valley:* Rosemount, Robson, Rothbury, Tyrrell, Tulloch, Lake's Folly, Lindeman.
Western Australia: Cullen, Leeuwin Estate, Moss Wood.
South Australia/Victoria: Petaluma, Kies, Wolf Blass, Mount Mary, Chateau Reynella, Balgownie.
Tasmania: Pipers Brook.

New Zealand

Perhaps New Zealand will come the closest of the New World regions to replicating the style and elegance of white Burgundy.

Recommended Producers Nobilo, Babich, Montana, Esk Valley, Vidal.

South Africa

Chardonnay has only been planted recently in the Cape although some forty producers now grow it.

Recommended Producers Backsberg, Blaauwklippen, Delaire, De Wetshof, Hamilton Russell, L'Ormarins, Nederburg, Overgaaw, Simonsig, Stellenryck.

Canada	Ontario produces the lion's share of Chardonnay and wineries such as Cave Springs and Stoney Ridge Cellars have been winning blind tastings against French and California wines. Ontario's style resembles Chablis although the use of new oak barrels can give the wines some exotic spicy flavours of clove and cinnamon.

Recommended Producers Cave Spring, Stoney Ridge, Inniskillin, Château des Charmes, Hillebrand, Vineland Estates, Stonechurch, Marynissen.
British Columbia: Divino, Mission Hill, Sumac Ridge.

Chile	This country is the best source of inexpensive, good Chardonnay. Its wines have rich fruit flavours and lots of extract, and are usually high alcohol.

Recommended Producers Cusiño Macul, Concho Y Toro, Viña Santa Carolina.

Chardonnay Substitutes	Tokay-Pinot Gris (Alsace)
	Pinot Blanc (Alsace)
	Weissburgunder (Germany)
	Cortese di Gavi (Italy)
	Rioja whites (Spain)

SAUVIGNON BLANC	This grape variety can masquerade under various names and appear in a variety of blends. The following list indicates where it is present in whole.

1 Varietally named Sauvignon Blanc. Examples: Sauvignon de St. Bris from Burgundy, Torres Santa Digna Sauvignon Blanc from Chile.
2 In California as Fumé Blanc. Examples: Robert Mondavi Fumé Blanc.
3 Under the Loire village name. Examples: Sancerre, Pouilly Fumé, Reuilly.
4 As a component with Sémillon in white Bordeaux, particularly from the Graves and Entre-Deux-Mers regions. Examples: Château La Louvière, Domaine de Chevalier.
5 As a lesser component with Sémillon in sweet dessert wines of Bordeaux. Examples: Sauternes, Barsac, Ste-Croix-du-Mont, Loupiac.
6 Also found in the dry and sweet wines of Bergerac, Monbazillac and Côtes de Duras.

Taste	Sauvignon Blanc can have a range of smells and flavours depending upon the soil and climate in which it is grown and the way it is vinified.
	The driest versions from the Loire will be sharply acidic and smell of asparagus or a freshly mown lawn. Examples: Ménétou-Salon, Quincy, Haut-Poitou.
	With more sunshine they exhibit herbaceous, smoky gooseberry or elderberry flavours. Examples: Sancerre, Pouilly-Fumé.
	In warm growing climates such as California and Chile the taste will be of ripe fig, pineapple and sweet grapefruit.
	Perhaps the variety's most persistent characteristic of the Sauvignon Blanc grape is a tendency to suggest the "cat's tray" on the nose when over-ripe and when given too much skin contact during fermentation.
	Sauvignon Blanc is grown around the world. The best dry expression of the grape is to be found in the Loire Valley and in New Zealand. For fruitier, more opulent versions try California's Sonoma Valley.
Sauvignon Blanc Substitutes	Ugni Blanc
	Vinho Verde
	Chenin Blanc (dry)
	New Zealand Chardonnay
	Ontario Chardonnay
	Vidal (dry)
RIESLING	Arguably Riesling is the world's most versatile wine grape. It can be made in a variety of styles ranging from bone dry to the unctuously sweet with every shade of dryness or sweetness in between. It can also be made in a light, low-alcohol style (German) or a full-bodied style (Alsace).
	There are, however, interloping clones of lesser breed who would parade themselves as the noble Riesling but are merely social climbers. Beware Emerald Riesling and Gray Riesling from California, the Cape or Paarl Riesling of South Africa, the Welschriesling of Austria, Hungary and Bulgaria and Riesling Italico grown in Italy, Czechoslovakia and Rumania. These make acceptable table wines, but none have the breed and quality of the true Riesling. In Australia's Hunter Valley they even call the Semillon grape Riesling which is weird although the wines age as magnificently as Riesling.

The true Riesling may also carry the name Johannisberg in front of it (which has nothing to do with South Africa but refers to Schloss Johannisberg in the Rheingau whose wines first established the primacy of the variety in Germany). It may also be called the Rhine Riesling (Australia, New Zealand) or the White Riesling (USA) or the Riesling Renano (Italy). Any reference to the Rhine attests to the real thing.

Riesling flourishes in cold, damp northerly climates, but as a vine it does not like to get its feet wet. That is why it is planted on torturously steep hillsides along the Rhine and Mosel valleys in northern Germany. It is here that Riesling produces one of the great wines of the world.

In Germany the quality of the wine (regardless of the grape variety used to produce it) is determined by the amount of sugar in the berries at the time of harvest. It is measured in Oechsle degrees. Theoretically, a single vineyard could produce seven different wines each designated by the sugar level of the grapes. Each of Germany's eleven wine-growing regions has its own ladder of quality which can vary for different grape varieties.

Let's take Riesling grown in the Rheingau as an example. To be classified as *Qualitätswein* (quality wine) the Riesling juice must have a minimum reading of fifty-three Oechsle degrees.

GERMAN LADDER OF QUALITY
(based on sugar in the grape)

```
                                        150 ——— Trockenbeerenauslese
                                  125 ————————— Beerenauslese/ Eiswein
                             95 ——— Auslese
                        85 ——— Spätlese
        73° OECHSLE ——————— Kabinett
```

The two most important German regions for growing Riesling are the Mosel and the Rheingau. There is a discernible difference in their taste profiles.

No other white grape, with the possible exception of Chenin Blanc, ages with such grace as Riesling. Sweet versions will last because of their sugar content. But dry ones will also enjoy a long life if they have a good backbone of acidity. This comes from cold nights so if you want to cellar Riesling for a decade or more make sure you choose wines of Kabinett quality or above from Germany, Alsace, Alto Adige, New Zealand, New York or Ontario.

When Riesling ages it takes on a petrol/kerosene nose with a touch of lime. The sweeter versions will become spicier, reminiscent of Muscat.

Qualitätswein (QbA) Riesling from the Mosel Almost water white, hints of green. The driest and lightest Riesling you will find. Racy acidity, fragrant floral quality, very elegant.

Qualitätswein (QbA) Riesling from the Rheingau Very pale straw. Very dry, more body than Mosel with fruity acidity.

This style difference holds true as you work up through the different sweetness levels. Ageing potential: 4–10 years.

Riesling Kabinett Pale straw colour. Very dry but with more fruit quality. More concentrated bouquet. Ageing potential: 6–10 years.

Riesling Spätlese Straw colour. Off dry. Floral with perceptible sweetness but good acidity. Ageing potential: 7–10 years.

Riesling Auslese Light gold. Medium sweetness. May have some *Botrytis* which will offer a lime or petrol/kerosene bouquet behind which you can smell a honeyed peachy quality. Ageing potential: 8–10 years.

Riesling Beerenauslese Orange-gold. Pronounced *Botrytis* character. Honeyed sweetness, dried apricots, peaches. Ageing potential: 9–10 years.

Eiswein Straw. Fresh acidity on the nose. Peachy, much crisper than *Beerenauslese* on the palate because of the high acidity. Ageing potential: 10–20 years.

Riesling Trockenbeerenauslese Burnished gold. Pronounced *Botrytis* nose; unctuous raisiny, toffee flavour. Very intense. Ageing potential: 10–20 years plus.

Other wine-growing regions, such as Australia, use the German terminology to describe the sweetness levels of their Rieslings as well. They also use the anglicized descriptors. In California these terms have been incorporated into the region's wine laws since 1981:

Early Harvest — equivalent to German *Kabinett*-style Rieslings.

Riesling (with no qualifying term) — will be *Spätlese* level.

Late Harvest — the same as *Auslese*.

Select Late Harvest — equivalent to *Beerenauslese*.

Special Select Late Harvest — *Trockenbeerenauslese*.

You may also see abbreviations of German wine terms on New World Rieslings as in Riesling TBA (which suggests Trockenbeerenauslese but the vintners will argue that it stands for Totally Botrytis Affected) and Riesling B.A. (Botrytis Affected).

Alsace Riesling

Alsace Riesling is sold in goose-necked green bottles similar to those used in the Mosel, but the style is as different as night and day. In France the sugar in the grapes is used to create alcohol, not to be left in the wine to give residual sweetness. As a result Alsatian Rieslings are very dry and full-bodied with a fine spine of acid. The best were once described to me by a local chef as tasting like "a naked sword"! Ageing potential: 5–10 years.

The Alsatians will also leave their grapes on the vine after the normal harvest date to get extra ripeness. Wines made from these grapes are called *Vendange Tardive* (late harvest), which is equivalent to Rheingau Riesling Auslese quality. Ageing potential: 7–10 years.

A sweeter version, when only the *Botrytis*-affected grapes are used is called *Selection de grains nobles* (selection of berries suffering from "noble rot") which is equivalent to *Beeren-auslese* or *Trockenbeerenauslese* quality depending on the final sugar reading of the grapes. Ageing potential: 10–20 years.

Riesling Substitutes

Edelzwicker (Alsace)

Dry Muscat (Alsace)

Müller-Thurgau (Germany, Alto Adige)

Liebfraumilch

Silvaner

CABERNET SAUVIGNON

This small blue grape is responsible for some of the greatest wine-drinking experiences you may ever have. Cabernet Sauvignon is one of the varieties used in the production of red Bordeaux which is among the longest-lived wines in the world. In great years it can survive and thrive for decades. Wines dating back to 1865 and earlier are still drinkable with pleasure.

What gives red Bordeaux (or claret as the British call it) its longevity is tannin. Because of the high ratio of skin to pulp, the juice will extract large amounts of tannin during the maceration and fermentation process.

Claret is the yardstick by which every other Cabernet Sauvignon the world over will be judged and whenever a New World winemaker wants to flex his muscles he will put on a blind tasting of his wines against the top growths of Bordeaux. If he stages the event properly, he will win. (Bordeaux wines take years to mature. Vintages vary substantially. A wine packed with sweet fruit can be more seductive in a blind tasting than one that is elegant and harmonious.) But for on-going drinking pleasure there is nothing to beat a fine Bordeaux. Californian and Australian winemakers are beginning to emulate the style by blending their Cabernet Sauvignon with the same grapes used in Bordeaux to balance the aggressive nature of this variety.

Red Bordeaux is made from three basic varieties:

1　Cabernet Sauvignon
2　Cabernet Franc (lower in tannin and acid)
3　Merlot (low tannin, more fruit sugar) with small additions of Malbec and Petit Verdot

Each Bordeaux château will have its own "recipe" in terms of percentages of these varieties, depending on their soil composition and exposure. On the left bank of the Gironde, the Cabernet Sauvignon is king — largely responsible for the great first growths, such as Lafite, Mouton-Rothschild, Latour, Margaux and Haut Brion. On the right bank, in St-Émilion and Pomerol, the earlier ripening and faster maturing Merlot predominates in the blend and Cabernet Sauvignon takes a back seat to Cabernet Franc.

Taste

The signature of Cabernet Sauvignon is black currants or cassis (in warmer growing regions) and cedarwood (cigar box). When young it will be harshly tannic with a leafy taste. As it ages the fruit aromas will change to more organic smells of leather, tobacco, chocolate, coffee beans and spices.

California

Napa and Sonoma Valley have produced Cabernet Sauvignons that may not rival the Bordeaux wines in longevity but certainly do in quality. The warmer growing regions produce sweeter fruit which can have blackberry, plum, green pepper and eucalyptus tones.

Australia	Stylistically, Australian Cabernets stand between Bordeaux and California although their bright fruit makes them more "New World" in style.
South Africa	This is a warm growing region. It produces dense wines that age well, especially the Cabernets and Pinotages. Sweet wines are also worth looking for.
Cabernet Sauvignon Substitutes	Merlot (California) Malbec (Chile, Argentina) Tempranillo (Rioja)
PINOT NOIR	Of all red wine grapes Pinot Noir is the most difficult to grow. It will only produce fine wines in the most marginal of climates. Too cold and it will not ripen, too warm and it will produce jammy, unstructured wines as in Chile, Argentina, Australia, South Africa and Central Europe. The hallmark region for Pinot Noir is Burgundy's Côte d'Or.
Côte de Nuits	This region is dominated by red wines. The Pinot Noir grown here makes denser, more full-bodied and spicier wines than those grown in the more southerly Côte de Beaune. As with Chardonnay the quality of the wines is designated by the nature of the vineyard in which the grapes are grown.
Taste	Burgundian Pinot Noir at its best is characterized by a fragrant bouquet of violets and raspberries or strawberries with a hint of barnyard — a vegetal/animal character that smells of mulch or undergrowth. The colour is deep cherry which goes slightly brickish or orange with age. Less tannic than Cabernet Sauvignon, it develops a silky mouth-feel.
Oregon	The climate of Oregon is very similar to that of Burgundy and the Pinot Noir does well here. The wines have a deeper colour than those of Burgundy, more apparent sweetness in the fruit and less acidity. While generally better structured than those of California (which tend to get jammy), they are not as long-lived as the Burgundian model. **Recommended Oregon Pinot Noir Producers** Adelsheim, Amity, Bethel Heights, Broadley, Eyrie, Knudsen-Erath, Ponzi.

Recommended California Pinot Noir Producers Acacia, Calera, Carneros Creek, Kalin Cellars, Robert Mondavi, Santa Cruz, Joseph Swann, Robert Stemmler.

Other regions which produce Burgundian-style Pinot Noir are Ontario, New York and New Zealand.

Light-bodied Pinot Noir can be found in:

France: Champagne, Alsace, Loire Valley

Germany: (Spätburgunder grape) Ahr, Assmannshausen

Switzerland: Dôle

Italy: Trentino-Alto Adige

Red Burgundy/Pinot Noir Substitutes

Italy: Pinot Nero

Spain: Rioja reds

Greece: Naoussis, Nemea

Hungary: Nagyburgundi

South Africa: Pinotage

SYRAH

Of all the grape varieties that are responsible for the world's great wines, Syrah is the least appreciated. In the Northern Rhône it is responsible for Hermitage, Crozes-Hermitage and Côte Rôtie as well as the lighter St. Joseph and Cornas. It is also a constituent grape in Châteauneuf-du-Pape.

Taste

Blackberry and pepper with a hint of smoke or tar. Usually very intense, deeply coloured and powerful. Needs bottle-ageing for several years. Will live as long as red Bordeaux.

Recommended Rhône Producers Jaboulet, Chapoutier, Délas, Guigal, Chave, (Côte Rôtie) Jasmin, Champet, (Cornas) Clape, Barjac, Michel.

Syrah or Sirah?

Petite Sirah grown in California is not the same variety as Syrah. In France they call it Duriff after the man who propogated the clone. In Australia and South Africa this particular grape is known either as Shiraz or Hermitage. The style of wine it produces is similar to the Syrah of the Rhône. Shiraz is also used as a blend with Cabernet Sauvignon and the major constituent will appear first on the label. Example: Brown Bros. Cabernet/Shiraz.

Just to confuse the issue, Australian wines labelled as "Claret" or "Burgundy" will be made from the Shiraz grape, not from Cabernet Sauvignon or Pinot Noir respectively.

Recommended California Petite Sirah Producers
Ridge, McDowell Valley Vineyard, Phelps.

Recommended Australian Shiraz Producers Grange
Hermitage (the finest Australian red), Penfolds, Taltarni, Hill-
Smith, Bailey, Brokenwood.

Syrah Substitutes

California: Red Zinfandel

Italy: Primitivo, Taurasi, Castel del Monte, Cannonau

Portugal: Dão garrafeira

Lebanon: Château Musar

France

The wines of France have become the yardstick by which every other growing country measures its progress. The classic Bordeaux and Burgundies, the white wines of the Loire, the dessert wines of Sauternes, Champagne and the exotic Gewürztraminers of Alsace are the model for every vintner who considers planting the noble European grapes. But French supremacy in quality wines is being challenged by the New World, especially when it comes to price.

RECOGNIZING FRENCH WINES

There are four regulated categories of wines based primarily on geographic principles. Other factors such as grape variety, alcoholic strength, traditional vineyard practices and wine-making techniques also play a part. These designations will appear on the label.

Vin de table (Table Wine) Invariably blended and sold under brand names. Examples: Piat d'Or, L'Epayrié.

Vin de pays (Regional Wines) Wines from a stated region, department or zone and grape variety or blend of varieties achieving a minimum of 9 percent, 9.5 percent or 10 percent alcohol by volume depending on the region. Examples: Vin de pays de l'Hérault, Vin de pays Charentais.

Delimited Wines of Superior Quality (VDQS) The minor league of Appellation Controlée wines. Regulated as to areas of production, permitted grape varieties, pruning, cultivation methods, maximum yields, minimum alcohol content, vinification practices and taste testing.

Controlled Appellation of Origin (AOC, Appellation d'Origine Controlée) The top quality French wines conforming to regulations similar to those of the VDQS, only more stringent, especially in terms of yield per hectare. The essential difference between the two is the superior quality of the soil in which AOC wines are grown. AOC wines account for about five percent of wine production in France.

WINE REGIONS OF FRANCE

BORDEAUX

Bordeaux produces dry red, dry white, dry rosé and sweet white wines.

In Bordeaux, perhaps more so than in any other of the world's wine regions, the combination of soil, microclimate and sunshine are so critical that neighbouring vineyards can produce wines of perceptibly different qualities. Given the unpredictability of the weather between spring and fall in this region, the smaller the area from which the grapes are obtained the greater the possibility of making fine wine. The best vineyards are those sited on great depths of gravel that allow the rainwater to drain away.

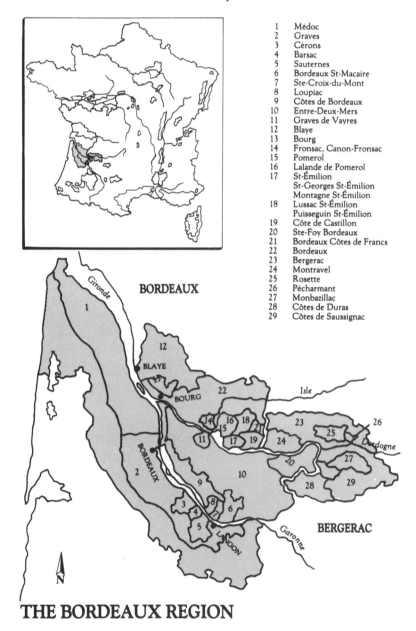

1   Médoc
2   Graves
3   Cérons
4   Barsac
5   Sauternes
6   Bordeaux St-Macaire
7   Ste-Croix-du-Mont
8   Loupiac
9   Côtes de Bordeaux
10 Entre-Deux-Mers
11 Graves de Vayres
12 Blaye
13 Bourg
14 Fronsac, Canon-Fronsac
15 Pomerol
16 Lalande de Pomerol
17 St-Émilion
    St-Georges St-Émilion
    Montagne St-Émilion
18 Lussac St-Émilion
    Puisseguin St-Émilion
19 Côte de Castillon
20 Ste-Foy Bordeaux
21 Bordeaux Côtes de Francs
22 Bordeaux
23 Bergerac
24 Montravel
25 Rosette
26 Pécharmant
27 Monbazillac
28 Côtes de Duras
29 Côtes de Saussignac

THE BORDEAUX REGION

THE QUALITY FACTOR

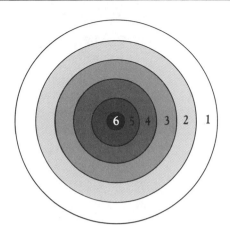

1 Bordeaux appellation — Wines made from grapes grown within the delimited region of Bordeaux. Invariably a blend. Examples: Mouton-Cadet, Beau Rivage.

2 Regional appellation — Wines from specified regions within Bordeaux. Examples: B & G Médoc, Schroeder & Schyler St. Émilion.

3 Commune wines — Wines from identified communes or villages. Examples: St-Julien, Margaux.

4 Cru Bourgeois wines — Appellations below the five classified growths of Bordeaux. Examples: Château Gloria, Château Greysac.

5 Château wines — Fifth to second growths. Examples: Château Lynch-Bages, Château Cos d'Estournel.

6 First Growths — Examples: Château Lafite, Château Haut-Brion.

Grape Varieties

Red   Cabernet Sauvignon, Cabernet Franc, Merlot and two lesser grapes, Malbec and Petit Verdot.

White   Sauvignon Blanc, Sémillon, Muscadelle.

The 1855 Classification of Red Médoc and Graves

To celebrate Bordeaux wines at the 1855 Universal Exhibition in Paris, the city's Chamber of Commerce asked brokers of the local stock exchange to classify the great red and white wines of the department. The brokers came back with two lists: Classified Red Wines of The Gironde and Classified White Wines of the Gironde.

Their decisions were based on the historic price and reputation of the châteaux and the quality of their soils. With minor changes this classification has remained intact to this day. The major difference was the elevation of Mouton-

Rothschild from the first-named of the second growths to a first growth in 1973.

Do not consider the Bordeaux Classification as a league table. The original intention was that the lists were an honour role based on past performance. Within each growth (*cru*) all the wines were to be equal. The brokers could have underlined this principle by listing the wines alphabetically.

Today the classification is more of an economic ladder. The first growths are very expensive, the seconds generally are more costly than the thirds, etc. The popularity of certain châteaux such as Palmer (third growth) and Lynch-Bages (fifth growth) have placed them in the price range of the second growths.

In 1855, only one wine outside the Médoc made the hallowed list of red wines: Château Haut-Brion from the Graves region.

Ironically, the most expensive red wine from Bordeaux today is not one of the *Premier Grand Crus* but a Pomerol, Château Pétrus, which has no Cabernet Sauvignon at all in the blend (95 percent Merlot, 5 percent Cabernet Franc).

Bordeaux Grape Mix

I offer the approximate proportions of the grapes in the blend as a guide to the length of time it takes for the wine to mature. The greater the proportion of Cabernet Sauvignon to Merlot and Cabernet Franc the longer you can expect the wine to take to lose its tannic astringency. Château Mouton-Rothschild for example, with its 85 percent Cabernet Sauvignon, will require longer ageing than a Château Lafite-Rothschild with 70 percent Cabernet Sauvignon. The higher the growth, generally speaking, the longer it will take to reach maturity.

Second Labels

Many châteaux now produce wines under a second label, for example, Les Forts de Latour is Château Latour's second label. These products will contain wines that the winemaker deems not quite up to the standard required to maintain the house's reputation in the marketplace. Such wines will generally be made from newly planted vines or from vats considered not suitable for blending into the best wine. In good vintage years they can offer great value for money.

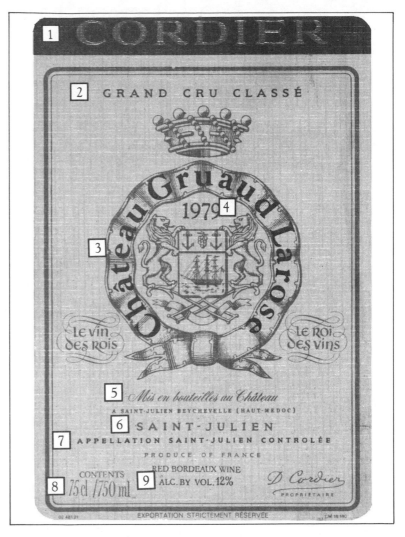

1   Cordier — Holding company name.
2   Grand Cru Classé — Classification: one of the five classified growths. The label will not tell you exactly which it is. Only first growths are stated as *Premier Grand Cru*.
3   Château Gruaud Larose — Property name including vineyards. Nearly all Bordeaux wines have a château name.
4   1979 — Vintage date (the year the grapes were harvested).
5   Mis en bouteilles au Château — Your guarantee the wine was bottled on the estate. This legend will also be branded on the cork with the vintage date.
6   Saint-Julien — The commune in which the château and its vineyards are situated.
7   Appellation Saint-Julien — The appellation of origin. The commune name will be bracketed by the terms *Appellation* and *Controlée*.
8   75cl/750 ml — The legal contents of the bottle.
9   Alc. By Vol. 12% — The alcohol content. This is a rough guide only. It can vary as much as 0.5% from time of bottling to opening.

1855 CLASSIFICATION OF BORDEAUX REDS

FIRST GROWTH CHÂTEAUX (PREMIERS CRUS)	COMMUNE	GRAPE PROPORTIONS
Lafite-Rothschild**	Pauillac	CS70%/Mer15%/CF13%/PV2% 2nd Label: Moulin des Carruades
Margaux**	Margaux	CS75%/Mer20%/PV & CF 5% 2nd Label: Pavillon Rouge du Château Margaux
Latour**	Pauillac	CS80%/CF10%/Mer10% 2nd Label: Les Forts de Latour*
Haut-Brion**	Graves	CS55%/Mer30%/CF15%
Mouton-Rothschild**	Pauillac	CS85%/Mer 8%/CF7%

SECOND GROWTH CHÂTEAUX (DEUXIÈME CRUS)	COMMUNE	GRAPE PROPORTIONS
Rausan-Ségla	Margaux	CS66%/Mer28%/CF4%/PV2%
Rausan-Gassies	Margaux	CS40%/Mer39%/CF20%/PV1% 2nd Label: Enclos de Moncabon
Léoville-Las-Cases**	St-Julien	CS65%/Mer/18%/CF14%/PV3% 2nd Label: Clos du Marquis
Léoville-Poyferré*	St-Julien	CS65%/Mer 35% 2nd Label: Château Moulin-Riche
Léoville-Barton*	St-Julien	CS70%/Mer15%/PV8%/CF7%
Dufort-Vivens	Margaux	CS80%/CF12%/Mer8% 2nd Label: Domaine de Cure-Bourse
Gruaud-Larose**	St-Julien	CS62%/Mer25%/CF9%/PV4% 2nd Label: Sarget du Gruaud-Larose
Lascombes*	Margaux	CS65%/Mer30%/CF3%/PV2% 2nd Label: Château Segonnes Brane-Cantenac
	Margaux	CS70%/CF13%/Mer15%/PV2% 2nd Label: Château Notton
Pichon-Longueville-Baron*	Pauillac	CS80%/Mer20%

KEY TO SYMBOLS
CS = Cabernet Sauvignon, Mer = Merlot, CF = Cabernet Franc, PV = Petit Verdot, Mal = Malbec, ** Highly recommended, * Recommended

SECOND GROWTH CHÂTEAUX (DEUXIÈME CRUS)	COMMUNE	GRAPE PROPORTIONS
Pichon-Longueville Comtesse de Lalande**	Pauillac	CS46%/Mer34%/CF12%/PV8% 2nd Label: Réserve de la Comtesse
Ducru-Beaucaillou**	St-Julien	CS65%/Mer25%/CF5%/PV5% 2nd Label: Château la Croix
Cos d'Estournel**	St-Estèphe	CS60%/Mer40% 2nd Label: Château de Marbuzet* (Mer56%/CS44%)
Montrose**	St-Estèphe	CS65%/Mer35%/CF10%

THIRD GROWTH CHÂTEAUX (TROISIÈME CRUS)	COMMUNES	GRAPE PROPORTIONS
Kirwan*	Margaux	CS40%/Mer30%/CF20%/PV10%
d'Issan*	Margaux	CS75%/Mer25%
Lagrange	St-Julien	CS65%/Mer35% 2nd Label: les Fiefs-de-Lagrange
Langoa-Barton*	St-Julien	CS70%/Mer15%/PV8%/CF7%
Giscours**	Margaux	CS75%/Mer20%/Cf3%/PV2%
Malescot-St-Exupéry*	Margaux	CS50%/Mer35%/CF10%/PV5% 2nd Labels: Château de Loyac, Domain du Balardin
Cantenac-Brown	Margaux	CS75%/Mer15%/CF8%/PV2% 2nd Label: Château la-Fontanelle
Palmer**	Margaux	CS55%/Mer40%/CF3%/PV2%
La Lagune**	Haut-Médoc	CS55%/CF20%/Mer20%/PV5% 2nd Label: Château Ludon-Pomiès-Agassac
Desmirail	Margaux	CS80%/Mer10%/CF9%/PV1%
Calon-Ségur**	St-Estèphe	CS60%/CF20%/Mer20% 2nd Label: Marquis de Ségur
Ferrière	Margaux	CS47%/Mer33%/PV12%/CF8%
Marquis d'Alesme-Becker	Margaux	CS40%/Mer30%/CF20%/PV10%
Boyd-Cantenac*	Margaux	CS67%/Mer20%/CF7%/PV6%

KEY TO SYMBOLS
CS = Cabernet Sauvignon, Mer = Merlot, CF = Cabernet Franc, PV = Petit Verdot, Mal = Malbec, ** Highly recommended, * Recommended

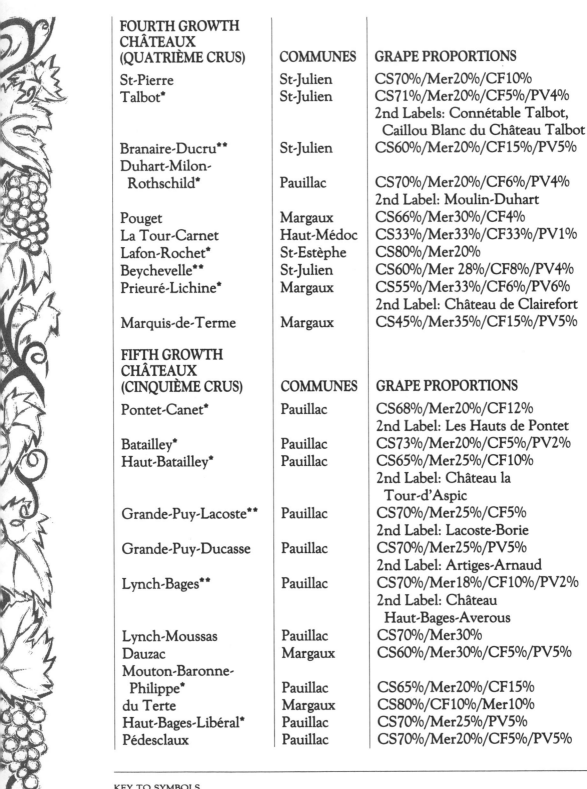

FOURTH GROWTH CHÂTEAUX (QUATRIÈME CRUS)	COMMUNES	GRAPE PROPORTIONS
St-Pierre	St-Julien	CS70%/Mer20%/CF10%
Talbot*	St-Julien	CS71%/Mer20%/CF5%/PV4%
		2nd Labels: Connétable Talbot, Caillou Blanc du Château Talbot
Branaire-Ducru**	St-Julien	CS60%/Mer20%/CF15%/PV5%
Duhart-Milon-Rothschild*	Pauillac	CS70%/Mer20%/CF6%/PV4%
		2nd Label: Moulin-Duhart
Pouget	Margaux	CS66%/Mer30%/CF4%
La Tour-Carnet	Haut-Médoc	CS33%/Mer33%/CF33%/PV1%
Lafon-Rochet*	St-Estèphe	CS80%/Mer20%
Beychevelle**	St-Julien	CS60%/Mer 28%/CF8%/PV4%
Prieuré-Lichine*	Margaux	CS55%/Mer33%/CF6%/PV6%
		2nd Label: Château de Clairefort
Marquis-de-Terme	Margaux	CS45%/Mer35%/CF15%/PV5%

FIFTH GROWTH CHÂTEAUX (CINQUIÈME CRUS)	COMMUNES	GRAPE PROPORTIONS
Pontet-Canet*	Pauillac	CS68%/Mer20%/CF12%
		2nd Label: Les Hauts de Pontet
Batailley*	Pauillac	CS73%/Mer20%/CF5%/PV2%
Haut-Batailley*	Pauillac	CS65%/Mer25%/CF10%
		2nd Label: Château la Tour-d'Aspic
Grande-Puy-Lacoste**	Pauillac	CS70%/Mer25%/CF5%
		2nd Label: Lacoste-Borie
Grande-Puy-Ducasse	Pauillac	CS70%/Mer25%/PV5%
		2nd Label: Artiges-Arnaud
Lynch-Bages**	Pauillac	CS70%/Mer18%/CF10%/PV2%
		2nd Label: Château Haut-Bages-Averous
Lynch-Moussas	Pauillac	CS70%/Mer30%
Dauzac	Margaux	CS60%/Mer30%/CF5%/PV5%
Mouton-Baronne-Philippe*	Pauillac	CS65%/Mer20%/CF15%
du Terte	Margaux	CS80%/CF10%/Mer10%
Haut-Bages-Libéral*	Pauillac	CS70%/Mer25%/PV5%
Pédesclaux	Pauillac	CS70%/Mer20%/CF5%/PV5%

KEY TO SYMBOLS
CS = Cabernet Sauvignon, Mer = Merlot, CF = Cabernet Franc, PV = Petit Verdot, Mal = Malbec, ** Highly recommended, * Recommended

FIFTH GROWTH CHÂTEAUX (CINQUIÈME CRUS)	COMMUNES	GRAPE PROPORTIONS
Belgrave	Haut-Médoc	CS60%/Mer35%/PV5%
Camensac*	Haut-Médoc	CS60%/CF20%/Mer20%
Cos-Labory	St-Estèphe	CS40%/Mer35%/CF20%/PV5%
Clerc-Milon*	Pauillac	CS70%/Mer20%/CF10%
Croizet-Bages	Pauillac	CS37%/CF30%/Mer30%/PV & Mal3%
Cantemerle	Macau	CS40%/Mer40%/CF18%/PV2%

1855 CLASSIFICATION OF BORDEAUX WHITES (SWEET: SAUTERNES & BARSAC)

FIRST GREAT GROWTH (PREMIER GRAND CRU)	COMMUNE	GRAPE PROPORTIONS
d'Yquem**	Sauternes	Sém80%/Sau20% 2nd Label: "Y" (dry)

FIRST GROWTH (PREMIERS CRUS)	COMMUNES	GRAPE PROPORTIONS
La Tour Blanche*	Bommes	Sém70%/Sau27%/Mus3%
Clos Haut-Peyraguey	Bommes	Sém83%/Sau15%/Mus2%
Lafaurie-Peyraguey*	Bommes	Sém90%/Sau5%/Mus5%
Rayne-Vigneau* (dry: Rayne Sec)	Bommes	Sém80%/Sau20%
Suduiraut**	Preignac	Sém80%/Sau20%
Coutet*	Barsac	Sém80%/Sau20%
Climens*	Barsac	Sém98%/Sau2%
Guiraud	Sauternes	Sém54%/Sau45%/Mus1% 2nd Labels: Le Dauphin de Lalague, "G" (dry) Cru St-Marc (sweet)
Rieussec*	Fargues	Sém80%/Sau18%/Mus2% 2nd Labels: Clos Labère, "R" (dry)
Rabaud-Promis	Bommes	Sém80%/Sau18%/Mus2% 2nd Label: Château Jauga
Sigalas-Rabaud*	Bommes	Sém90%/Sau10%

KEY TO SYMBOLS
CS = Cabernet Sauvignon, Mer = Merlot, CF = Cabernet Franc, PV = Petit Verdot, Mal = Malbec, Sém = Sémilion, Sau = Sauvignon, Mus = Muscadelle
** Highly recommended, * Recommended

SECOND GROWTH (DEUXIÈME CRUS)	COMMUNES	GRAPE PROPORTIONS
Doisy-Daëne*	Barsac	Sém100%
		2nd Labels: Vin Sec de D-D, Cantegril
Doisy-Védrines*	Barsac	Sém80%/Sau20%
d'Arche	Sauternes	Sém80%/Sau15%/Mus5%
Filhot*	Sauternes	Sém60%/Sau37%/Mus3%
Broustet	Barsac	Sém63%/Sau25%/Mus12%
Nairac*	Barsac	Sém90%/Sau6%/Mus4%
Caillou*	Barsac/ Sauternes	Sém90%/Sau10%
Suau*	Barsac	Sém80%/Sau10%/Mus10%
de Malle*	Sauternes	Sém75%/Sau22%/Mus3%
		2nd Labels: Ste-Hélène, Chevalier de Malle
Romer-du-Hayot*	Fargues	Sém70%/Sau25%/Mus5%
Lamothe*	Sauternes	Sém70%/Sau20%/Mus10%
Doisy-Dubroca	Barsac	Sém90%/Sau10%

Recommended *Crus Bourgeois* Bastor-Lamontagne, Raymond-Lafon, de Fargues.

GRAVES REGION CLASSIFIED GROWTHS (1959)

CHÂTEAU	COMMUNE	GRAPE PROPORTIONS
RED WINES		
Bouscaut	Cadaujac	Mer55%/CS35%/CF5%/Ma15%
Haut-Bailly*	Léognan	CS60%/Mer30%/CF10%
		2nd Label: Parde de Haut-Bailly
Carbonnieux*	Léognan	CS50%/Mer30%/CF10%/PV & Mal10%
Domaine de Chevalier**	Léognan	CS65%/Mer30%/CF5%
Fieuzal	Léognan	CS65%/Mer30%/PV & Mal5%
Olivier	Léognan	CS65%/Mer35%
Malartic-Lagravière	Léognan	CS44%/CF31%/Mer25%
La Tour-Martillac	Martillac	CS60%/Mer25%/CF6%/Mal & PV9%
		2nd Label: La Grave-Martillac
Smith-Haut-Lafitte	Martillac	CS73%/Mer16%/CF11%

KEY TO SYMBOLS
CS = Cabernet Sauvignon, Mer = Merlot, CF = Cabernet Franc, PV = Petit Verdot, Mal = Malbec, Sém = Sémillon, Sau = Sauvignon, Mus = Muscadelle
** Highly recommended, * Recommended

CHÂTEAU	COMMUNE	GRAPE PROPORTIONS
Haut-Brion**	Pessac	CS55%/Mer30%/CF15%
La Mission- Haut-Brion**	Talence	CS60%/Mer35%/CF5%
Pape-Clément*	Pessac	CS60%/Mer40%
La Tour-Haut-Brion**	Talence	CS70%/CF15%/Mer15%

WHITE WINES (DRY)

CHÂTEAU	COMMUNE	GRAPE PROPORTIONS
Bouscaut	Cadaujac	Sém52%/Sau48%
Carbonnieux**	Léognan	Sau65%/Sém30%/Mus5%
Domaine de Chevalier**	Léognan	Sau70%/Sém30%
Malartic-Lagravière*	Léognan	Sau100%
Olivier*	Léognan	Sém65%/Sau30%/Mus5%
La Tour-Martillac*	Martillac	Sém55%/Sau30%/Mus15%
Laville-Haut-Brion**	Talence	Sém60%/Sau40%
Couhins	Villenave d'Ornon	Sau50%/Sém50%

Also Highly Recommended Château La Louvière from Léognan with grape proportions Sau75%/Sém15%

ST-ÉMILION CLASSIFICATION 1985

The wines of St-Émilion are divided into two classifications: *premiers grands crus classé* (A) and (B) above the *grands crus classés*.

(A) CHÂTEAU	GRAPE PROPORTIONS
Ausone*	Mer50%/CF50%
Cheval Blanc**	CF66%/Mer33%/Mal1%

(B) CHÂTEAU	GRAPE PROPORTIONS
Beauséjour	Mer50%/CF25%/CS25%
Belair*	Mer60%/CF40%
Canon*	Mer55%/CF40/CS5%
Clos Fourtet	Mer60/CF20%/CS20%
Figeac**	CS35%/CF35%/Mer30%
la Gaffelière*	Mer65%/CF and CS25%
Magdelaine	Mer80%/CF20%
Pavie*	Mer55%/CF25%/CS20%
Trottevieille	Mer60%/CF25%/CS15%

KEY TO SYMBOLS
CS = Cabernet Sauvignon, Mer = Merlot, CF = Cabernet Franc, PV = Petit
Verdot, Mal = Malbec, Sém = Sémillon, Sau = Sauvignon, Mus = Muscadelle
** Highly recommended, * Recommended

Next on the St-Émilion scale are sixty-three *grands crus classés* wines. Highly recommended among them are l'Angélus, l'Arrosée, Belair, Berlinquet, Cadet-Piola, Clos des Jacobins, Grand-Corbin-Despagne, Pavie, Soutard, La Tour-du-Pin-Figeac.

POMEROL CLASSIFICATION

The Pomerol region neighbouring St-Émilion has yet to be classified officially, but it is generally accepted that the leading wine (and most expensive Bordeaux red) is Château Pétrus (Mer95%/CF5%). Other recommended Pomerol Châteaux include:

CHÂTEAU	GRAPE PROPORTIONS
Certan-de-May**	Mer65%/CF25%/Mal10%
la Conseillante	Mer45%/CF45%/Mal10%
l'Evangile**	Mer65%/CF35%
la Croix de Gay*	Mer80%/CF15%/CS5%
l'Enclos*	Mer80%/CF20%
la Fleur du Gay**	Mer100%
la Fleur Pétrus**	Mer75%/CF25%
Le Gay*	Mer50%/CF and CS50%
Gazin	Mer80%/CF15%/CS5%
Latour-à-Pomerol*	Mer80%/CF20%
Nenin	Mer50%/CF30%/CS20%
Petit-Village*	Mer80%/CF10%/CS10%
Trotanoy**	Mer85%/CF15%
Vieux-Château-Certan**	Mer50%/CF25%/CS20%Mal15%

KEY TO SYMBOLS
CS = Cabernet Sauvignon, CF = Cabernet Franc, Mer = Merlot, Mal = Malbec
** Highly recommended, * Recommended

Recommended Bourgeois Châteaux

Some of the best values of the Médoc and Graves are to be found in the ranks of the *crus bourgeois* or unclassified wines. They do not have the same concentration of flavour and lasting power of the classified growths, except in certain instances (marked with an asterisk in the following list), but they are well worth seeking out.

D'Angludet*	Larose-Trintaudon
Brillette	Loudenne
Chasse-Spleen*	La Louvière* (red and white)
Cissac	Maucaillou
Coufran	Meyney*
De Pez*	Les Ormes de Pez*
Ferrande (white)	Pichon
De Fieuzal (white)	Pontensac*
Fonbadet	Poujeaux
Fourcas-Hosten*	Ramage La Batisse
Gloria*	St-Georges*
Greysac	Smith-Haut-Lafitte (white)
Haut-Marbuzet*	Sociando-Mallet*
Labégorce-Zédé	La Tour St-Bonnet
Lamarque*	La Tour de By
Lanessan*	Tronquoy Lalande

BURGUNDY (BOURGOGNE)

Burgundy as a region is much more appealing to tourists than Bordeaux. While Bordeaux is a sea of vines punctuated by occasional châteaux of varying degrees of architectural interest, Burgundy is a patchwork of small holdings, sloping vineyards and wine villages. What we call Burgundy is actually an archipelago of six different wine regions beginning in the north with the isolated Chablis separated by 120 kilometres from the Côte d'Or (which is made up of the Côte de Beaune and Côtes de Nuits). The Côte d'Or runs into the Côte Chalonnais, Mâconnais and Beaujolais to the south. Because of the region's length — stretching 300 kilometres from the cool Chablis region to the sunny Beaujolais region — the wine styles vary radically.

Over the years Burgundian inheritance laws have had the effect of carving up the vineyards to the point where one grower may own a mere three rows of vines in a world famous vineyard such as Clos de Vougeot.

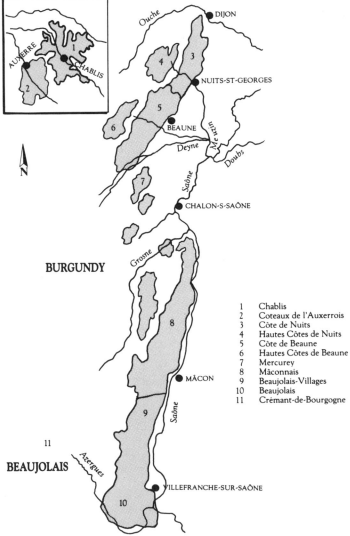

1	Chablis
2	Coteaux de l'Auxerrois
3	Côte de Nuits
4	Hautes Côtes de Nuits
5	Côte de Beaune
6	Hautes Côtes de Beaune
7	Mercurey
8	Mâconnais
9	Beaujolais-Villages
10	Beaujolais
11	Crémant-de-Bourgogne

THE BURGUNDY REGION

Because of these subdivisions, choosing a Burgundian wine can be problematic. Instead of relying on the integrity of a château-bottled wine as we do in Bordeaux, we have to put our faith in the person who either grows or selects the wine, rather than the plot of ground that produced the grapes.

So, in Burgundy, the name of the vineyard or the village is not as important as the name of the shipper. Clos de Vougeot, an enclosed vineyard of fifty hectares, has nearly eighty different owners each of whom could legally make his own wine and sell it as Clos de Vougeot. Yet the location of their holding in the vineyard may be unfavourable and their growing or winemaking practices less competent than their neighbours.

The Quality Factor

The essential Burgundian soil is limestone and marl. The best vineyards offering good drainage and the best exposure to the early morning and late afternoon sun are to be found on east and southeast facing slopes.

Chardonnay is planted where there is a preponderance of limestone in the soil (as in Champagne) and Pinot Noir in richer ground which features higher concentrations of clay.

Grape Varieties

White   Chardonnay, Aligoté.

Red   Pinot Noir, Gamay.

BURGUNDY WINE

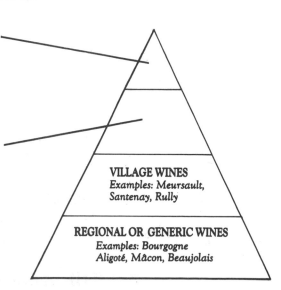

GRANDS CRUS (*Great Growths*), the 30 finest wines of Burgundy which carry only the name of the vineyard
Examples: Corton, Chambertin, Montrachet

PREMIERS CRUS (*First Growths*), named vineyards of quality (*Clos des Mouches*) from a specified village (*Beaune*), Beaune Clos des Mouches
Examples: Fixin Clos du Chapitre, Pommard Les Rugiens

VILLAGE WINES
Examples: Meursault, Santenay, Rully

REGIONAL OR GENERIC WINES
Examples: Bourgogne Aligoté, Mâcon, Beaujolais

VIN DE BOURGOGNE
PRODUCE OF FRANCE

BURGUNDY WINE
PRODUIT DE FRANCE

1 Récolte   1974

2 Mis en bouteilles au Domaine

3 **MEURSAULT**

4 **LES GENEVRIÈRES**

5 Appellation Contrôlée

6 DOMAINE A. ROPITEAU-MIGNON

7 Propriétaire à Meursault, Côte-d'Or, France

8 730 ml   25,7 fl oz liq   9 13 % alc./vol.

1   Récolte 1974 — Year of the harvest.

2   Mise en bouteilles au Domaine — Bottled on the property.

3   Meursault — Village name.

4   Les Genevrières — The vineyard name.

5   Appellation Contrôlée — A designated first growth wine of Meursault.

6   Domaine A. Ropiteau-Mignon — Part-owner of the property.

7   Propriétaire à Meursault, Côte-d'Or, France — Address.

8   730 ml 25,7 fl oz liq — Capacity of bottle in millilitres and ounces. (Under EEC law now all wines have to be in 750 mL or 750 cL bottles.)

9   13% alc./vol. — Alcoholic strength.

Mis En Bouteilles and Other Bottling Jargon

Printed on French wine labels and branded on corks you will find a bewildering number of expressions which explain under what circumstances the wine was put into the bottles. These can be a clue to the wine's quality.
Mis en bouteilles par le propriétaire — *bottled by the* grower who cannot bottle anyone else's product.
Mis à la propriété *or* Mis en bouteilles au Domaine — *bottled on the estate by the grower or by a mobile bottler visiting the estate.*
Mis en bouteilles dans nos caves — *bottled in our cellars, which means nothing. It could be your cellar or my* cellar. It hides the fact that the wine was not bottled on the estate.
Mis en bouteilles au Château — *for Bordeaux wines this means the wine was bottled on the estate and is a guarantee of quality. In Burgundy it could mean that the shipper has a bottling line in a château he owns.*

Chablis — Crisp and Fresh	There are four levels of quality for Chablis: 1 Grands Crus: seven vineyards situated north of the town of Chablis — Blanchots, Bourgros, Les Clos, Grenouilles, Preuses, Valmur and Vaudésir. Maximum production: forty-five hectolitres per hectare. Can age several years. 2 Premiers Crus: thirty-odd vineyards in seven communes ringing the town of Chablis. The most widely available names are La Fourchaume, Montmains and Montée de Tonnerre. Maximum production: fifty hectolitres per hectare). Can age three to four years. 3 Chablis: wines grown in nineteen communes within the delimited area of Chablis. Maximum production: fifty hectolitres per hectare. Drink within two years of the vintage. 4 Petit Chablis: a delimitated area in the Yonne region outside Chablis. Less favoured limestone soil producing wines lighter in flavour, concentration and alcohol. This appellation will disappear and will be replaced by a name such as Hautes Côtes de Chablis. Drink as young as possible.

Recommended Chablis Shippers   Moreau, Régnard et fils, Drouhin, de Ladoucette.

Recommended Producers   René Dauvissat, Paul Droin, William Fèvre (known for his oak-aged Chablis), Long-Depaquit, Louis Michel, Louis Pison, François Ravenvau, Guy Robin, Rottiers-Clothilde, Philippe Testut, Robert Vocoret.

Côte d'Or — The Quintessential White Burgundy	The Slope of Gold is well named. In the fall when the vine leaves turn colour, the landscape becomes golden. The cost of the most expensive Chardonnays such as Montrachet Marquis de Laguiche will leave you little change from an ounce of gold and the real estate here is the most costly agricultural land in the world. The Côte d'Or is made up of two areas: Côte de Nuits (some Chardonnay is planted here but mainly Pinot Noir) and the Côte de Beaune where the great white wines are grown around the three villages where only Chardonnay is grown — Meursault, Puligny-Montrachet and Chassagne-Montrachet.
Grands Crus	The finest white wines of Burgundy come from seven vineyards whose name they will carry on their label. These vineyards on the slopes, by virtue of their soil, exposure to sunshine and overall microclimate, produce the best Chardonnay grapes in the region:

Corton-Charlemagne

Charlemagne

Montrachet

Bâtard-Montrachet

Chevalier-Montrachet

Bienvenue-Bâtard-Montrachet

Criots-Bâtard-Montrachet

These wines are expensive and in limited supply. In good years they can be aged for a decade or more.

Premiers Crus

These are wines from very good single vineyard sites on the slopes. The label will bear the village name followed by the name of the vineyard. Examples: Meursault "Les Perrières," Puligny-Montrachet "Les Caillerets," Chassagne-Montrachet "Les Ruchottes."

These wines too are costly and will age well in good vintages.

Recommended Shippers Bichot, Bouchard Père et Fils, Champy, Chartron & Trebuchet, Joseph Drouhin, Louis Jadot, Maison Jaffelin, Louis Latour, Moillard, Remoissenet Père et Fils.

Recommended Producers The following are recommended.

Corton-Charlemagne: Bonneau du Martray, Bouchard Père et Fils, Coche-Dury, Louis Chapuis, Faiveley, Louis Jadot, Louis Latour, Domaine Dubreuil, Michel Voarick, Roland Rapet, Remoissenet.

Meursault: Coche-Dury, Jean Germain, Albert Grivault, François Jobard, Domaine Comtes Lafon, Leroy, Château de Meursault, Michelot-Buisson, Pierre Morey, Guy Roulot.

Puligny-Montrachet: Chartron & Trebuchet, Louis Carillon, Joseph Drouhin, Domaine Leflaive, Paul Pernot, Etienne Sauzet.

Chassagne-Montrachet: Bachelet-Ramonet, Blain-Gagnard, Marc Colin, Colin-Deleger, Delagrange-Bachelet, Fontaine-Gagnard, Louis Jadot, Jean Marc Morey, Michel Niellon, Domaine André Ramonet.

Le Montrachet: Domaine de la Romanée-Conti, Marquis de Laguiche, Baron Thénard, Domaine Comte Lafon.

Chevalier-Montrachet: Domaine Leflaive, Louis Jadot, Louis Latour, Jean Chartron, Michel Niellon.

Bâtard-Montrachet: Domaine Leflaive, Domaine Morey, Domaine Pierre Morey, Blain-Gagnard, J.N. Gagnard, Gagnard-Delagrange, Michel Niellon, Etienne Sauzet.

Bienvenue-Bâtard-Montrachet: Domaine Leflaive, Domaine Carillon, Lequin Frères.

Criots-Bâtard-Montrachet: Delagrange-Bachelet.

Village Wines

These will bear the name of the village or commune where the vineyards are sited. Example: Meursault, Monthélie, Santenay (without any qualifying vineyard added to the place name).

They are more affordable. Look for good vintage years and reliable growers and recommended producers.

Côte de Beaune-Villages

A wine or blend of wines from any of the seventeen communes around the Côte de Beaune region.

This is a good value wine in fine vintage years. Not for ageing.

Côte d'Or Chardonnay Style Dry, full-bodied with an oaky apple character which blossoms into rich nutty and buttery tones in the village and single vineyard wines.

Chalonnais and Mâconnais — The Cheaper Alternative

South of the Côte d'Or are two regions that offer Chardonnays which will not cause financial hardship. Look for these village names and producers:

Rully

These are the best wines in the region.

Charton & Trebuchet

Chanzy Frères

Jean Daux

Raymond Bêtes

Pierre Cogny

Jean Coulon

Georges Duvernay

Domaine de la Folie

Domaine de Rully

Mercurey	Château de Chamirey
	Chanzy Frères
	Faiveley
Givry	J. P. Ragot
	Veuve Steinmaier
Montagny (very dry)	Cave de Buxy
	Château de la Salle
	Vachet
	Veuve Steinmaier

Chalonnais Style Closer in character to the Côte d'Or, but lacks the concentration of flavour and intensity. However, their price compensates for that. Newest appellation: Bourgogne Côte Chalonnaise. Drink within three years of the harvest.

The Mâconnais marks the southern part of Burgundy where it joins Beaujolais. The region owes its success to the popularity of one of its village wines: Pouilly-Fuissé. As the largest Chardonnay producing region in Burgundy it offers a reliable though non-spectacular white under the generic label, Mâcon Blanc. One step up in quality, and perhaps the best value in white Burgundy, is Mâcon-Villages.

The best wines are named after the villages. Look for such names as:

St-Véran

Pouilly-Fuissé

Pouilly-Vinzelles

Pouilly-Loché (Vinzelles and Loché are usually cheaper and equally as good as Fuissé)

Mâcon-Clessé

Mâcon-Viré

Mâcon-Lugny

Mâcon-Prissé

Mâconnais Style More solid and earthy than Côte d'Or. Very dry with pineapple and honey flavours. Very full-bodied.

Look for the following recommended Mâconnais producers:

André Bonhomme

Domaine de Bellenand

Domaine de Roally

Georges Duboeuf

Jean Thévenet

Cave de Viré

Madame Ferret

Bernard Léger-Plumet

Roger Luquet

Château de Fuissé

Generic White Burgundy

Chardonnay grown on the poorest vineyard sites will be classified as simple "Bourgogne Blanc."

Red Burgundy

The finest red Burgundies are grown in *grands crus* vineyards around the following villages. The name of the vineyard will be prominently displayed on the label.

Côte de Nuits
Gevrey-Chambertin

Chambertin

Chambertin-Clos de Bèze

Chapelle-Chambertin

Charmes-Chambertin

Griotte-Chambertin

Latricières-Chambertin

Mazis-Chambertin

Ruchottes-Chambertin

Recommended Gevrey-Chambertin Producers   Domaine Drouhin, Drouhin-Laroze, Domaine Dujac, Maison Faiveley, Jean-Claude Fourrier, Philippe Leclerc, Bernard Maume, Joseph Roty, Armand Rousseau, Louis Trapet, Domaine des Varoilles.

Morey-St-Denis

Bonnes Mares

Clos des Lambrays

Clos de la Roche

Clos St. Denis

Clos de Tart

Recommended Morey-St-Denis Producers Domaine Arlaud Père et Fils, Domaine Daujac, Domaine des Lambrays, Georges Lignier, Domaine Ponsot, Roumier, Bernard Serveau, J. Truchot-Martin.

Chambolle-Musigny	Bonnes Mares
	Le Musigny

Recommended Chambolle-Musigny Producers Bernard Amiot, Gaston Barthod-Noëllat, Domaine Clair-Daü, Georges Clerget, Alain Hudelot-Noëllat, Maison Leroy, Daniel Moine-Hudelot, J-Frédéric Mugnier, Georges Rumier, Bernard Serveau.

Vougeot	Clos de Vougeot

Recommended Vougeot Producers Château de la Tour, Georges Clerget, Joseph Drouhin, Domaine Drouhin-Laroze, Faiveley, Jean Gros, Domaine Mongeard-Mugneret, Maison Pierre Ponnelle, Domaine Daniel Rion.

Vosne-Romanée	La Romanée
	Romanée-Conti
	Romanée-St-Vivant
	Richebourg
	La Tâche
	Echézeaux
	Grands Echézeaux

Recommended Vosne-Romanée Producers Robert Arnoux, Philippe Engel, Jean Grivot, Gros Frère et Soeur, Henri Jayer, Domaine Lamarche, Méo-Camuzet, Cathiard Molinier, Mongeard/Mugneret-Gibourg, Domaine de la Romanée-Conti, Jean Tardy. (Négociants) Bouchard Père et Fils, Drouhin, Remoissenet.

Nuits-St-Georges	No *grands crus*.

Recommended Nuits-St-Georges Producers Robert Chevillon, Robert Dubois, Domaine Faiveley, Domaine Henri Gouges, Bernard de Gramont, Machard de Gramont, Alain Michelot, Henri Remoriquet, Domaine Daniel Rion.

Côte de Beaune

Aloxe-Corton

Le Corton

Corton-Bressandes

Corton-Clos du Roi

Corton-Renardes

Les-Maréchaudes (part)

Recommended Aloxe-Corton Producers Pierre André, Domaine Adrien Belland, Domaine Chandon de Briailles, Domaine Louis Chapuis, Domaine Antonin Guyon, G. & P. Ravaut, Daniel Senard, Tollot-Beaut, Tollot-Voarick.

Grands Crus

These wines are expensive and will age from ten to fifteen years depending on the vintage.

Premiers Crus

These wines will be labelled with the village name followed by that of the vineyard. Examples: Nuits-St-Georges "Les St. Georges," Gevrey-Chambertin "Clos St. Jacques," Aloxe-Corton "Les Valozières," Volnay "Caillerets." These are also quite expensive with an ageing potential of up to ten years.

Village Wines

The products of one or several vineyards with a named village or commune. Examples: Pommard, Beaune, Nuits-St-Georges. Best values come from the lesser-known villages. Examples: Côte de Nuits — Fixin; Côte de Beaune — Ladoix-Serrigny, Pernand-Vergelesses, Savigny-Lès-Beaune, Chorey-Lès-Beaune, Santenay, Auxey-Duresses and Monthélie. Reasonably priced. Will age up to eight years.

Fixin Recommended Producers André Bart, V & D Berthaut, Bruno Clair, Pierre Gelin, Gelin-Molin, Philippe Joliet, Mongeard-Mugneret.

Ladoix-Serrigny Recommended Producers Chevalier Père et Fils, Edmond Cornu, Michel Mallard et Fils, Prince Florent de Mérode, André Nudant et Fils.

Pernand-Vergelesses Recommended Producers Bonneau de Martray, Chandon de Briailles, Domaine Chanson, Delarche Père et Fils, Denis Père et Fils, Dubreuil-Fontaine, Laleure-Piot, Louis Latour, Rapet Père et Fils, Maurice Rolland.

Savigny-Lès-Beaune Recommended Producers Simon Bize, J-M Capron-Manieux, Chandon de Briailles, Ecard, Girard-Vollot et Fils, Pierre Guillemot, Antonin Guyon, Pavelot-Glantenay, Jean Pichenet, Rapet Père et Fils.

Chorey-Lès-Beaune Recommended Producers Jacques Germain, Tollot-Beaut.

Beaune Recommended Producers Arnoux Père et Fils, Besancenot-Mathouillet, Bichot-Clos Frantin, Bouchard Aîné, Bouchard Père et Fils, Champy Père, Chanson Père et Fils, Joseph Drouhin, Jacques Germain, Louis Jadot, J. Guitton, Albert Morot.

Pommard Recommended Producers Comte Armand, Billard-Gonnet, Domaine de Courcel, Michel Gaunoux, Armand Girardin, Domaine Lejeune, Domaine de Montille, Domaine Mussy, Jacques Parent, Pothier-Rieusset.

Volnay Recommended Producers Marquis d'Angerville, Henri Boillot, Domaine Y. Clerget, Bernard Glatenay, Michel Lafarge, Comtes Lafon, Hubert de Montille, Domaine de la Pousse d'Or.

Monthélie Recommended Producers Jacques Boigelot, Eric Boussey, Armand Douhairet, Henri Potinet-Ampeau, Robert de Suremain.

Auxey-Duresses Recommended Producers J-P Diconne, Henri Latour, Domaine Leroy, Duc de Magenta, Bernard Roy, Michel Prunier.

Blagy Recommended Producers Robert Ampeau, Domaine de Blagny, Jospeh Matrot.

Chassagne-Montrachet Recommended Producers Bachelet-Ramonet, Domaine Carillon, Gagnard-Delagrange, Lamy-Pillot, Château de la Maltroye, Domaine Morey, Ramonet-Prudhon.

Guy Accad Burgundies

A Lebanese oenologist named Guy Accad has created a furor in Burgundy by advocating a winemaking technique which, say the traditionalists, completely changes the character of what has become recognized as red Burgundy. Accad advises his clients to allow the freshly pressed juice to macerate on the skins for up to two weeks before a long, cool fermentation. The resulting wines are densely coloured, very aromatic and have masses of extract. Whether they will age as well as the traditional Burgundies which are fermented at high temperatures remains to be seen.

Producers who favour the Guy Accad method are Château de la Tour in the Clos de Vougeot; Vosne-Romanée — Henri Jayer, Jean-Jacques Confuron, Etienne Grivot and Pernin-Rossin; Aloxe Corton — Daniel Senard; Nuits St. Georges — Georges Chictot; Savigny-les-Beaune — Chandon de Briailles.

Saint Aubin Recommended Producers Raoul Clerget, Hubert Lamy, Henri Prudhon, Domaine Roux Père et Fils, Gérard Thomas.

Santenay Recommended Producers Adrien Belland, Château de la Charrière, Michel Clair, Lequin-Roussot, Mestre Père et Fils.

Côte de Nuits-Villages

Wines from five communes — Brochon, Comblanchien, Corgoloin, Fixin and Prissey — bottled under the generic name, Côte de Nuits. Worth looking for in good years. Ageing potential: three to five years.

Recommended Producers Bourée Père et Fils, Bernard Chevillon, André Chopin, Robert Dubois, Maurice Fornerol, Jean Petitot, Domaine de la Poulette.

Côte de Beaune-Villages

Pinot Noir wines from any of the seventeen communes making up the Côte de Beaune. Simple reds can be excellent buys in fine vintages. However, there is a tendency for the wines to be thin, acidic and lacking colour in poor years. Ageing potential: three years.

Recommended Producers Bernard Bachelet, Paul Chevrot, Clos des Langres, Maison Leroy, Tollot-Beaut.

Hautes Côtes de Nuits and Beaune

The Hautes Côtes de Nuits and Beaune are extensive hilly areas lying to the west of the Côte d'Or. These slopes have become a cheaper source of Burgundian wines than those grown on the expensive real estate along the Route N 74, the road that takes you through all the famous wine villages.

Haut Côtes de Nuits Recommended Producers Claude Cornu, Domaine Fribourg, Geisweiler et Fils, Bernard Hudelot, Jayer-Gilles, Henri Naudin-Ferrand, Simon Fils, Thévenot-le-Brun, Alain Verdet.

Haut Côtes de Beaune Recommended Producers Jean-Claude Bouley, Denis Carre, François Charles, Château de Mercey, Lucien Jacob, Jean Joliot, Domaine des Vignes des Demoiselles.

The Côte Chalonnaise and the Mâconnais

Red wines from these regions south of the Côte d'Or have less finesse, but can offer a cheaper alternative to the big names of Burgundy.

Chalonnaise Recommended Producers The following are recommended.

Bouzeron: Chanzy Frères

Rully: Jean-Claude Brelière, Domaine de la Folie, H & P Jacqueson, Guy Mugnier, Domaine du Prieuré, Domaine de la Renarde.

Mercurey: Luc Brintet & Frédéric Charles, Domaine Flaively, Jeanin-Naltet, Michel Juillot, Y & P de Launay, Louis Menand, Domaine de la Monette, Domaine Saier, Domaine de Suremain.

Givry: Jean Chofflet, Propriété Desvignes, Domaine du Gardin, Domaine Jobolot, Lumpp Frères, Gérard Mouton, Domaine Thénard.

Mâconnais Recommended Producers Domaine de Chervin, Guffens-Heynen, Pierre & Veronique Janny, Henri Lafarge.

Bourgogne Rouge	The basic red wine of the Burgundy region. Lower in alcohol and not worth ageing.

BEAUJOLAIS

Ask anyone to name the first wine that comes into their mind and I'll lay odds that it's Beaujolais. No other wine so perfectly expresses the region where it is grown and the attitude to life of the people who make it. Beaujolais is an uncomplicated, easy-drinking wine, full of fruit and the sensation of being outdoors on a sunny afternoon. It is a daylight wine, while its betters — red Burgundy and Bordeaux — wake up with the night.

The Beaujolais region stretches for fifty-five kilometres between Mâcon and Lyon abutting the southern end of the Burgundy region. At its widest point it is fifteen kilometres across. Over 120,000 hectares of land are under vine.

Although Beaujolais is a simple wine made from a single grape variety (Gamay), there are four different Beaujolais to contend with.

1 **Beaujolais** (minimum alcohol content nine degrees) — wines grown in the southern half of the region on flat land the soil of which is a mix of clay and limestone. Fifty-nine communities south of the town of Villefranche produce wines entitled to the basic appellation, Beaujolais.
2 **Beaujolais-Villages** (minimum alcohol content ten degrees) — wines grown in the northern half of the region on hillsides which contain granitic soil. Thirty-eight villages produce wines that can be called Beaujolais-Villages.
3 **The Named Growths (*crus*)** — wines from specific villages or communes selected for their favourable growing sites.

Ten such sites are identified by their place name (see page 160). You will not find the term "Beaujolais" on these labels, only "Product of Burgundy."

4   **Beaujolais Nouveau (Primeur)** — wines produced by the quick carbonic maceration technique for release on the third Thursday of November. Only the wines of Beaujolais or Beaujolais-Villages can be produced as Nouveau.

You may also find Beaujolais rosé and white Beaujolais (made from Chardonnay grapes or Aligoté).

The term *Beaujolais Supérieur* on a label has nothing to do with the wine being better quality. If the wine contains one degree of alcohol over the minimum permissible nine degrees, the producer can call his wine *Supérieur*.

Beaujolais Nouveau

In North America, the Far East, anywhere in fact where it is necessary to fly Beaujolais Nouveau
so that it will be available for release on the third Thursday of November, the price will be inflated by the cost of air-freight.

A misconception exists that if Beaujolais Nouveau is not consumed by the end of December it goes off. Admittedly, the wine is made for obsolescence. But don't throw those unopened bottles out in January. The wine will go dormant in the early spring and will hibernate until the following September. It will still be drinkable then but rounded and less firm in style. I would not recommend, however, laying down Nouveau wines for longer than one year.

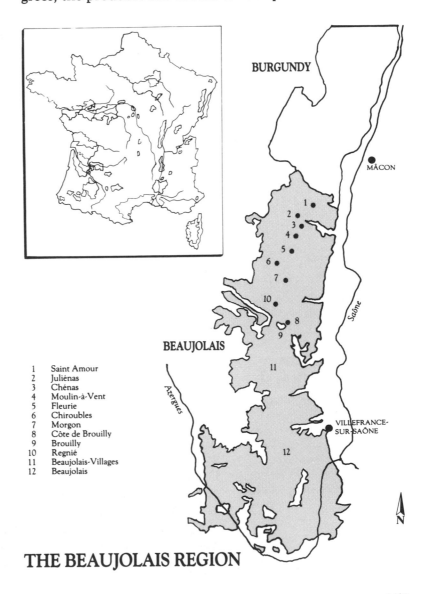

1   Saint Amour
2   Juliénas
3   Chénas
4   Moulin-à-Vent
5   Fleurie
6   Chiroubles
7   Morgon
8   Côte de Brouilly
9   Brouilly
10 Regnié
11 Beaujolais-Villages
12 Beaujolais

THE BEAUJOLAIS REGION

Beaujolais Taste Profile	Beaujolais is a simple, gulpable wine. Tannin and acidity are not pronounced. The accent is on the fruit. The wine should smell of soft fruit — black cherries, plums, strawberries as well as violets. The taste should be light and fruity with a hint of pepper on the finish.

Recommended Shippers Paul Beaudet, Bouchacourt, Caves de Champclos, Chevalier Fils, Joseph Drouhin, Georges Duboeuf, Pierre Ferraud, Jaffelin, Prosper-Maufoux, Sarrau, Louis Tête, Trenel Fils, Thomas la Chevalière.

Serving Beaujolais	All Beaujolais wines, even the named growths, should be served slightly chilled (but not as chilled as white wine) to enhance their fruity quality.

Basic Beaujolais and Beaujolais-Villages go well with cold cuts, *charcuterie* and simple meat dishes such as hot dogs and hamburgers. Try them with roasted chestnuts as the French do around Beaujolais Nouveau release time. The named growths can be consumed with more sophisticated meat dishes which are not too heavy or overly spiced.

Beaujolais Substitutes	Burgundy: Passe-Tout-Grains (A mix of two-thirds Gamay and one-third Pinot Noir crushed together)

Loire: Gamay de Touraine, Anjou Gamay, Haut-Poitou Gamay

Rhône: Gamay de l'Ardèche

Switzerland: Dôle

California: Gamay Beaujolais, Napa Gamay

Ontario: Gamay Beaujolais

Italy: Valpolicella, Bardolino, Grignolino

The Ten Beaujolais Crus

The finest Beaujolais are the ten named growths. These wines have more concentration of flavour and will last longer than Beaujolais or Beaujolais-Villages. From the lightest to most full-bodied the wines are:
Chiroubles
Brouilly
Côte de Brouilly
Juliénas

Fleurie
Regnié
Saint Amour
Chénas
Morgon
Moulin-à-Vent
    In great years such as 1947 and 1976, the most full-bodied crus will last for many years and with bottle-ageing take on the character of an old Pinot Noir from the

Côte d'Or. I have tasted a 1947 Moulin-à-Vent forty years later and it was still alive and delicious!
    Apart from the village or commune name you may also see the name of a property or a single vineyard — such as Château de Briante Brouilly or Saint Amour Domaine de Monrêve.

ALSACE	Of all French wine regions, Alsace is the easiest to understand since its wines are labelled by grape type, not by village or vineyard name. Apart from a small amount of rather insipid Pinot Noir, all Alsatian wines are white.
	This ninety-six kilometre stretch from Mulhouse to Strasbourg, in the shelter of the Voges Mountains, is France's most easterly wine-growing area, bordering on the Rhine. Its bottle shape may look German, but the wines are very French.
Wine Style	Dry, medium to full-bodied, flowery with good fruit extract. Usually around twelve percent alcohol by volume.

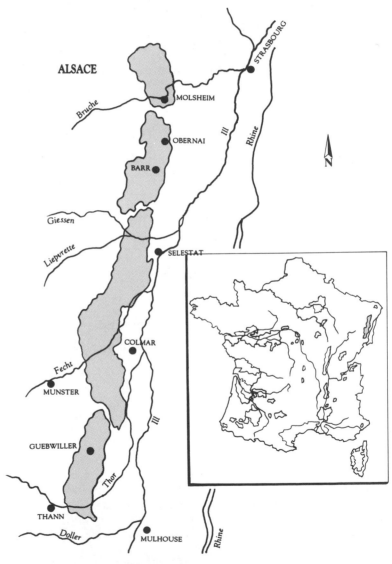

THE ALSACE REGION

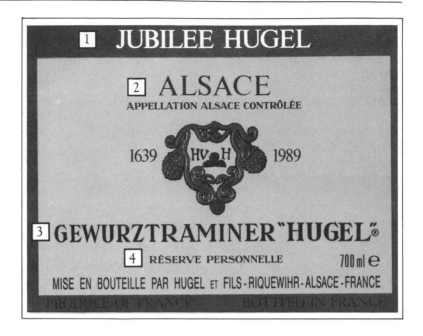

1 Jubilee Hugel — Special anniversary label marking the company's 350th anniversary.
2 Alsace, Appellation Alsace Contrôlée — Appellation of origin.
3 Gewürztraminer "Hugel" — The grape variety and producer's name.
4 Réserve Personnelle — Quality designation by Hugel.

Best Wines

Riesling (ages well, five to ten years)

Tokay-Pinot Gris (ages well, five to ten years)

Gewürztraminer (drink young, unless Vendanges Tardives)

Muscat (vinified in dry style, drink young)

Inexpensive Wines

To be consumed when purchased.

Silvaner

Pinot Blanc (also called Klevner)

Pinot Noir

Edelzwicker (blend of Chasselas with Silvaner, Pinot Blanc, Riesling and Gewürztraminer)

Grands Crus

Certain favoured vineyard sites growing Riesling, Gewürztraminer, Tokay-Pinot Gris and Muscat have been granted the appellation *Grand Cru*. Not all the producers are in favour of this distinction and though they may own vineyards which would qualify for this status they choose not to use the term on their labels.

Label Terminology

Producers have developed their own individual terms for differentiating quality among their wines. Terms such as *Réserve Personnelle* and *Réserve Particulière* or *Cuvée Tradition* and *Cuvée Speciale* on the label have no legal definition but merely designate levels of quality within particular houses.

While most Alsatian wines are dry in certain years the four top grapes can develop high levels of sugar. If these are left on the vine to maximize the sugar they can be labelled *Vendanges Tardives* (Late Harvest) and *Sélection de Grains Nobles* (corresponding to Germany's Auslese sweetness level and above).

Crémant d'Alsace

This is champagne-method sparkling wine which can be made from the following grape varieties: Riesling, Pinot Blanc, Pinot Noir, Pinot Gris, Auxerrois and Chardonnay. Rosé is made from Pinot Noir. It is a good champagne substitute. Do not age.

Recommended Alsace Producers Leon Beyer, Marcel Deiss, Dopff au Moulin, Josmeyer, Gisselbrecht, Hugel, Kuentz-Bas, Schlumberger, Trimbach, Domaine Weinbach, Willm, Zind-Humbrecht.

LOIRE

The Loire Valley produces an enormous range of wines from very crisp dry whites (Muscadet), off-dry whites (Vouvray), sweet whites (Coteaux du Layon) to light reds (Chinon) and even some fuller-bodied reds.

Grape Varieties

White Muscadet, Chenin Blanc, Sauvignon Blanc.

Reds Cabernet Sauvignon, Cabernet Franc, Gamay, Pinot Noir.

Wine Style Fresh, lively whites with high acidity. Off-dry and sweet wines also have good acidity. Reds are light in colour, fresh and fruity with lively acidity. Can be served chilled.

Muscadet

Grown in the Pays Nantais in the west of the region near the Atlantic seaboard. The best comes from the stony-clay soil around the two rivers Sèvre et Maine whose names will appear on the label.

163

Muscadet-sur-lie means that the wine has been left on its lees in the barrel or tank until the spring. This technique extracts more fruit and can impart a slight prickling quality on the tongue. Drink young.

Another wine grown in this region is Gros Plant which lacks the fruit of the Muscadet. Drink young.

Recommended Muscadet Producers   André-Michel Bergeon, Château de Chasseloir, Château du Cléray, Domaine des Dorices, Joseph Drouard, Domaine de la Févrie, Marquis de Goulaine, Château de la Mercredière, Louis Métaireau, Domaine de la Mortaine, Domaine des Mortiers-Gobin, Château La Noë, Domaine la Quila, Sauvion et Fils (les Découvertes).

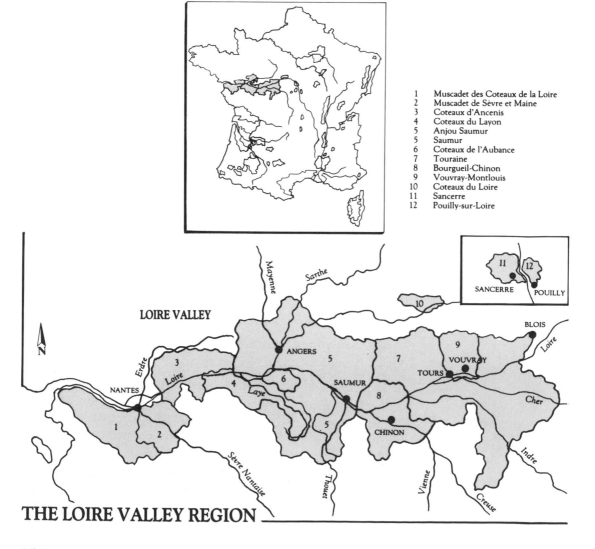

1	Muscadet des Coteaux de la Loire
2	Muscadet de Sèvre et Maine
3	Coteaux d'Ancenis
4	Coteaux du Layon
5	Anjou Saumur
5	Saumur
6	Coteaux de l'Aubance
7	Touraine
8	Bourgueil-Chinon
9	Vouvray-Montlouis
10	Coteaux du Loire
11	Sancerre
12	Pouilly-sur-Loire

THE LOIRE VALLEY REGION

Anjou/Saumur	Known for its rosés and off-dry and sweet white wines and sparkling wines. Some of its finest wines are dry Chenin Blancs from Savennières.
	The region's most important appellations are Anjou, Bonnezeaux, Coteaux du Layon, Quarts de Chaume and Savennières.
Grape Varieties	**White** Chenin Blanc, up to twenty percent Chardonnay, Sauvignon Blanc.
	Red Cabernets, Pineau d'Aunis, Gamay, Cot, Groslot.
	Recommended Anjou/Saumur Producers The following are recommended.
	Bonnezeaux: Domaine de la Croix de Mission, Château de Fesles.
	Coteaux d'Anjou: (rosé) Château de Tigné, Domaine des Maurières.
	Coteaux du Layon: Jacques Beaujeau, Philippe Delesvau, Château de Plaisance, Château de la Roulerie.
	Quarts de Chaume: Domaine des Baumard, Château de Belle Rive.
	Savennières: Coulée de Serrant (dry), Château de la Bizolière, Domaine du Closel, Château de Chamboureau, Château d'Epiré.
Vins du Haut-Poitou	The red, white, rosé and sparkling wines from this area can be very good value, especially the very dry Sauvignon Blanc and the rosé.
Sparkling Wine	Saumur produces some excellent champagne-method sparkling wines based on the Chenin Blanc grape with a maximum of twenty percent Chardonnay or Sauvignon Blanc.
	Recommended Producers Ackerman, Bouvet-Ladubay, Gratien et Meyer, Langlois.
Touraine	Sauvignon Blanc and Gamay provide easy-drinking light white and red wines from this region that are less costly than neighbouring Pouilly-Fumé and Sancerre and Beaujolais. The best reds in the Loire are grown from Cabernet Franc around the towns of Chinon and Bourgueil, but the major name in this region is Vouvray. The Chenin Blanc grape can be fermented dry, off-dry or sweet and sparkling.

Recommended Producers The following are recommended.

Bourgueil: Georges Audebert, Caslot-Galbrun, Pierre-Jacques Drouët, Gustav Goré, Marc Mureau, Domaine de Raguenières, Lamé-Delille-Bouchard.

Chinon: Gérard Chaveau, Pierre Jacques Druet, Charles Joguet, Couly-Dutheil, Gratien-Ferrand, Domaine du Roncée.

Vouvray: Jean Bertrand, Marc Brédif, Sylvain Gaudron, Gaston Huët, Prince Poniatowski.

Montlouis: Berger, Délétang, Moyer.

Pouilly-Fumé/ Sancerre	The finest expression of dry Sauvignon Blanc. Pouilly-Fumé is generally fatter and more concentrated in fruit than Sancerre. Slightly more spare in style are those Sauvignons from the villages of Ménétou-Salon, Quincy and Reuilly. Red and rosé wines are also made in Sancerre from Pinot Noir.

Recommended Pouilly-Fumé Producers Bailly Père et Fils, Domaine du Buisson-Menard, Domaine des Coques, Serge Dagueneau, Domaine Masson-Blondelet, Patrick de Ladoucette, Domaine Sarget.

Recommended Reuilly Producers Gérard Cordier, Didier Martin

Recommended Sancerre Producers Paul Cotat, Lucien Crochet, Vincent Delaporte, Gitton Père et Fils, Roger Neveu, Jean Reverdy, Jean-Max Roger, Jean Vacheron.

RHÔNE	From Vienne to Avignon, a distance of some 200 kilometres, the Rhône River provides a microclimate for wines of extraordinary quality in a hot growing region. The region is divided into the northern and southern ends.
Grape Varieties	Different grape varieties are used in the north than in the south.
North	**Red** Syrah. **White** Viognier, Roussanne, Marsanne.
South	**Red** Grenache, Syrah, Cinsault, Mourvèdre, Carignan. **White** Clairette, Roussanne, Marsanne, Grenache Blanc, Bourboulenc, Ugni Blanc.

Wine Style	Powerful, deep-coloured reds with high alcohol. Lots of spicy fruit. Whites are equally powerful and are dry with a tendency to be hot.
Northern Rhône	With its single red grape, Syrah, and three whites, Viognier, Roussanne and Marsanne, the Northern Rhône is relatively easy to understand.
Château Grillet	The second smallest appellation in France, Château Grillet produces a lovely peachy, honeysuckle and quince, dry white from the Viognier grape. Expensive. Can age, but best at four years old.

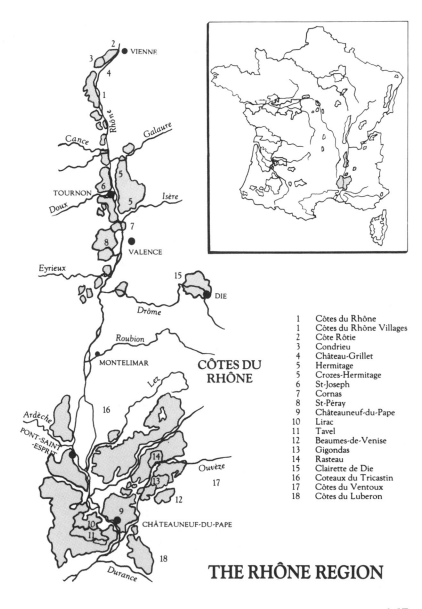

1   Côtes du Rhône
1   Côtes du Rhône Villages
2   Côte Rôtie
3   Condrieu
4   Château-Grillet
5   Hermitage
5   Crozes-Hermitage
6   St-Joseph
7   Cornas
8   St-Péray
9   Châteauneuf-du-Pape
10   Lirac
11   Tavel
12   Beaumes-de-Venise
13   Gigondas
14   Rasteau
15   Clairette de Die
16   Coteaux du Tricastin
17   Côtes du Ventoux
18   Côtes du Luberon

THE RHÔNE REGION

Condrieu	The Condrieu produces wines similar to Château Grillet. Worth looking for. Grape: Viognier.

Recommended Condrieu Producers André Dezormeaux, Pierre Dumazet, Paul Multier, Etienne Guigal, Georges Vernay. |
| *Cornas* | Deep-coloured, long-lived wines with concentrated blackberry flavours and lots of tannin. Grape: Syrah.

Recommended Producers Auguste Clape, Guy de Barjac, Marcel Juge, Robert Michel, Alain Voge, Noël Verset. |
| *Côte Rôtie* | Smoky, full-bodied, rich wine that ages beautifully. Grapes: Syrah and up to twenty percent Viognier.

Recommended Producers Pierre and Gilles Barge, Emile Champet, Dervieux-Thiaze, Gentaz-Dervieux, Etienne Guigal, Bernard Guy, Robert Jasmin, René Rostaing, Vidal-Fleury, Paul Jaboulet. |
| *Crozes-Hermitage* | Not as fine as Hermitage, less concentrated and elegant but good value, firm, big reds. Drink within five to eight years. Grape: Syrah.

Recommended Crozes-Hermitage Producers Caves des Clairmonts, Albert Desmeure, Emile Florentin, Alain Graillot, Paul Jaboulet, Tardy et Ange, Robert Michelas, GAEC de la Syrah, Bernard Gripa. |
| *Hermitage Red* | One of the finest red wines in the world. Full-bodied, tannic, rich fruit, long-lasting. Blackberry fruit with herbs and spices. Grape: Syrah.

Recommended Producers Max Chapoutier, Jean Louis Chave, Bernard Chave, Delas Frères, Etienne Guigal, Paul Jaboulet, Henri Sorrel. |
| *Hermitage White* | Bouquet of apricots, powerful, full-bodied, dry. Grapes: Marsanne and Roussanne.

Recommended Producers Chapoutier, Jaboulet, J.L. Chave, Jean-Louis Grippat. |
| *St. Joseph* | The Beaujolais of the Rhône, ready younger, fruitier than its neighbours. Grape: Syrah.

Recommended Producers Chave, Maurice Courbis, Pierre Coursodon, Pierre Gonon, Jean-Louis Grippat, Jean Marsanne, Paul Jaboulet. |

St-Péray	Solid rather cumbersome whites (still) and full-bodied sparklers with not much finesse. Grapes: Roussanne and Marsanne. **Recommended Producers** Jean-François Chaboud, Pierre Darona, Paul Etienne, René Milliand, Auguste Clape, Marcel Juge, Alain Voge, Delas.
Southern Rhône	The southern growing region of the Rhône offers a real fruit salad of grapes, particularly in Châteauneuf-du-Pape. Because of the high temperature here the wines have high alcohol.
Gigondas	Red and rosé wines. Their chunky, dense reds are much undervalued. Can be terrific. Grapes: Grenache Noir, Syrah, Mourvèdre, Cinsault. **Recommended Producers** Domaine Saint-Gayan, Les Pallières, Domaine Raspail, Domaine les Goubert, Domaine de Cayron (Michel Faraud), Clos des Cazeaux, Domaine de Longue-Toque, Domaine du Gour de Chaule, Domaine l'Ostau Fauquet.
Châteauneuf-du-Pape	Red and white wines. Massive, dense reds that can be long-lived. Grapes: Grenache, Syrah, Mourvèdre, Picpoul, Terret noir, Counoise, Muscardin, Vaccarèse, Picardin, Cinsault, Clairette, Roussanne, Bourboulenc. **Recommended Producers** Château Beaucastel, Vieux Télégraph, Château Fortia, Château Rayas, Château de la Nerthe, Clos des Papes, Château de Mont-Redon, Domaine du Vieux-Lazaret, Bosquet des Papes, Château des Fines Roches.
Lirac	Red, rosé and white wines made from the same grapes as Châteauneuf-du-Pape. Lighter reds than Gigondas and Châteauneuf and excellent dry rosés. **Recommended Producers** Château Saint-Roch, Château de Ségriès, Domaine La Fermade, Domaine du Devoy, Château de Clary.
Tavel	The finest rosés of France which should be consumed within a year of the vintage. Grapes: Grenache, Cinsault. **Recommended Producers** Château de Trinquevedel, Domaine de la Génestière, Château d'Aquéria, Domaine du Vieux Moulin, Domaine de la Forcadière, Domaine de la Mordorée.

Côtes du Rhône-Villages	Red, rosé and white wines made from the same grapes as Châteauneuf-du-Pape. Good rosés and good quality inexpensive reds. Of the seventeen named villages the best are Vacqueyras, Rasteau, Cairanne, Sablet and Beaumes-de-Venise (for sweet white).

Recommended Producers The following Côte du Rhône-Villages producers are recommended.

Beaumes de Venise: Domaine Durban, Jaboulet, Domaine de Coyeux, Château Redortier, Château des Applanats, Caves Co-operative.

Vacqueyras: Domaine des Lambertins, Clos des Cazaux, Château des Roques, Domaine La Fourmone (Roger Combe), Le sang des Cailloux, Jaboulet.

Rasteau: Domaine de la Grangeneuve, Maurice Charavin, Domaine La Soumade, Domaine des Girasols, Caves des Vignerons.

Cairanne: Domaine Rabasse-Charavin, Domaine du Banvin, Domaine Brusset, Domaine Richaud, Domaine de l'Oratoire Saint-Martin.

Sablet: Château du Trignon, Domaine de Verquière, Paul Roumanille, René Bernard, Domaine du Parandou.

Other Recommended Producers *Laudun* — Domaines Pelaquié; *Saint-Gervais* — Domaine Ste-Anne; *Séguret* — Domaine de Cabasse, Domaine des Grands Devers; *Vinsobres* — Domaine les Aussellons; *Visan* — Domaine de la Cantharide, Clos du Père Clément.

Recommended Producers For other appellations:

Coteaux de Baronnies: Domaine de la Rosière

Côtes du Lubéron: Château de Mille, Val Joanis

Lesser Known Rhône Wines	The Côtes du Vivarais, Coteaux du Tricastin and Côtes du Ventoux are up-and-coming areas for fast-maturing red wines.

Recommended Producers The following are recommended.

Vivarais: Domaine de Belvezet, Domaine Gallety, Domaine de Viguier, Vignerons de St-Montant.

Tricastin: Domaine de la Tour d'Elyssas, Château des Estubiers, La Suzienne, Domaine du Vieux Micocoulier, Domaine de Grange Neuve.

Ventoux: Domaine des Anges, La Vieille Ferme, Domaine Vieux Lazaret.

SOUTHWEST FRANCE

Most wine lovers will be able to tell you the major French regions (Bordeaux, Burgundy, Loire, etc.) but wines of high quality and good value can be found in the lesser known regions of Bergerac, Cahors, Gaillac, Monbazillac and Pécharmant.

Bergerac

Bergerac uses the same grape types as Bordeaux. The reds are lighter than Bordeaux and not as long lasting. The whites are fresh and lively and should be consumed young.

Recommended Producers Château de Belingrad, Château Court-les-Mûtes, Château de la Jaubertie (highly recommeded), Château Michel de Montague, Château les Plaquettes.

THE SOUTHWEST, SOUTH AND EASTERN REGIONS

Cahors	This region is famous for its "black" wines of old. Density and power are the keynotes of red wines from some of France's oldest vineyards. Grapes: seventy percent Malbec (locally called Cot), twenty percent Merlot and Tannat, ten percent Jurançon Noir. Age the better wines up to ten years.
	Recommended Producers Château du Cayrou, Château de Chambert, Château de Haut-Serre, Château St-Didier Parnac, Clos de Triguedina.
Côtes de Buzet	The same style of red and white wine as made in Bordeaux. The use of carbonic maceration for reds makes them light and early-drinking wines.
	Recommended Producers Château de Padère, Vignerons Réunis des Côtes-de-Buzet.
Côtes de Duras	Similar in style to Côtes de Buzet. Produces good white wines.
	Recommended Producers Berticot, Domaine de Durand, Domaine de Ferrant, Domaine Las-Brugues Mau-Michau.
Côtes du Frontonnais	Reds and rosés from Negrette, Cabernets, Malbec, Cinsault, Syrah, Mauzac and Gamay. Drink young.
	Recommended Producers Domaine de Baudare, Château Bellevue La Forêt, Domaine de la Colombière, Château Cransac, Château Montauriol, Château Flotis.
Gaillac	Fruity, aromatic reds and dry and sweet whites. Reds are made from a fruit salad of grapes: Fer, Negrette, Duras, Gamay, Syrah, Cabernets and Merlot. Whites are made from Len de L'El, Mauzac, Mauzac rosé, Muscadelle, Ondenc, Sauvignon and Sémillon.
	Recommended Producers La Croix Saint-Salvy, Domaine Jean Cros, Mas d'Aurel, Domaine de Labarthe, Domaine de Roucou Cantemerle.
Irouléguy	Hard by the Spanish border. Full-bodied, peppery acidic reds and ho-hum rosés. Grapes for reds: Tannat, Cabernet Franc, Cabernet Sauvignon. Grapes for whites: Petit Marseng, Gros Marseng, Corbu.
	Recommended Producer Cave Co-op St. Etienne-de-Baïgorry.
Madiran	Similar to Cahors for reds. Can be consumed young and can age up to ten years.

	Recommended Producers Château d'Aÿdie-Laplace, Domaine Boucassé, Château Montus, Plaimont Co-operative.
	Interesting aromatic whites from this region are called Pacherenc du Vic-Bilh and are made from Sauvignon, Sémillon and the local Arrufiat, Marseng and Corbu.
	Recommended Producers Domaine Bouscasse, Château d'Aÿdie, Domaine de Teston, Vignerons Reunis du Vic-Bilh.
Tursan	Madiran style. Grapes for reds: Tannat, Cabernet Franc, Cabernet Sauvignon. Grapes for whites: Barroque plus ten percent Sauvignon, Marseng, Clairette, etc.
	Recommended Producer Château de Bachen.
Monbazillac	This region produces a cheaper version of Sauternes made from the same grapes, Sémillon and Sauvignon Blanc. Medium-dry and sweet white wines. Will age eight to ten years.
	Recommended Producers Château le Fagé, Château Treuil-de-Nailhac.
Jurançon	Rich, spicy, honeyed wines made from the local Petit Marseng, Gros Marseng and Corbu grapes.
	Recommended Producers Clos Cancaillau, Domaine de Bellegarde, Domaine Bru-Baché, Domaine Cauhape, Cru Lamouroux, Clos Uroulat.
Pécharmant	Bordeaux-style reds that have a tendency towards fruitiness. Best consumed between three and six years old.
	Recommended Producers Château Champerel, Domaine du Haut Pécharmant, de Tiregand.

---

*The Naturally Sweet
Wines of the South*

The French call them Vins Doux Naturels which is something of a misnomer since they are fortified with grape spirit to stop the fermentation and leave residual sugar in the wine. Because they are fortified they do not improve in the bottle and should be consumed young and well chilled. These wines can either be white or red depending on the grape used.
Whites: *Muscat, Malvoisie, Maccabeo.*
Reds: *Grenache (with the white grapes).*

The taste is sweet and grapey with a minimum alcoholic strength of fifteen percent (usually around eighteen percent). They are produced in the following appellations: red — Banyuls, Maury and Rasteau; white — Muscat Beaumes-de-Venise, Muscat de Frontignan and Rivesaltes (red, white and rosé).

| PROVENCE | The amount of sunshine in the south of France makes for powerful wines. Once the source of rough, cheap wine, new vineyard techniques and better winemaking skills are producing some excellent reds, whites and rosés that are still inexpensive. |

Bandol: full-bodied, tannic reds that can age ten years. Recommended Producers are Domaine de Frégat, Domaine le Gallatin, Domaine de l'Hermitage, La Laidière, Moulin des Costes, Château Pradeaux, Château Romasson, Domaine Tempier.

Bellet: recommended producers are Château de Bellet, Château de Crémat.

Cassis: recommended producers are Clos Boubard, Château de la Ferme Blanche, Château de Fontblanche, Clos Ste-Magdeleine.

Coteaux d'Aix-en-Provence: recommended producers are Château de Beaulieu, Château de Calissanne, Château La Coste, Château de Fonscolmbe, Domaine de la Grande Seouve, Mas de la Dame, Château Vignelaure (highly recommended).

Coteaux des Baux-en-Provence: recommended producers are Mas de Cellier, Mas de Gogonnier, les Terres Blanches, Domaine Trévallon.

Côtes de Provence: recommended producers are Domaine des Aspras, Château Barbeyrolles, Domaine de la Bernarde, Domaine Gavoty, Domaine de l'Ile de Porquerolles, Domaine Ott, Commanderie de Peyrassol, Château St. Pierre, Domaine Richeaume, St-André de Figuière, Château Ste-Roseline.

Palette: recommended producer is Château Simone (highly recommended).

| LANGUEDOC-ROUSSILLON | Known collectively as The Midi, these two provinces arc around the Mediterranean from the mouth of the Rhône to the Spanish border. The vineyards were established by the Greeks eight centuries BC. Quality varies greatly, depending on the altitude of the vineyard, the soil and proximity to the sea. |

| **Grape Varieties** | **Red** Carignan, Cinsault, Grenache, Mourvèdre, Syrah. |
| | **White** Carignan, Grenache Blanc, Picpoul, Bourboulenc, Clairette. |

Vin jaune: *This wine is indigenous to the Jura and Arbois regions where the Savignin grape is late-picked and fermented like fino sherry (which it resembles in flavour). Jaune refers to the yellow colour it acquires through ageing.*

Vin de paille: A rare dessert wine produced from grapes that have been left to dry on straw mats following the harvest. After three months the dehydration process concentrates the sugars and acids (rather like the effect of Botrytis cinerea). The liqueur-like wine produced from these grapes will have spent some three to four years in oak. Both wines will last for many years.

Highly Recommended Blanquette de Limoux, the region's sparkling wine produced from Mauzac (locally called Blanquette), Chardonnay and Chenin Blanc by the champagne method.

Costières du Gard: recommended producers are Domaine de l'Amarine, Château Belle-Coste, Château de Campuget, Domaine St-Louis-La Perdrix.

Hérault: recommended producer is Mas de Daumas Gassac (expensive but great).

Faugères: Gilbert Alquier, Domaine du Fraisse, Château de Grezan, Château Haut-Fabreges.

Fitou: Paul Colomer, Caves des Producteurs de Fitou, Caves du Mont-Tauch.

Minervois: Co-operative du Haut-Minervois, Château de Gourgazaud, Domaine des Homs, Domaine de Mayranne, Domaine Ste-Eulalie, Château Villerambert-Julien.

St-Chinian: Domaine des Calmette, Château Cazals-Viel, Château de Coujan, Domaine de Jougla.

Collioure: Château des Abelles, Domaine de la Rectorie.

Corbières: Château de la Baronne, Château L'Etang des Colombes, Château Lastours, Domaine de Mandourelle, Château de Queribus, Domaine de Villemajou, Domaine de la Voulte-Gasparets.

Côtes du Roussillon: Calvet-Marty, Cazes Frères, Jaubert-Noury, Château de Jau, Domaine de Rombeau, Domaine St-Luc, Domaine Sarda-Malet, Viticulteurs Catalans.

CORSICA

This mountainous island has some 28,000 hectares under vine, more than in all of Canada. The simple wines are produced from such local varieties as Niellucio and Sciaccarello. Reds are in the style of the southern Rhône and the whites (made from Vermentino and Ugni Blanc) are fruity and short lived.

Recommended Producers Clos Capitoro, Comte Peraldi, Domaine de Torraccia, Clos Valle-Vecchia.

JURA

This mountainous region with cold winters and unpredictable summers produces two indigenous oddities, *vin jaune* and *vin de paille*.

Wine Style	Full-bodied dry whites and early-drinking, deep-coloured reds.
Grape Varieties	**Red/Rosé** Trousseau, Poulsard and Pinot Noir. **White** Savagnin (*vin jaune*), Chardonnay and Pinot Blanc. The four appellations of the region are Arbois, Château-Châlon, Côtes du Jura and L'Étoile. *Arbois*: recommended producers are Fruitière Vinicole d'Arbois, Lucien Aviet, Jacques Forêt, Rolet Père et Fils, Henri MaireAndré et Mireille Tissot. *Château-Châlon*: This region's wines are expensive and difficult to obtain. Recommended producers are Château-Châlon, Jean-Marie Courbet, Jean Macle, Marius Perron. *Côte de Jura*: recommended producers are Chartreux de Vaucluse, Jean Bourdy, Gabriel Clerc, Château Gréa, Caveau des Jacobins. *L'Étoile*: recommended producers are Château l'Étoile, Domaine de Montbourgeau.
SAVOIE	The Alpine slopes provide a variety of microclimates for the region which produces very dry, lean wines for early consumption preferably in the region. One of the glories of Savoie is its sparkling wine from Seyssel. Other appellations are Crépy, Roussette de Savoie and Vin de Savoie.
Wine Style	Reds are similar to a light Beaujolais; whites are tart and fresh.
Grape Varieties	**White** Roussette, Jacquière, Altesse, Roussanne, Chasselas. **Red** Gamay, Mondeuse. **Recommended Producers** Caves Cooperative des Vins Fins Cruet, Claude Delalex, La Plantée, Château Monterminod, GAEC Les Perrières, Coteau de Tormery.
Sparkling Wine	**Recommended Producers** Clos de la Peclette, Royal-Seyssel, Varichon-et-Clerc.

Italy

WINE REGIONS OF ITALY

Labels on map: Valle d'Aosta, Trentino-Alto Adige, Lombardy, MILAN, Friuli-Venezia-Giulia, Piedmont, Veneto, Liguria, Emilia-Romagna, FLORENCE, Marches, Tuscany, Umbria, ROME, Abruzzi, Latium, Molise, Sardinia, Puglia, NAPLES, Campania, Basilicata, PALERMO, Sicily, Calabria, N

*I*taly is one vast vineyard. Wines are grown the length and breadth of the country. No other wine-growing nation produces as much wine, as many different wines and as many unique wines as do the Italians. Both reds and whites have a flavour all their own (except for the plethora of Chardonnays and Cabernets which have been planted lately to take advantage of the worldwide demand for these varietals).

Italian wine laws don't help the consumer. Some of the very best Italian wines and many of the very worst are labelled *Vino da Tavola* (Table Wine). This anomaly came about because of the frustration of producers who were locked into using traditional

grape varieties under the governing regulations, or who introduced new varieties into their vineyards which were not recognized by the authorities, or aged their wines in small French barrels as opposed to the traditional large vats or stainless steel containers.

Denominazione di Origine Controllata e Garantita (DOCG) The highest category for Italy's most prestigious wines, currently accorded to the red Barolo, Barbaresco, Chianti, Brunello di Montalcino, Vino Nobile di Montepulciano and the white Albano di Romagna. The wines have to be tasted by a special panel. Waiting in the wings to be elevated to DOCG with the attendant price rise are another three reds — Carmignano, Torgiano Rosso Riserva and Gattinara.

Denominazione di Origine Controllata (DOC) Similar to the French AOC laws governing grape variety, yield, minimum alcohol, acidity and extract, tipicity of taste and minimum ageing. Currently there are some 250 DOCs.

Vino da Tavola This can be a simple table wine of varying quality or it can be the most expensive Italian wine you'll ever purchase. In Tuscany and Piedmont many producers prefer to use non-traditional grapes to enhance their wines or to bottle them as varietals.

Vino Tipico The Italian equivalent of *vin de pays*. This category has not been fully defined yet nor the name formally adopted.

READING THE LABEL

The Italians have many words to describe wineries and estates. You will see the following descriptions on wine labels: *Castello* (castle); *Villa* (manor); *Azienda Agraria, Azienda Agricola, Tentimento, Podere, Fattoria, Tenuta* (all meaning farm or agricultural holding); *Cantina(e)* (winery or cellars); *Stabilimento* (company).

Wine Language

Abboccato — semi-sweet

All'annata — of the year

Amabile — sweeter than Abboccato

Amaro — bitter

Annata — year

Asciutto — dry

Azienda Agricola — wine estate

Bianco — white

Bottiglia — bottle

Cantina Sociale — co-operative

Chiaretto — rosé

Consorzio — a consortium of winemakers who band together to protect the integrity of their wine by setting production standards (e.g., Chianti Classico Gallo Nero)

Classico — the classical heart of the region

Dolce — sweet

Enoteca — wine library

Etichetta — label

Fiasco — straw-covered bottles

Frizzante — lightly sparkling

Governo — dried grapes or must added to Chianti to produce a secondary fermentation to enrich and freshen the wine

Liquoroso — very sweet dessert wine

Nero — black

Passito — wine made from grapes left to dry for many weeks

Produttore — producer

Riserva — long ageing in oak and bottle. Varies according to region. Chianti, Vino Nobile — 3 years; Barbaresco — 4; Brunello, Barolo — 5. Riserva Speciale is longer.

Rosato — rosé

Rosso — red

Secco — dry

Spumante — sparkling

Stravecchio — very old

Superiore — the wine has met higher production and ageing standards and will be higher in alcohol strength

Vecchio — old

Vendemmia — vintage

Vigna, Vignetta — single vineyard

Vino da Tavola — table wine

Vino Locale, del Paese — local wine

Vino Novello — Italian equivalent of Beaujolais Nouveau

V.Q.P.R.D (Vin de qualité produit en régions déterminées) — quality wine produced in specific region, a Common Market category

---

PIEDMONT

Arguably, the best red wines of Italy come from Piedmont. Certainly the longest-living wines are grown on slopes that are shrouded in morning fog. The Italian name for fog is *nebbia*, which has given its name to the grape variety grown here, Nebbiolo.

Grape Varieties

Red Nebbiolo, Barbera, Dolcetto.

White Muscat, Arneis, Cortese di Gavi, Erbaluce di Caluso.

The Nebbiolo grape is king in Piedmont, producing red wines of austere majesty that take years to soften up. The location of the vineyard in the region will determine the name of the wine. The best come from Barolo and Barbaresco. Gattinara, Ghemme, Spanna (a synonym of Nebbiolo) and Nebbiolo d'Alba or Nebbiolo delle Langhe are less concentrated. Other Nebbiolo wines from Piedmont are Boca, Lessona, Sizzano, Carema and Fara. (In neighbouring Valle d'Aosta to the north, Nebbiolo is used in the wines of Donnaz.)

Recommended Red Wines

Piedmont's great red wines are based on a single grape type and the noblest of them all is Nebbiolo.

Barolo

Taste Profile   Earthy, full-bodied and powerful with a nose and flavour of truffles, leather, black cherries and herbs. Bitter, tannic finish. Can be cellared up to fifteen years.

Recommended Producers   Elio Altare, Ceretto, Clerico, Aldo Conterno, Giacomo Conterno, Fontanafredda (single vineyards), Bruno Giacosa, Giuseppe Macarello, Prunotto, Renato Ratti, Vietti. From 1993 Angelo Gaja.

Barbaresco

Taste Profile   Not quite as big as Barolo, with more evident plummy fruit. Cedar and chocolate tones. Matures faster than Barolo.

Recommended Producers   Angelo Gaja, Castello di Neive, Ceretto, Bruno Giacosa, Marchesi di Gresy, Produttori di Barbaresco, Pio Cesare, Prunotto, Secondo Pasquero-Elia, Vietti.

Barbera

Light, acidic red that requires ageing to soften up. Drink at four to five years old. New experiments in oak are producing better wines.

Recommended Producers   Altare, Giacomo Bologna, Damonte, Bruno Giacosa, Giuseppe Macarello, Scarpa, Vietti.

Dolcetto

Deep coloured, spicy, dry cherry-like flavour, low acidity. Drink young.

Recommended Producers   Castello di Neive, Chionetti, Giacomo Conterno, Mascarello, Ratti, Valentino, Vietti.

Recommended White Wines	Unlike the long-lasting reds of Piedmont, the whites should be enjoyed young and fresh.
Arneis	Rich, pear-like nose, dry fruity flavour and very soft on the palate with lingering notes of spice and nuts. An intriguing wine. Age two to three years.
Gavi	(Cortese di Gavi) Crisp, lemony, stony flavour. Good Chardonnay substitute. Age two to four years.
Erbaluce di Caluso	A zesty, acidic wine with a bitter, herby taste. Age one to two years.
Moscato d'Alba	The still white made from Muscat grapes. Fresh and grapey, slightly sweet. Drink young.

TUSCANY	Tuscany is home to three of Italy's greatest red wines, Chianti, Brunello di Montalcino and Vino Nobile di Montepulciano. They are all based on clones of the Sangiovese grape. The original recipe for Chianti called for Sangiovese and Canaiolo with small amounts of Trebbiano and Malvasia. The addition of white wine to red not only lightened the colour but made it susceptible to oxidation. When certain producers stopped using white grapes in their Chianti and included Cabernet Sauvignon instead, new wines were born outside the DOC laws, such as Tignanello. Other producers went the whole hog and made 100% Cabernets, such as Sassicaia.
Grape Varieties	**Red** Sangiovese, Canaiolo, Cabernet Sauvignon.
	White Trebianno, Malvasia, Grechetto, Vernaccia, Chardonnay, Sauvignon Blanc.
Tuscan Reds	The reds of Tuscany are based on the Sangiovese grape blended with another red variety, Canaiolo, and a token amount of Trebbiano and Malvasia.
Chianti	Chianti can be a hit or miss proposition depending upon the producer. A good Chianti should have evident red berry fruit with a fine spine of acidity, slightly bitter on the finish with a tannic bite. Too often they are sour and weak-kneed.
	The Chianti region is divided into two: Chianti Classico (the area between Florence and Siena) and the six smaller

satellite regions. Wines are bottled under the Black Rooster symbol of the Consortium in the Chianti Classico region.

There are six satellite regions in the hills around the classical zone: Rufina, Colli Fiorentini, Colli Senesi, Montalbano, Colli Arentini and Colline Pisane. (Apart from Rufina which can live for many years, the other Chiantis will not last as long as those from the Classico zone.) These wines are bottled under the Cherub symbol of the Consortium.

Recommended Producers   Antinori, Badia a Coltibuono, Castella di Ama, Castellare, Castello di Volpaia, Fattoria Selvapiana, Felsina Berardenga, Fontodi, Il Palazzino, Isole e Olena, Monsanto, Montesodi, Monte Vertine, Nipozzano, Pagliarese, Peppoli, Riecine, Ruffino, Savignola Paolina.

Age three to twelve years.

Brunello di Montalcino	Grape variety: Sangiovese Grasso. Longer lived than Chianti, very expensive. Rich and powerful flavours of blackberries, smoke and spices. A less expensive and faster maturing version is Rosso di Montalcino.	

Recommended Producers Altesino, Biondi-Santi, Caparzo, Case Basse, Col d'Orcia, Lisini, Il Poggione, Pertimali, San Felice, Talenti, Villa Banfi, Val di Suga.

Vino Nobile di Montepulciano

Similar to Chianti but unwarrantedly more expensive.

Recommended Producers Avignonesi, Boscarelli, De Ferrari-Corradi, Fanetti, Fattoria di Gracciano, Fognano, Montenero, Poliziano, Vecchia Cantina.

Carmignano

A Chianti which has ten to fifteen percent Cabernet Sauvignon in the blend. The resulting wine is well-structured with a hint of black currant in the taste.

Recommended Producers Ambra, Artimino, Bacchereto, Cappezzana, Il Poggiolo, Trefiano.

Tuscan Vini da Tavola — A Grape Profile

Some of the most expensive Tuscan wines are those that have defied the DOC laws and must bear the *Vino da Tavola* appellation. Since they are labelled under proprietary names it is not easy to find out what grapes are used. Here is a guide to the top wines.

WINE	PRODUCER	GRAPE
Alte d'Altesi	Altesino	Sangiovese/ Cabernet
Ania	Gabbiano	Cabernet Sauvignon
Balifico	Castello di Volpaia	Sangiovese/ Cabernet
Barco Reale	Cappezzana	Cabernet Sauvignon
Brunesco di San Lorenzo	Montagliari	Sangiovese
Bruno di Rocca	Vecchie Terre Montefili	Sangiovese/ Cabernet
Brusco di Barbi	Barbi	Sangiovese
Ca' del Pazzo	Caparzo	(50/50) Sangiovese/ Cabernet
Capannelle Rosso	Capannelle	Sangiovese
Cetinaia	San Polo in Rosso	Sangiovese

Vin Santo

In Tuscany and Umbria farmers will harvest their Malvasia, Grechetto and Trebbiano grapes and then leave them to dry on mats or in trays for three months before pressing and fermenting over the winter. The wine is racked off its lees at Easter (hence the name "holy wine"), then sealed in barrels and left to age under the roof for three to six years. The producer never knows quite what he will get when he opens the barrel. The best Vin Santo such as those produced by Avignonesi and Isole e Olena are like nectar. Also recommended are Antinori, Badia a Coltibuono, Tenuta di Capezana, Castellare, Felsina, Frescobaldi, Monte Vertine, Tenuta Il Poggione and Castello di Volpaia.

WINE	PRODUCER	GRAPE
Coltassala	Castello di Volpaia	Sangiovese
Concerto	Fonterutoli	Sangiovese
Elegia	Poliziano	Sangiovese
Flaccianello della Piave	Fontodi	Sangiovese
Fontalloro	Felsina	Sangiovese
Ghiaie della Furba	Cappezzana	Cabernet Sauvignon
Grifi	Avignonesi	Sangiovese/ Cabernet Franc
Grosso Senese	Il Palazzino	Sangiovese
Il Querciolaia	Castello di Quercato	Sangiovese/ Cabernet Sauvignon
Il Sodaccio	Monte Vertine	Sangiovese/ Canaiolo
La Corte	Castello di Quercato	Sangiovese
I Sodi di San Niccolo	Castellare	Sangiovese/ Malvasia Nera
Monte Atico	Monte Atico	Sangiovese
Mormoreto	Frescobaldi	Cabernet Sauvignon
Ornellaia	L. Antinori	Cabernet Sauvignon/ Merlot
Palazzo Altesi	Altesino	Sangiovese
Percarlo	San Giusto	Sangiovese
le Pergole Torte	Monte Vertine	Sangiovese
Quercigrande	Podere Capaccia	Sangiovese
Ripa della Morro	Castello Vicchiomaggio	Sangiovese
Sammarco	Castello di Rampolla	Cabernet Sauvignon/ Sangiovese
Sangioveto	Badia a Coltibuono	Sangiovese
Sangioveto Grosso	Monsanto	Sangiovese
Sassicaia	Incisa della Rocchetta	Cabernet Sauvignon/ Cabernet Franc
Ser Gioveto	Rocca delle Macie	Sangiovese

184

WINE	PRODUCER	GRAPE
Solaia	Antinori	Cabernet Sauvignon
Solatio Basilica	Villa Cafaggio	Sangiovese
Tavernelle	Villa Banfi	Cabernet Sauvignon
Tignanello	Antinori	Sangiovese/ Cabernet Sauvignon
Vigneti di Geografico	Chianti Georgrafico	Cabernet Sauvignon/ Sangiovese
Vigorello	San Felice	Sangiovese
Vinattieri Rosso	Maurizio Castelli	Sangiovese

In order to make some sense of Italian wine law, Tuscan producers have come up with new appellations for their fine wines made outside the DOC regulations. You may see the following descriptions on *vino da tavola* wines which will alert you that they are not simple plonk — even if the price has not already informed you!

Reds

Predicato di Cardisco: The wine contains at least ninety percent Sangiovese with red grapes other than Cabernet or Merlot.

Predicato di Biturica: The wine contains a minimum of thirty percent Cabernet with Sangiovese and up to ten percent other red varieties.

Whites

Predicato del Muschio: Chardonnay-based wines containing at least eighty percent of the named varietal.

Predicato del Selvante: Sauvignon Blanc-based wines containing at least eighty percent of the named varietal.

Tuscan Whites

Vernaccia di San Giminiano is the only dry white of quality in the region. Vernaccia is the name of the grape variety. Michelangelo described it as a wine that "kisses, licks, bites, tingles and stings." What more can I say?

Recommended Producers Riccardo Falchini, Fugnano, Guicciardini-Strozzi, di Panchole, Pietrafitta, Pietraserena, Teruzzi & Pothod, Vagnoni, Vigna a Solatio.

Galestro	Made from the Trebbiano and Malvasia that used to go into Chianti before the producers banished them from the recipe. Fresh, dry and light, it's a pleasant fruity wine to drink young.
	Recommended Producers Antinori, Frescobaldi, Ruffino, Frattoria Fonti, Rocca del Macie, Barone Ricasoli.
	Other Recommended Whites Frescobaldi Pomino, Avignonesi Malvasia.
VENETO	The home of three of Italy's best-known wines — Soave, Valpolicella and Bardolino — Veneto is one of the largest wine-producing regions in Italy.
Grape Varieties	**Red** Corvina, Rondinella, Molinara, some Negrara, Sangiovese and Barbera.
	White Garganega, Trebbiano, Grechetto.
Wine Styles	Light reds and heavy, full-bodied reds (Recioto della Valpolicella, Amarone); crisp medium-bodied whites and sweet whites (Recioto di Soave).
Veneto Red Wines *Bardolino*	A light, dry red wine with a hint of bitterness on the finish. Also in rosé style as Chiaretto. Grapes: Corvina, Molinara, Rondinella and Negrara.
	Recommended Producers Bertani, Bolla, Boscaini, Ca' Furia, Cavalcina, Girasole, Guerrieri-Rizzardi, Il Colle, Masi, Montecorno, Santa Sofia, Scamperle, Tedeschi, Tommasi, Zenato.
Valpolicella	This wine is made from the same grapes as Bardolino. It has a ruby, cherry and banana nose, a fresh, dry, fruit flavour and a bitter finish.

The Recioto Phenomenon

Simple Valpolicella is a light, fresh wine somewhat similar to Beaujolais. But if only the ripest grape clusters are selected (what the Venetians call the recie, or ears of the bunches), the resulting wine will be richer in extract and alcohol. If these grapes are left to dry until the end of January, their sugars are further concentrated. The wines will be of high alcohol especially if all the sugar is fermented out. This dry version is called Amarone, from the Italian amaro meaning bitter, and it can reach 16.5% degrees of alcohol. If the sugar is not fully fermented out the sweet wine will be called Recioto della Valpolicella and will reach 13 degrees.

The same procedure is used for the production of sweet Recioto di Soave and Recioto di Gambellara.

Recommended Producers Alighieri, Allegrini, Anselmi, Bertani, Bolla, Boscaini, Girasole, Guerrieri-Rizzardi, Le Ragose, Masi, Scamperle, Speri, Tedeschi, Zenato.

Some producers enrich their Valpolicella by pouring the newly fermented wine onto the lees of their Amarone or Recioto grapes. The result is a fruitier wine with greater body.

Recommended Producers Bolla (Jago), Masi (Campofiorin), Quintarelli, Le Ragose (Le Sassine), Santi (Castello d'Illasi), Tedeschi (Capitel San Rocco).

Recioto della Valpolicella, Amarone Serègo Alighieri, Allegrini, Masi (highly recommended), Quintarelli (highly recommended), Le Ragose, Tedeschi (highly recommended), Venturini.

Worth Looking For Cabernet Sauvignon produced by Bortoluzzi e Pajer, Maculan, Venegazzu and Villa Sceriman.

Bianco di Custoza

Simple, light, aromatic wine. Grapes: Garganega, Trebbiano, Tocai, Cortese.

Recommended Producers Arvedi d'Emilei, Cantine Sociale di Custoza, Gorgo, Le Tende, Menegotti, Piona, Scamperle, Tebaldi.

Sparkling Wines

Veneto produces sparkling versions of Soave and Valpolicella in both dry and Recioto versions. The best sparkler is, however, Prosecco made from the grape of the same name. It may also be labelled Cartizze after the Classico zone of production.

Recommended Prosecco Producers Canevel, Cantina Colli de Soligo, Carpenè Malvolti, Nino Franco (highly recommended), Torre Collalto, Pino Zardetto.

Veneto White Wines
Soave

A pale, delicate wine, dry with a herbal flavour and a bitter almond finish. Drink young. Grapes: 80 percent Garganega, 20 percent Trebbiano.

Recommended Producers Aldegheri, Anselmi, Bolla, Boscaini, Guerrieri-Rizzardi, Masi, Pegaso, Pieropan, Scamperle, Tedeschi, Tommasi, Villa Girardi, Zenato.

Recioto di Soave Aldegheri, Anselmi (highly recommended), Pieropan, Tedeschi, Zenato.

Gambellara

Similar to Soave. Tends to be softer, more aromatic and less delicate.

Recommended Producers Cantine Sociale di Gambellara, Cavazza, Menti, Zonin.

TRENTINO-ALTO ADIGE

Italy's most northerly wine region produces some of the most elegant whites in a tradition that owes much to its Austrian neighbour. Many of the wines will look Germanic from their labels, but their style is very Italian.

Grape Varieties

Red Schiava, Lago di Caldaro, St. Magdalener, Blauburgunder (Pinot Noir), Cabernet Sauvignon, Lagrein Dunkel, Lagrein Kretzer, Merlot (Trento), Teroldego.

White Silvaner, Gewürztraminer, Pinot Bianco, Pinot Grigio, Riesling, Terlano, Grauernatsch.

Wine Styles

This region produces light, chillable reds that are not for ageing and aromatic, elegant whites.

Trentino Recommended Producers Barone de Cles, Cavit, Conti Martini, Dolzan, Donati, Foradori, Gaierhof, C.P. Mezzacorona, C.S. Mezzolombardo, Moser, Pojer e Sandri (highly recommended), Simoncelli, Zeni.

Alto Adige Recommended Producers (red wines): Bellendorf (highly recommended), Brigl, Hofstätter (highly recommended), Hirschprunn, Kettmeir, Kuenburg, Lageder, Neidermeir, Rottensteiner (Hans and Heinrich), Schloss Schwanburg, Tiefenbrunner (highly recommended), Walch.

FRIULI-VENEZIA-GIULIA

This hilly region divided into three zones — Collio, Colli Orientali and Grave del Friuli — borders on Yugoslavia. Some of the finest Italian whites are produced here.

Grape Varieties

Red Cabernet Franc, Merlot, Pinot Nero, Refosco.

White Picolit, Ribolla Gialla, Malvasia, Tocai, Pinot Bianco, Pinot Grigio, Riesling Italico, Sauvignon, Chardonnay, Tocai, Verduzzo.

Wine Styles

Whites Dry with good acidity. Drink young.

Reds Deep coloured, very dry. Drink within five years.

Recommended Producers Abbazia di Rosazzo, Angoris, Collavini, Livio Felluga, Marco Felluga, Gradnick, Gravner, Jermann (highly recommended), Pighin, Plozner, Russiz Superiore, Schiopetto (highly recommended), La Viarte, Volpe Pasini (highly recommended).

Picolit	This rare dessert wine from Friuli is named after the grape. Difficult to find and expensive, Picolit does not share the unctuousness of a Sauternes although it can reach fifteen percent alcohol. The taste is delicate and medium-sweet with hints of almond. A less expensive substitute is sweet Verduzzo or Ramandolo. The top producers of both wines are Abbazia di Rosazzo, Giovanni Dri, Pighin, Graziano Specogna and Volpe Pasini.

LIGURIA

This narrow crescent of coast immediately south of Piedmont is known as the Italian Riviera since it begins at Monte Carlo. There is nothing special about Ligurian wines which are best consumed in the local cafés and restaurants. Two worth looking for are Rosso di Dolceaqua and Cinqueterre.

Rosso di Dolceaqua

A light, dry red with a wild strawberry taste and a bitter finish. Grapes: Rossese plus Dolcetto, Massarda, the white Vermentino.

Recommended Producers Anfosso, Croesi, Tenuta Giuncheo.

Cinqueterre

A dry and a semi-sweet version is made. Deep golden in colour, very aromatic. Grapes: Bosco, Vermentino, Vernaccia.

Recommended Producers Calleri, Crespi, Vairo.

Vermentino

A light, dry and crisp wine that goes best with seafood.

Recommended Producers La Colombiera, Musetti, Tognoni.

LOMBARDY

Lombardy, home of Gorgonzola cheese, produces a range of red wines from the Nebbiolo grape, locally known as the Chiavennasca. They are not as fine as Barolo or Barbaresco from Piedmont, but the Valtellina Superiore wines (ninety-five percent Chiavennesca from the higher slopes) can be worthy substitutes. Wines from the valley floor are simply called Valtellina (Chiavennasca plus thirty percent Pinot Nero, Brugnola, Merlot, Pignola or Rossola.)

Subzones of the wine will also be labelled Valgella, Fracia, Inferno, Grumello and Sassella (in order of ageing potential).

Red

Taste Profile Bright garnet colour, earthy-violet bouquet, very dry with a bitter finish. Age *riservas* five to ten years.

Recommended Producers Bettini, Enologica Valtellinese, Negri, Nera, Rainoldi, San Carlo, Tona, Fratelli Triacca.

Sfursat

One hundred percent Nebbiolo, made from dried grapes like Amarone in Veneto. Intense, sweet, high alcohol wine. Decant and allow to breathe for several hours.

Groppello

This wine is named after the grape it is made from. It is dry red and full-bodied. Also made in Amarone style.

White

Lugano (Trebbiano), light, very dry and fresh.

Rosé

Chiaretto del Garda (Groppello, Sangiovese, Barbera, Marzemino). Deep rosé colour, light dry, slightly bitter flavour. Drink young.

Worth Looking For Ca' del Bosco's spumante, Cabernet and Franciacorta Rosso.

MARCHES

One of Italy's best-loved wines comes from this region on the Adriatic coast — Verdicchio. Marches also offer some serviceable reds from Sangiovese and Montepulciano grapes.

Verdicchio

Verdicchio is a pale straw colour with a dry fruity flavour and a peach-pit aftertaste. Drink it young. Wines from the classical zone (Castelli di Jesi) will be superior to those labelled Verdicchio di Matelica.

Recommended Producers Bianchi, Brunoria, Bucci (highly recommended), Castelfiora, Cantine Sociale di Cupramontana, Fabrini, Fazi Battaglia, Garofoli (highly recommended), MecVini, Monte Sciavo, Torelli, Umani Ronchi (highly recommended), Zaccagnini.

Reds

Rosso Conero, Rosso Piceno (chillable) — light, dry, drink young.

Worth Looking For Château Frecciarossa (La Vigne Blanche — white, Grand Cru — red).

UMBRIA

This land-locked province has long been the domain of the Lungarotti family who produce excellent red wines. The most widely noted white is Orvieto in dry and off-dry style. Lately

Chardonnay and Sauvignon Blanc have been planted and several producers are offering oak-aged blends.

Whites
Orvieto

The dry version is pale coloured and medium-bodied with a bitter almond finish. Grapes: Trebbiano, Verdello, Malvasia, Grechetto, Drupeggio. The sweeter version is called Abbocatto. It is peachy, round and fuller-bodied.

Recommended Producers Antinori (highly recommended), Barberani, Bigi, Cotti, Decugnano dei Barbi (highly recommended), Dubini Locatelli, Papini, Le Velette, Conte Vaselli.

Other Recommended Whites Lungarotti Chardonnay, Lungarotti Torre di Giano (Grechetto, Trebbiano). Good value.

Reds

Recommended Reds Lungarotti Rubesco (Sangiovese, Canaiolo). The *riserva* is one of the great Italian wines. Lungarotti San Giorgio (Sangiovese, Canaiolo, Cabernet Sauvignon); Lungarotti Cabernet Sauvignon; Andanti Sagratino de Montefalco.

Recommended Rosé Lungarotti Castel Grifone.

EMILIA-ROMAGNA

As the culinary heart of Italy, this region does not produce the most distinguished of wines. Its best-known export is the fizzy red Lambrusca produced by Riunite. The best wine of the region is Albana di Romagna (dry and sweet) which is the only DOCG white.

Grape Varieties

Red Lambrusco, Barbera, Bonardo, Sangiovese, Cabernet Sauvignon.

White Albana di Romagna, Scandiano Bianco, Trebbiano di Romagna.

Wine Styles

Red Light, chillable. Not for ageing.

White Medium-bodied, dry to medium-sweet.

Albana di Romagna Full-bodied, rich fruit flavours, lively acidity. The dry version nutty with a bitter finish. The sweet one is golden with a rich honeyed flavour. Drink young.

Recommended Producers Fattoria Paradiso (highly recommended), Ferrucci, Pasolini dall'Onda, Tenuta Panzacchia, Tenuta Zerbina, Valeriano Trere, Vallunga.

Other Varieties   Castelluccio, Frattoria Paradiso (highly recommended), Monsignore, Spalletti, Zanetti.

Worth Looking For   Enrico Vallania's Cabernet Sauvignon, Paradiso's Pagadebit, Catelluccio Ronco del Re.

LATIUM (LAZIO)	The Alban hills south of Rome produce Colli Albani and Castelli Romani which have long been a staple source of house wines for Italian restaurants abroad. The whites are better than the reds, the best of them being the light and fragrant Frascati. Drink both red and white young and fresh. Quaffing wines.
Grape Varieties	**White** Malvasia, Trebbiano, Bellone, Bonvino, Cacchione.
	Red Sangiovese, Montepuciano, Canaiolo, Cesanese, Nero Buono di Cori, Barbera,
Whites	Frascati, Est! Est!! Est!!!, Castelli Romani, Colli Albani, Colli Lanuvi, Marino, Velletri.
Reds	Castelli Romani, Marino Rubino, Veletri, Torre Ercolana, Colle Picchioni.
	Frascati Recommended Producers Colli di Catone, Colli di Tuscolo, Cantine Sociale di Monteporzio Catone, Fontana Candida, Conte Zandotti, Gotto d'Oro, Paolo di Mauro, C.S di Montecompatri, Villa Simone.

Est! Est!! Est!!!

This innocuous white wine vinified in dry, off-dry and sweet style around the town of Montefiascone today lives off its name and the legend that inspired it. In 1110, Bishop Johann Fugger of Augsberg was on his way to the coronation of Henry V in Rome. Fond of the pleasures of the table, he sent his servant ahead to check out the inns on the way and note where the wines were particularly good. His instructions were to chalk on the doorpost the code word "Est" (short for vinum bonum est meaning "the wine is good"). At Monte-fiascone the servant was bowled over by what he found and marked the inn door with the hyperbolic, Est! Est!! Est!!! The Bishop must have concurred with these tasting notes because he took up residence in Montefiascone. History does not record whether he made it to the coronation or not since he was buried in the church of San Flaviano there and directed in his will that on the anniversary of his death a barrel of Est! Est!! Est!!! be poured over his grave. His successor decided that the local wine was too good to be wasted and ordered the annual barrel to be sent over to the local seminary so that the priests could toast the town's benefactor.

The wine that so enchanted Johann Fugger was not the wine we know today. Back then it was made with the Muscat grape. Today it is fermented from the ubiquitous Trebbiano.

Recommended Producers
Antinori, Cantine Sociale di Montefiascone, Italo Mazziotti.

ABRUZZI AND MOLISE	The reds in these Adriatic coastal regions are produced from Montepulciano and the whites from Trebbiano (blended with Bombino).

In Molise, Montepulciano and Trebbiano are called Biferno or Pentro. |
| **Wine Style** | **White** Fuller bodied and softer than most Trebbianos.

Red Broad fruit flavours, mouth-filling. Drink within five years. Not to be confused with Tuscany's Vino Noblie di Montepulciano.

Recommended Producers Casal Thaulero, Duchi di Castelluccio, Baron Cornacchia, Lucio di Giulio, Dino Illuminati, Emedio Pepe (highly recommended and expensive but great), Scialletti, Tenuta Sant' Agnese, Cantina Tollo, Valentini (highly recommended and expensive but great). |
| **CAMPANIA** | The volcanic soil of this region produces powerful, firm, full-flavoured wines. The star producer here is Mastroberadino — two brothers Antonio and Walter who have done much to rescue ancient Greek grape varieties such as Greco di Tufo and Fiano di Avellino from extinction. Their Taurasi Riserva made from Aglianico grapes is one of the longest lasting Italian wines, not unlike a Barolo. |
| **Grape Varieties** | **White** Coda di Volpe, Greco di Torre, Greco di Tufa, Fiano di Avellino, Biancolella, Forastera.

Red Aglianico, Guarnaccia, Piedirosso, Barbera.

Mastroberadino Wines These wines are expensive but are of high quality.

White: Greco di Tufo (with Coda di Volpe, "fox tail")
       Fiano di Avellino
       Lacryma Christi
Red: Taurasi
Rosé: Lacrimarosa d'Irpinia

Other Recommended Producers Antonio Pentangelo, D'Ambra Vini d'Ischia, Saviano. |
| **BASILICATA** | On the volcanic slopes of Monte Vulture, Aglianico grapes produce a fine red called Aglianico del Vulture. Like Taurasi it is a long-lived wine. After three years of ageing (two in barrel) it will carry the designation *vecchio* (old). |

Recommended Producers D'Angelo (highly recommended), Botte, Paternoster, Sasso.

PUGLIA

Northern winemakers used to order deeply coloured, high-alcohol Puglia wines to beef up their blends, both white and red. However, modern winemaking techniques have produced local wines of more finesse and style.

Grape Varieties

White Bombino Bianco, Trebbiano, Malvasia, Verdea, Pampanuto.

Red Aleatico, Bombino, Montepulciano d'Abruzzo, Sangiovese, Negroamaro, Primitivo di Manduria, Nero di Troia.

Best Red Castel del Monte produces a powerful, dark red, that is high in alcohol, dry and tannic. It will age ten years. Grapes: Bombino, Nero di Troia, Montepulciano. (Also an undistinguished white and a good rosé).

Recommended Producers Bruno, Cantine Sociale di Locorotondo, Rivera (Riserva Il Falcone) (highly recommended), Strippoli, Taurino, Conti Zecca.

Other Reds Alezio, Brindisi, Copertino, Leverano, Rosso di Cerignola, Salice Salentino, San Stefano, Squinzano.

Whites Locorotondo, San Severo Bianco.

Worth Looking For Attilio Simonini Chardonnay.

CALABRIA

The mountainous toe of Italy produces wines as rugged as the men who work the vineyards. Don't look for finesse and elegance here but strapping powerful reds and a rosé with a name worthy of a German label — Sant' Anna Isola di Capo Rizzuto Rosato. The main red grape is the delightfully named local variety, Gaglioppo, and the white, Greco.

Best Red Cirò — deep ruby, high in alcohol, peppery, reminsicent of Châteauneuf-du-Pape. Capable of long ageing. (Also vinified as rosé and white — Greco.)

Other Reds Donnici, Pollino, Savuto.

Whites Cirò Bianco, Greco di Bianco, Lamentino, Melissa.

Worth Looking For Umberto Ceratti's sweet Greco di Bianco.

SICILY	This Mediterranean island is best known for Marsala but some well-priced, assertive table wines (Corvo, Regaliali) and dessert wines (Moscato, Malvasia) are to be found here today.

Grape Varieties

White Cataratto, Inzolia, Carricante, Minnella, Trebbiano, Malvasia, Moscato.

Red Nerello, Nocera, Perricone, Catanese.

Recommended Producers Giuseppe Camillieri, Rapitalà, Rincione, Duca di Salaparuta, Rallo, Conte Tasca d'Almerita.

Sweet Whites (Moscato) De Bartoli, Cantina Sociale di Pantellaria (Tanit), (Malvasia delle Lipari) Hauner (highly recommended), Lo Schiavo, Moccotta.

SARDINIA	One winery dominates the island's production, Sella and Mosca (highly recommended), while other producers have gathered together in co-operatives. The quality of Sardinia's inexpensive sweet wines, both red and white, are a well-kept secret.

Grape Varieties

Red Cannanou, Girò, Monica.

White Malvasia, Moscato, Nasco, Vernaccia di Oristano.

The reds and whites tend to be heavy and short-lived, but the sweet versions are worth exploring.

Sweet Reds Anghelu Ruju (Sella & Mosca) (highly recommended), Cannonau Capo Ferrato (Cantina Sociale Castiadio), Cannonau di Alghero, Cannonau del Parteolla, Cantina Sociale di Dorgali, Gir di Cagliari, Monica di Cagliari.

Sweet Whites Nasco, Malvasia di Bosa, Malvasia di Cagliari. Dry versions — Vernaccia di Oristano (Fratelli Contini)

Worth Looking For Cantina Sociale di Dolianova Vermentino di Sardegna — a light, crisp white reminiscent of Muscadet.

Germany

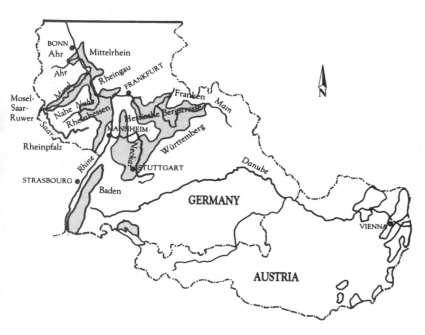

WINE REGIONS OF GERMANY

The vineyards of Germany are the most northerly in the world, which means the ripeness and quantity of the grapes will vary considerably from vintage to vintage compared with warmer growing regions. This is probably why the German growers have traditionally prized high sugar readings in their grapes above all else. Unlike France and Italy, the quality of the wine is judged on the amount of sugar in the berries prior to fermentation and the products are priced accordingly. The best wines are grown along the river valleys.

German labels may look daunting at first sight but they are a model of efficiency in describing the exact location and quality of the wine. Once you have broken the code you will know exactly what you are getting. But there are pitfalls. Because of the worldwide demand for drier wines to be consumed with food, German producers are no longer leaving the sugar in their wines and more adventurous vintners are challenging accepted ideas by ageing their wines in French oak (as opposed to large old casks or stainless steel tanks) and putting their high-acid wines through a malolactic fermentation (see page 20) to soften them.

Grape Varieties	**White** Riesling, Müller-Thurgau, Bacchus, Kerner, Gewürztraminer, Silvaner, Rülander, Morio-Muskat, Scheurebe.
	Red Blau Portugieser, Spätburgunder, Trollinger, Limberger.
Wine Style	**White** Light in alcohol, fragrant and floral, generally good acidity, varying degrees of residual sugar according to the designation, from bone-dry to honey-sweet.
	Red Light, deep rosé colour, good acidity, dry to medium-sweet.

GERMAN WINE LAW

The wine-producing area is divided into eleven growing regions:

- Ahr — known for its red wines
- Mittelrhein — very crisp and dry
- Mosel-Saar-Ruwer — light, racy, elegant whites
- Rheingau — great breed and balance
- Nahe — grapey with steely acidity
- Rheinhessen — softer, fruitier wines
- Rheinpfalz — aromatic, full-bodied
- Hessische-Bergstrasse — hearty, simple dry wines
- Franken — earthy, steely dry
- Württemberg — powerful, earthy, fruity
- Baden — aromatic, strong whites; full-bodied reds

Each region is further divided into thirty-four districts encompassing many wine-growing villages. These are called *Bereiche* and take their name from the most famous village in the area, for example, Bereich Bernkastel (Mosel), Bereich Johannisberg (Rheingau), Bereich Nierstein (Rheinhessen).

There are thirty-four *Bereiche* throughout Germany — districts which are further broken down into *Gemeinde* or parishes (1,387 in all). These parishes are split up into vineyard sites, either collectively as *Grosslagen* (152) or as single vineyards known as *Einzellage* of which 2,597 are named. These individual vineyards generally produce a higher quality wine than those from the larger *Grosslagen* sites.

THE QUALITY SCALE

The degree of ripeness of the grapes at picking time is recorded on the label. The two broad categories are *Tafelwein* (Table Wine) and *Qualitätswein* (Quality Wine).

Tafelwein

1   *Deutscher Tafelwein* (German Table Wine) — simple everyday fare. If the word Deutsche is not on the label this means the grapes were grown outside Germany.
2   *Deutscher Landwein* (German Country Wine) — simple table wine made from riper grapes.

Qualitätswein

1   *Qualitätswein bestimmter Anbaugebeite* (QbA for short, thank heavens) — means quality wine of designated areas of origin, similar to the French AOC or Italian DOC. The wine will come from one of the eleven specified growing regions.
2   *Qualitätswein mit Prädikat* (quality wine with pedigree) — a category that specifies six different wines based on the ripeness of the grapes.
    Kabinett — literally "cabinet," what the farmers originally kept back for their own consumption.
    Spätlese — late-picked. Grapes are left on the vine at least two weeks after the harvest to increase their sugars.
    Auslese — specially selected bunches, usually with some noble rot (what the Germans call *Edelfäule*).
    Beerenauslese (BA) — selected over-ripe berries (*Beeren*).
    Eiswein — the same concentration of sugar as BA but pressed while the grapes are frozen.
    Trockenbeerenauslese (TBA) — selected over-ripe berries which have dried (*Trocken*) to raisins. You don't get any sweeter than this!

Because German wines are qualified by the amount of sugar in the grapes, a vineyard may produce an *Auslese* or *Beerenauslese* in one vintage and only a QbA or *Kabinett* the next. As well, different parts of the same vineyard may produce wines of different qualities.

READING THE LABEL

Usually the most prominent words on a German label are the village name followed by the name of the individual vineyard.

Below you will see Geisenheimer Rothenberg. This means the grapes were grown in the Rothenberg vineyard which is located within the town boundaries of Geisenheim.

READING THE LABEL

1 Rheingau — The region where the grapes were grown.

2 1982 — The vintage date.

3 Geisenheimer Rothenberg — The village name and the vineyard name.

4 Riesling Kabinett — The grape variety and the level of ripeness (Kabinett).

5 Qualitätswein mit Prädikat — The quality category.

6 A. P. Nr. — The official quality control number. No wine of QbA level or above can be exported without being tasted and approved by a local panel.

7 Erzeugerabfüllung — Bottled on the estate.

8 Bottled by/mis en bouteilles par — The name of the bottler.

9 Deinhard — The company that owns the property or merchandises the wine.

10 Oestrich/Rheingau — The regional address of company.

11 750 ml — Contents of the bottle.

12 8% alc./vol. — Alcoholic strength of the wine.

DRIER AND DRIER	In an effort to compete with dry French and Italian wines in the world market, German wine producers are "drying out" many of their wines, that is, leaving less residual sugar in them.

GERMAN WINE SEALS

Trocken	The driest category of German wine, from QbA to *Auslese* level. This term will appear on the label, usually after the grape variety. It will denote that the wine does not contain more than four grams per litre of residual and fermentable sugar. The higher the designation, the richer the wine's flavour. (I find that anything below *Spätlese Trocken* is too spare for my taste.) The bottle will carry a yellow seal bearing the term *Trocken*.
Halbtrocken	Semi-dry. Not exceeding eighteen grams per litre. The bottle will carry a lime-green seal with the term *Halbtrocken*.
Lieblich	Medium-sweet, traditional style. Does not exceed forty-five grams per litre. The bottle will have a red seal with no designation.

Wine Language

Aus Eigenem Lesegut — estate-bottled

Bocksbeutel — Franconian bottle shape modelled apparently after a goat's scrotum

Edelfäule — noble rot (*Botrytis cinerea*)

Kellerei — cellars or winery

Rotwein — red wine

Spritzig — lightly effervescent

Steinwein — stone-wine, descriptive of Franconian wines

Weinbau — wine growing

Weingut — vineyard owner

Weinkellerei — winery

Weissherbst — white wine made with red grapes

Weisswein — white wine

Winzer — grower

Winzergenossenschaft — a growers' cooperative winery

Winzerverein — small producers' cooperative

AHR

This is Germany's most northerly region. The best reds come from here and from Baden.

Best Wine Villages   Ahrweiler, Bad Neuenahr.

Recommended Producers   J.J. Adenauer, Jakob Sebastian, Staatliche Weinbaudomän Kloster Marienthal, Jean Stodden.

MITTELRHEIN

Mittlelrhein produces very dry, sharp Rieslings.

Best Wine Villages   Bacharach, Oberwesel, St. Goarshausen.

Recommended Producers   Wilhelm Wasum (shipper), Heinrich Weiler, Toni Jost.

MOSEL-SAAR-RUWER

Arguably the purest expression of German Riesling.

Best Wine Villages   *Mosel* — Bernkastel, Brauenburg, Erden, Graach, Piesport, Wehlen, Zeltingen; *Saar* — Okfen, Saarburg, Serrig, Wiltingen; *Ruwer* — Eitelsbach, Kasel, Grünhaus, Trier.

Recommended Mosel Producers   Deinhard, Friedrich-Wilhelm Gymnasium, Graf zu Hoensbroech, von Kesselstatt, von Landenburg, J. Lauerburg, Peter Nicholay, Dr. Pauly-Burgweiler, J.J. Prüm, S.A. Prüm-Erben, Dr. Thanisch, Fritz Haag, Dr. Loosen, Max Ferd. Richter, Selbach Oster.

Recommended Saar Producers   Dr. Fischer, Egon Müller, Edmund Reverchon, Geltz Zilliken.

Recommended Ruwer Producers Bishöflichen, Karthäuserhof, Dr. H. Wagner, von Hüvel, von Nell, von Schubert Maximin Grünhaus, Staatliche Weinbaudomänen.

RHEINGAU

The most consistently high quality German wines come from the Rheingau.

Best Wine Villages Hochheim, Eltville, Rauenthal, Erbach, Hattenheim, Winkel, Rüdesheim. Good reds from Assmannhausen.

Recommended Producers Aschrottsche Erban, Baron von Brentano, Deinhard, Domdechant Werner, Königin Victoria Berg, Landgraf von Hessen, Licht-Kilburg, Dr. Nagler, Schloss Groensteyn, Schloss Johannisberg, Schloss Reinhardtshausen, Schloss Schönborn, Schloss Volrads, von Schubert Maximin Grünhaus, Staatsweingüter Eltville, von Kanitz, von Mumm, Langwerth von Simmern, Dr. Weil.

NAHE

The Nahe wines are similar in style to the Mosel.

Best Wine Villages Schlossböckelheim, Neiderhausen, Bad Kreuznach, Münster-Sarmsheim.

Recommended Producers Anheuser, Hans Crusius, Carl Finkenauer, Schloss Plettenberg, Schlossgut Diel auf Berg Layen, Dr. Höfer Schlossmühle, Staatliche Weinbaudomänen Bad Kreutznach and Niederhausen, Erbhol Tesch.

Liebfraumilch

Even non-wine drinkers have heard of Liebfraumilch, Germany's largest exported wine. The name translates as "The Milk of Our Lady." Today the wine can come from one of four regions — Rheinhessen, Rheinpfalz, (less likely) Rheingau or the Nahe — and is a blend of Silvaner, Müller-Thurgau and maybe some Riesling. Liebfraumilch originated from a single vineyard belonging to the Liebfrauenkirche, a church on the Rhine in the town of Worms. Such was its popularity that other producers got in on the act and blended a similar wine until its provenance was lost.

By law Liebfraumilch must have more than eighteen grams per litre of residual sugar, which puts it outside the Halbtrocken designation. Its label will not tell you what grapes are in the blend or in what proportion or offer any vineyard name, only the region where the grapes were grown, most often Rheinhessen or Rheinpfalz.

Usually, the producers will give the wine a proprietary name to distinguish it from the competition. The most reliable are Sichel's Blue Nun, Lagenbach's Crown of Crowns and Deinhard's Hanns Christof.

RHEINHESSEN	This is Germany's largest wine-growing region, producing soft whites and some inexpensive quaffing products.

Best Wine Villages Bingen, Bodenheim, Nierstein (highly recommended), Oppenheim (highly recommended), Dienheim, Guntersblum.

Recommended Producers Balbach Erban, Baumann, Gunderloch, L. Guntrum, Freiherr Heyl zu Herrnsheim, Alfred Müller, Dr. Muth, Franz Karl, Schmitt, Gustav Schmitt, Heinrich Seip, Dr. A. Senfter, J.& H. Strub.

RHEINPFALZ	The Rheinpfalz, known as Palatinate or Pfalz for short, produces well-rounded wines in warm years.

Best Wine Villages Wachenheim, Forst, Deidesheim, Ruppersberg.

Recommended Producers Basserman-Jordan, von Bühl, Bürklin-Wolf, Deinhard, Fitz-Ritter, Hanhof, Kurfürstenhof, Lingenfelder, Pfeffingen, Thomas Siegrist, Eugen Spindler, Stumpf-Fitz'sches Weingut Annaberg, Wegeler-Deinghard, Winzergenossenschaft Deutsches Weintor.

HESSISCHE-BERGSTRASSE	This is Germany's smallest region. Wines are more full-bodied and richer in fruit than those of the Rheingau, but are usually difficult to find.

Best Wine Villages Bensheim, Heppenheim.

Recommended Producers H. Freiberger, Weingut der Stadt Bensheim, Staatsweingut Bergstrasse.

FRANKEN	Full-bodied Silvaner wines are the specialty here.

Best Wine Villages Würzburg, Thüngersheim, Iphofen, Randersacker, Rodelsee, Sommerach, Sommerhausen, Escherndorf.

Recommended Producers Bügerspital zum Heiligen Geist, Fürstlich Castell'sches Domaine, Fürstlich Löwenstein-Wertheim-Rosenberg, Juliusspital, Ernst Popp, Staatlicher Hofkeller, Hans Wirsching.

WÜRTTEMBERG	Much red and rosé wine is produced in this region dominated by co-operatives.

Recommended Producers Wrütt. Hofkammer-Kellerei, Graf Adelmann, von Bentzel-Sturmfede, Fürst zu Hohenlohe-Öhringen, Fürstlich Hohenloe Langenburg, Staat. Lehr u. Versuchsanstalt für Wein u. Obstbau Weinsberg, Drautz-Able, Graf von Neipperg.

BADEN

As Germany's warmest region, the whites and reds have good body and extract.

Best Wine Villages Durbach, Ihringen, Meersburg, Salem, Nekarzimmern.

Recommended Producers Franz Keller, von Baden, von Gemmingen-Hornberg, von Gleichenstein, von Neveu, Wolff Metternich, Schloss Staufenberg, Blankenhornsberg, Staatsweingut Meersburg, Karl Heinz Jöhner.

GERMAN WINE AND FOOD

The natural combination of low alcohol and evident acidity makes German wine an ideal companion for a variety of dishes. The following wine styles will match the named dishes:

- Smoked fish — Riesling/Kerner Trocken Kabinett
- Pâté, melon — Müller-Thurgau/Scheurebe Spätlese
- Cream soups — Riesling/Weissburgunder Halbtrocken Kabinett, Spätlese
- Seafood, cream sauce — Riesling/Kerner Halbtrocken Kabinett
- Fowl, turkey — Riesling/Weissburgunder Kabinett, Halbtrocken Spätlese
- Red meat — Weissburgunder/Spätburgunder Spätlese Trocken
- Fruit desserts — Auslese, Beerenauslese
- Cheeses
    soft — Riesling/Weissburgunder Spätlese Halbtrocken
    sharp, ripe — Gewürztraminer/Morio-Muscat Spätlese
    blue — Riesling/Kerner Beerenauslese
- Oriental dishes — Liebfraumilch/Gewürztraminer QbA

Spain
and
Portugal

SPAIN

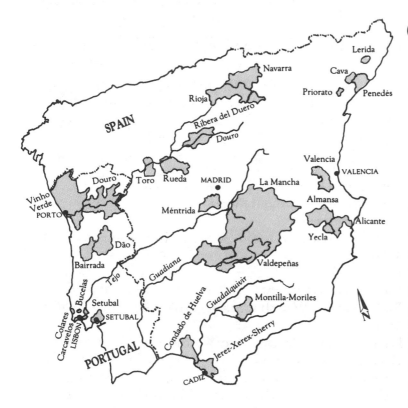

WINE REGIONS OF SPAIN AND PORTUGAL

Think of Spain and the beverage that immediately springs to mind is Sherry. But the country's enormous expanse of vineyards (second only to Russia's in size) produces table wines and sparkling wines of high quality at prices worthy of the budget-minded wine-lover's attention. Currently, there are thirty-six wine regions, the best known being Rioja, Penedes, Ribera del Duero and the sherry-growing area around Jerez de la Frontera (see under Sherry).

Traditionally, the best Spanish wines have come from the cooler growing regions of Rioja and Penedes, but with a new understanding of vineyard techniques and a more scientific approach to winemaking (especially in cool fermentation) other regions are beginning to produce wines of great quality. The white wines in particular used to be kept too long in oak casks which gave them an oxidized flavour, not unlike the Spaniards' beloved dry sherry, but the economic imperative to export has ensured fresher, younger wines for the world market.

Wine Style

White   Old style — oak-ageing subdues youthful fruit giv- ing honey, peach and almond flavours.

New style — light, clean and sharp with hints of citrus, easy- drinking without predominant character.

Red   Oaky, coconut nose; soft, full strawberry, raspberry flavours. Ages well.

Spanish Wine Laws

Like France and Italy, Spanish wines have a denomination of origin (D.O.) which states where the grapes must be grown, the number of vine plants per hectare, the amount of wine produced and other procedures relating to vineyard care, vinification and ageing of the wine. The back labels will tell you how long the wine has been aged and how. The Spanish talk about the upbringing of a wine in terms of nurseries, which shows a very human approach to the subject.

- *Sin Crianza* — "without nursery." One-year-old wine, proba- bly not aged in oak.
- *Con Crianza* — "with nursery." The wines must be aged at least two years, one year in barrel for reds and six months for whites.
- *Reserva* — reds: good-quality wine aged three years in oak and bottle (minimum one year in oak); whites: two years in oak and bottle (minimum six months in oak).
- *Gran Reserva* — high-quality wine aged at least two years in oak and three in bottle (for reds) and six months in oak and four years in bottle for whites.

Wine Language

Blanco — white
Cava — sparkling wine (champagne method)
Criado por — matured and/or blended by
Dulce — sweet
Elaborado por — matured and/or blended by
Embotellado por — bottled by
Espumoso — sparkling wine
Generoso — dessert wine

Gran-vas — sparkling wine made in tank rather than bottle
Rosado — rosé
Seco — dry
Tinto — red wine
Vendimia — vintage
Viña, Vinedo — vineyard

Rioja

The best red wine region with a few classic whites.

Grape Varieties

Red Tempranillo, Graciano, Mazuelo, Garnacha.

White Viura, Malvasia, Garnacha Blanca.

Ageing Potential The Gran Reserva and Reserva wines of the top producers can last for decades, both red and white. Other reds should be consumed within five years and whites within two.

Recommended Producers Berberana, Beronia, Martinez Bujanda, Bilbainas, Campo Viejo, CVNE, Muga, Faustino Martinez, Lopez de Heredia, Marques de Caceres, Marques de Murrieta, Marques de Riscal, Montecillo, Muga, Federico Paternino, La Granja Remelluri, Rioja Alavesa, La Rioja Alta, Riojanas.

Worth Looking For The long-lived whites of Castillo de Ygay (Murrieta) and Viña Tondonia (Lopez de Heredia).

Navarra

The neighbouring region to Rioja produces some excellent reds and is the place to look for *rosados* (rosés).

Recommended Producers Chivite, Irache, Monte Ory, Ochoa, Senorio de Sarria, Castillo de Tiebas.

Penedes

The Torres family created the reputation of this region around Barcelona for table wines with their red and white wines. Here the Tempranillo grape is called Ull de Llebre and the Viura, Macabeo.

Large plantings of Cabernet Sauvignon, Pinot Noir and Chardonnay have produced excellent results for growers here.

Penedes is also the home of Spain's sparkling wine industry centred at San Sadurní de Noya. These sparklers are created in the same fashion as champagne and are called *cava*. They represent excellent value.

Recommended Producers Masia Bach, Castell del Remei, Jean Leon, Marques de Monistrol, Torres.

Worth Looking For Torres Gran Coronas Black Label Reserva.

Sparkling Wines The grape varieties used are Macabeo, Xarel-lo and Parellada.

Recommended Producers Castellblanch, Cavas Hill, Codorniu, Freixenet, Juvé & Camps, Marques de Monistrol, Castillo de Perelada, Segura Viudas.

Ribera del Duero

This region produces two of the finest and longest-lived Spanish reds — Pesquera and the legendary and expensive Vega Sicilia (Bordeaux grapes blended with Spanish).

Other Regions

Recommended Producers in other Spanish wine-producing regions are as follows:

Almansa — Bodegas Piqueras

Galicia — Marques de Figueroa, Bodegas Chaves

New Castile-La Mancha — Hijos de Jesús Diaz

Old Castile-Léon — Palacio de Arganza, Valdeobispo, VILE

Lérida — Raimat (Chardonnay, Cabernet Sauvignon)

Priorato — Cellers de Scala Dei

Rueda — Marques de Grigñon

Tierra de Barros — Lar de Barros

Toro — Bodegas Farina, Luis Mateos

PORTUGAL

There is more to Portugal than Port and Mateus rosé. This often-overlooked wine region offers some of the best bargains in well-aged reds and refreshing summer whites. The best wines — Vinho Verde, Dão and Bairrada — come from the north of the country where the Port vineyards are also to be found. But there are treasures to be found south as well.

Vinho Verde

Vinho Verde means "green wine" but it comes only in red and white.

Wine Style

Fresh, tangy and needle-sharp with a faint prickle on the tongue. We don't see the red variety which mercifully is consumed by the people who grow it. The white is an ideal aperitif wine. Green, incidentally, refers to the freshness of the wine although it could well attest to the landscape of the Minho region where Vinho Verde grows.

Grape Varieties	**Red** Vinhão, Cainhos, Doçar, Brancelho.
	White Alvarinho, Loureiro, Azal Branco.
	Recommended Producers Quinta da Aveleda, Fonseca, Grinaldi, Real Co. Vinicola do Norte de Portugal, Borges & Irmão, Caves Aliança, Ribeiro & Irmão.
Dão	The most reliable region for red wines.
Grape Varieties	**Red** Touriga Naçional, Alfrocheiro Preto, Tinta Amarela, Tinta Pinheira, Alverelho, Jaen.
	White Arinto do Dão, Borrado das Moscas, Cerceal, Marcelo, Encruzado, Verdelho.
Wine Style	**Red** Earthy, deeply coloured, full-bodied, capable of long ageing especially *garrafeiras*.
	White Heavy, somewhat dull, woody.
	Recommended Producers Vinícola do Vale do Dão (Grao Vasco), J.M. da Fonseca (Terras Altas), Caves Império, Caves Aliança, Caves Dom Teodósio, Carvalho Ribeiro & Ferreira, Caves Sao Joao.
	Worth Looking For Conde de Santar (Cabernet Sauvignon).
Bairrada	A relatively new region with reds of a slightly lighter style than Dão and some good sparkling wines.
Grape Varieties	**Red** Baga, Tinta Pinheira, Joao de Santarém.
	White Bical, Maria Gomez.
	Recommended Producers Aliança, S. Domingos, Solar de Francesas, Império, Sao Joao, Barrocao, Borlido.
	Sparkling Wine Aliança, Neto Costa, Caves de Raposeira.
	Worth Travelling to Portugal For Buçaco — the white and red wine of the Buçaco Hotel, an exquiste summer palace set in its own gardens. This must be the only hotel in the world to have its own appellation!

Garrafeira

For red and white wines capable of ageing look for the term garrafeira on the label. This means that the wine has been specially selected for its ability for long bottle-ageing. A wine so labelled must have had at least two years of ageing in cask before bottling and will be cellared for many years before it is released for sale. Labels will bear the name Garrafeira, the vintage date and the producer's name.

Other Regions

Colares (phylloxera-free sandy vineyards) — Antonio Paulo da Silva

Setúbal — Recommended Producer: Fonseca (look for the fortified Moscatels, the red Periquita, Camarate and red and white Pasmodos — all excellent value).

Worth Looking For Portugal's most illustrious and expensive red, Barca Velha, produced from three Port grapes (Tinta Roriz, Amarela and Touriga Francesca) in the Upper Douro Valley.

The
United States

CALIFORNIA

WINE REGIONS OF CALIFORNIA

*N*o other wine region has imposed itself upon the map with such authority in such a short period of time as California. Its white, red, sparkling and dessert wines now rival the quality of their French models and if its young vintners have yet to emulate the best of the Rhône it is only because those varieties are only coming into fashion. Italian and Spanish grapes are also being planted which suggests that California could, all by itself, provide the world with virtually every wine style, except the light, crisp Rieslings of the Mosel and Rheingau.

The image of the state is one of constant sunshine, but the range of temperatures during the growing season in its eighteen designated regions can vary dramatically. The amount of sunshine hours has been tabulated to distinguish five ranges which has proven that California can replicate the climates of every wine growing country of Europe and North Africa.

While California has built its reputation on Chardonnay and Cabernet Sauvignon, lately winemakers have been concentrating on Sauvignon Blanc, Merlot and Pinot Noir. Ultimately you can find just about any grape variety you want from California's 770 (and growing!) bonded wineries.

Most Californian wines will be labelled with the name of the grape. Some are still called after the European appellations (e.g., Chablis, Burgundy, Champagne, etc.), but will bear no similarity in taste, style or price to their progenitors.

Grape Varieties

White Chardonnay, Sauvignon Blanc, Chenin Blanc, Pinot Blanc, White Riesling, Gewürztraminer, small amounts of Muscat, Roussanne, Marsanne, Viognier and Silvaner; also, lesser quality French Colombard, Emerald Riesling, Gray Riesling.

Red Barbera, Cabernet Sauvignon, Merlot, Cabernet Franc, Pinot Noir, Zinfandel, Syrah, Petit Sirah (Duriff); *lesser quality*: Alicante Bouschet, Carignane, Charbono, (Napa) Gamay, Gamay Beaujolais, Grenache, Grigolino, Ruby Cabernet.

Blush for Zinfandel

It is said that Zinfandel, a black grape now native to California, was introduced into Sonoma County by Count Agoston Haraszthy in 1861. The original cutting was purported to be from the Primitivo vines of Abruzzi in southern Italy. Zin, as it's affectionately known, makes a powerful, blackberry flavoured wine not unlike a Rhône; but when the switch to white occurred in the late 1970s, Zinfandel growers found they had a lot of unwanted grapes on their hands. With minimum skin contact a white Zinfandel was produced which had the faint tinge of a rosé. To give it consumer appeal some residual sugar was left in the wine. But rosé was not a category that sold, so the marketing men took over and by a stroke of genius christened it Blush. A new wine was born — White Zinfandel. (Haraszthy, incidentally, met his ultimate end when he fell from his horse into a crocodile-infested river in Nicaragua.)

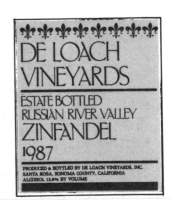

DE LOACH VINEYARDS
ESTATE BOTTLED
RUSSIAN RIVER VALLEY
ZINFANDEL
1987
PRODUCED & BOTTLED BY DE LOACH VINEYARDS, INC.
SANTA ROSA, SONOMA COUNTY, CALIFORNIA
ALCOHOL 13.5% BY VOLUME

Recommended Producers By Grape Variety	Unlike European wine enterprises who will produce one, two or maybe three wines, California and other New World producers will have a range of wines to offer. Seeking the best grape for their microclimate, they will plant several varieties until they settle on the right one.

Chardonnay

Napa County Acacia, Beringer, Chateau Montalena, Château Potelle, Far Niente, Flora Springs, Grgich Hills, William Hill, Iron Horse, Mayacamus, Robert Mondavi, S. Anderson, Sterling, Stony Hill, Trefethen, ZD.

Sonoma County Arrowood, Buena Vista, Chateau St. Jean, Clos du Bois, De Loach, Dry Creek, Ferrari-Carano, Fischer, Glen Ellen, Jordan, Kistler, Matanzas Creek, Simi, Sonoma-Cutrer.

Other Regions Au Bon Climat (Santa Barbara), Chalone (Monterey), Edna Valley (San Luis Obispo), Kalin (Marin), Kendall-Jackson (Mendocino), Mount Eden (Santa Clara), Talbott (Monterey), Tiffany Hill (Edna Valley), Calera (San Benito).

Sauvignon Blanc (Fumé Blanc)

Sonoma Carmenet, Château St. Jean, Dry Creek, Glen Ellen, Hidden Springs, Matanzas Creek, Preston, Simi.

Napa Concannon, Duckhorn, Flora Springs, Long, Mondavi, St. Clement, Spottswoode, Sterling.

Other Regions Congress Springs (Santa Cruz), Fetzer (Mendocino), Kalin (Marin), Kendall-Jackson (Lake County).

Cabernet Sauvignon

Napa Beaulieu, Beringer, Caymus, Diamond Creek, Dunn, Far Niente, Heitz, William Hill, Mayacamus, Mondavi, Phelps, Shafer, Silver Oaks, Silverado, Spottswoode, Stag's Leap, Sterling, Viansa.

Sonoma Arrowood, Bellerose, B.R. Cohn, Carmenet, Fisher, Jordan, Kistler, Gundlach-Bundschu, Laurel Glenn, Ravenswood, Simi.

Other Regions Boeger (El Dorado), David Bruce (Santa Cruz), Durney (Monterey), Fetzer (Mendocino).

Pinot Noir

Acacia, Bonny Doon, Calera, Chalone, Edna Valley, Robert Mondavi, Joseph Swan, Robert Stemmler.

| The Regions | California can be confusing because of the growing number of regional names. Basically, the state is divided into four growing areas: |

The Regions

California can be confusing because of the growing number of regional names. Basically, the state is divided into four growing areas:

1 **North Coast** — made up of Lake County, Mendocino, Napa Valley and Sonoma Valley where most of California's finest wines are grown. This area also includes new plantings in the Sierra Foothills.

2 **Central Coast** — composed of Alameda County, Amador, Monterey, San Benito, San Luis Obispo, Santa Barbara County, Santa Clara and the Santa Cruz Mountains. Less fashionable but good wines are to be found here.

3 **San Joaquin Valley** — a vast, hot, inland growing region that stretches from Lodi to Bakersfield in a valley between the coastal range and the Sierra Mountains. Huge tonnages of grapes are grown here, mainly for blending purposes.

4 **Southern California** — around Los Angeles and stretching down to the Mexican border, including Riverdale, San Diego and Imperial Valley.

Mendocino and Lake County

The most northerly growing region in California consists of these two counties.

Recommended Producers   Fetzer, Guenoc, Hidden Cellar, Kendall-Jackson, Konocti, McDowell Valley Vineyards.

Sonoma

Ocean breezes and fog from the San Francisco Bay make this a cool growing region. Identified growing areas are Alexander Valley, Russian River Valley, Sonoma Valley, Knight's Valley, Los Carneros (shared with Napa under the appellation Carneros Quality Alliance) and the coastal Bodega Bay area.

Recommended Producers   Arrowood, Bellerose, Buena Vista, Château St. Jean, Clos du Bois, De Loach, Dry Creek, Jordan, Kistler, Lyeth, Lytton Springs, Mantanzas Creek, Preston, Simi.

Meritage

The recently coined term Meritage refers to a red wine blended in the style of Bordeaux, that is, with Cabernet Sauvignon, Cabernet Franc, Merlot and maybe some Petit Verdot and Malbec. The wine will carry a fantasy name and will generally cost more than a varietal Cabernet Sauvignon which can contain up to fifteen percent Cabernet Franc and/or Merlot.
   Examples: Opus One (Mondavi-Rothschild), Dominus (John Daniel Society), Insignia (Joseph Phelps), Alexandre (Geyser Peak), Marlestone (Clos du Bois), Rubicon (Niebaum-Coppola).

Napa	Napa is separated from Sonoma by the Mayacamas Mountains and is the home of the best Cabernets. It has a bewildering number of wineries. Napa is the most concentrated wine experience in the world.

Recommended Producers Acacia, Beaulieu Vineyard, Burgess, Cakebread, Carneros Creek, Chateau Montalena, Clos du Val, Cuvaison, Diamond Creek, Duckhorn, Freemark Abbey, Heitz, Mayacamas, Mondavi, Phelps, Spring Mountain, Stag's Leap, Sterling, Trefethen.

San Francisco Bay

This region includes the Santa Clara ("Silicon Valley") and Santa Cruz counties, as well as Livermore Valley.

Recommended Producers Concannon, Kalin, Mount Eden, Ridge, Wente.

Monterey Bay

From Santa Cruz to the town of Gilroy which is the garlic capital of America.

Recommended Producers Bonny Doon, David Bruce, Calera, Chalone, Jekel, Monterey Peninsula, Santa Cruz Mountain.

South Central Coast

This area consists of San Luis Obispo, Santa Barbara and Ventura counties.

Recommended Producers Eberle, Edna Valley, Firestone, Meridian, Sandford, Qupé.

Central Valley

Gallo's empire is located at Modesto. Great dessert wines are produced in this region.

Recommended Producers Ficklin, Quady.

Southern California

This warm growing area is between Los Angeles and San Diego.

Recommended Producers Callaway, Maurice Carrie.

Sierra Foothills

Old gold-rush territory now being planted with vines make up this region.

Recommended Producers Baldinelli, Boeger, Granite Springs, Montevina, Stevenot, Story.

OREGON

This region in the Pacific Northwest has the distinction of not using French appellations for any of its wines.

The cooler growing climate of the Willamette Valley produces a leaner, more acidic style than California. They can also be longer lived. Chardonnay in a Chablis style, dry Riesling and a Burgundian-style Pinot Noir do well in this region.

Recommended Chardonnay Producers Adams, Cameron, Eyrie, Girardet, Oak Knoll, Ponzi, Shafer, Tualatin, Yamhill Valley.

Recommended Pinot Noir Producers Adelsheim, Amity, Bethel Heights, Eyrie, Knudsen-Erath, Ponzi, Rex Hill.

WINE REGIONS OF OREGON AND WASHINGTON

| WASHINGTON | The Yakima Valley enjoys a more consistent climate than Oregon. Cabernet and Merlot are the region's strengths, although some fine Sauvignon Blancs are also to be found. |

Recommended Producers Arbor Crest, Columbia, Chateau Ste. Michelle, Hogue, Latah Creek, Leonetti, Woodward Canyon, Zillah Oakes.

| NEW YORK | The Finger Lakes and Long Island produce wines in European style from both *vinifera* and hybrid grapes. Erie-Chautauqua and the Hudson River areas are not quite up to this standard. New York whites are better than the reds, although some fine Cabernet Sauvignon is grown in favourable years by Hargrave Vineyard on Long Island. Late Harvest Riesling and Icewine are also worth looking for. |

Recommended Producers Bridgehampton, Casa Larga, Glenora, Hargrave, Knapp, Millbrook, Pindar, Rivendell, Wagner, Weimer, Woodbury.

| OTHER REGIONS | Forty-one states of the Union produce wine! Some are better at it than others. |

Recommended Producers *Connecticut* — Crosswoods, Haight; *Idaho* — Ste. Chapelle; *Maryland* — Basignani, Boordy, Byrd Vineyard, Catoctin, Montbray Vineyard; *Massachusetts* — Commonwealth Winery; *New Jersey* — Tewkesbury; *Ohio* — Markko Vineyard; *Pennsylvania* — Allegro Vineyards; *Rhode Island* — Sakonnet; *Texas* — Fall Creek, Llano, Pheasant Ridge; *Virginia* — Meredyth, Mont Domaine, Piedmont Vineyards.

Australia
and
New
Zealand

AUSTRALIA

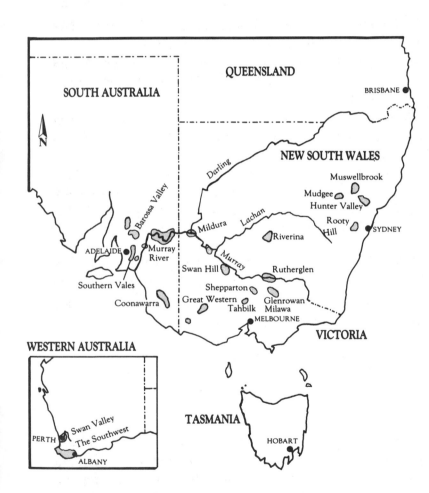

WINE REGIONS OF AUSTRALIA

*I*n the southern hemisphere the grape harvest takes place in March and April and, like California, you can find just about every wine style your heart desires — from bone dry Rieslings and oaky Chardonnays to elegant Cabernet Sauvignons and lusciously rich Muscat liqueurs. No other country produces wines that so closely mirror the personality of its people: Australian wines are extroverted, easy to like and mostly uncomplicated with masses of fruit and bold, broad flavours.

No other wine-growing country or region, not even California, has had such an impact on the world wine scene in so short a time as Australia. Its finest reds and whites rival the best wines of Europe and lately its sparkling wines have proved to be excellent too. Australian winemakers are constantly experimenting in the vineyard and in the cellar, breaking old rules to come up with better wines.

Labelling

Australian wines are generally labelled by the varietal and when two grapes are used, as in Cabernet/Shiraz, the first named will be the preponderant one. The Aussies still persist in using some French designations, such as Burgundy, Chablis, Sauternes and Champagne, to describe their wines and the loose definition of Riesling can be misleading. A wine labelled Riesling without any geographical qualification will be a blend of white grapes. Hunter Riesling is really the Semillon grape; Cruchen masquerades as Clare Riesling. The real thing is called Rhine Riesling down under.

Another complicating factor is the use of Bin numbers (as in Lindeman Chardonnay Bin 65). This practice denotes a specially selected or reserve wine.

Blended wines may also have a proprietary name, such as Tyrrell's Long Flat Red (named after the "paddock" in which the grapes are grown).

Geographical designations are less important since Australian winemakers can ship in grapes for blending from any state they want. Label information attests to the frantic transportation of grapes on Australian highways.

Grape Varieties

White   Chardonnay, Riesling, Sauvignon Blanc, Semillon, Gewürztraminer, Colombard, Muscat, Marsanne, Chasselas.

Red   Cabernet Sauvignon, Shiraz (also called Hermitage), Pinot Noir, Pinot Meunier.

Ageing Potential

- Chardonnays — three to five years
- Semillons — eight to fifteen years
- Cabernets, Cabernet/Shiraz — seven to eight years
- Shiraz (Hermitage)— ten or more

Wine Language

The Aussies are the antidote to the wine bore. They refer to wine with a very basic vocabulary. James Hardy, head of the firm that bears his family name, once described the difference between a white and a red in these terms: "Put two fingers behind the glass and hold it up to the light. If you can't see your fingers, it's a red wine."

The Australians have an engaging habit of referring to their dessert wines as "stickies." If you get some on your fingers you'll understand why. The sweetest ones they call "ultra stickies."

Vintages   Because of the evenness of the Australian climate there is not as much vintage variation as you will find in Europe.

WINE REGIONS BY STATE

If you look at the map of Australia you'll see that the wine growing areas are concentrated in the coolest parts of the country to the south and west along the river valleys.

New South Wales
The Hunter Valley

Divided into the Lower Hunter and the Upper Hunter by the river of the same name this region is Australia's Napa and Sonoma. It produces full-bodied Cabernet and Shiraz plus good Chardonnay and Semillon.

Recommended Producers Allandale, Arrowfield, Château François, Hungerford Hill, Lake's Folly, Lindeman, Robson, Rosemount, Rothbury, Saxonvale, Tyrrell, Wyndham Estate.

Worth Looking For Brokenwood Cabernet Sauvignon and Shiraz (Hunter-Coonawarra blends) and "Graveyard Vineyard" Cabernet Sauvignon.

Mudgee

Mudgee is a small area producing gutsy Chardonnays and Cabernets.

Recommended Producers Allandale, Craigmoor, Huntingdon Estate, Miramar, Montrose.

Murrumbidgee Irrigation Area

Generally inexpensive, uninteresting wines apart from some good sweet offerings from De Bartoli and fine reds from McWilliams.

Victoria
Central Goulburn Valley

Chunky reds and full-bodied, fleshy whites are produced in the Central Goulburn Valley.

Recommended Producers Michelton, Chateau Tahbilk, Tisdall.

Pyrenees

This region northwest of Melbourne produces well-structured reds and good Sauvignon Blanc.

Recommended Producers Chateau Remy, Mount Avoca, Redbank, Taltarni, Warrenmang.

Great Western	Good sparkling wines and medium-bodied reds come from Great Western.
	Recommended Producers Best's, Cathcart Ridge, Mount Langi Ghiran, Seppelt's.
Northeast	This area includes Rutherglen, Milawa and Glenrowan and the best fortified and dessert wines come from here. Sherries, ports and dessert wines are this area's mainstay with one or two outstanding small producers of massive reds.
	Recommended Producers Bailey's, Brown Brothers, Campbells, Morris, Stanton and Killeen.
Murray River	Mainly bulk wines are produced but some good reds and whites are made in this hot growing area.
	Recommended Producers Best's, St. Andrews, Lindeman's, Mildara.
Bendigo	One producer has put this new region on the map — Balgownie. First-rate Cabernet Sauvignon and Pinot Noir comes from this region.
	Also Recommended Chateau Le Amon, Jasper Hill.
Geelong	This area southwest of Melbourne is one of the coolest growing areas.
	Recommended Producers Bannockburn, Hickinbotham, Prince Albert.
Macedon	This windy growing region is located north of Melbourne.
	Recommended Producers Knights' Granite Hills, Virgin Hills.
Yarra Valley	The Yarra Valley northeast of Melbourne is the most promising region for Pinot Noir.
	Recommended Producers Coldstream Hills, Lillydale, Mount Mary, Seville, Yarra Yering, Yeringberg.
	Worth Looking For Wantirna Estate, east of Melbourne (Pinot Noir, Cabernet/Merlot, Chardonnay) and Main Ridge Estate, south of Melbourne (Cabernet, Chardonnay, Pinot Noir).

South Australia

Adelaide Hills

A cool climate supports good Chardonnay and Riesling and grapes for "champagnes."

Recommended Producers D.A. Tolley's Pedare, Mountadam, Petaluma.

Barossa Valley

Solid reds and very good whites are grown in the hills of the Barossa Valley.

Recommended Producers Wolf Blass, Leo Buring, Heggies Vineyard, Henschke, Krondorf, Peter Lehmann, Penfolds, Saltram, Seppelt.

Clare Valley

Wonderful Chardonnay and Riesling and elegant Cabernets come from this region.

Recommended Producers Jeffrey Grosset, Tim Knappstein, Lindemans, Mitchells, Quelltaler, Stanley Leasingham, Taylors.

Coonawarra, Padthaway, Keppoch

This region produces the finest Cabernet Sauvignons, very Bordeaux in style. Chardonnay and Sauvignon Blanc also do well here.

Recommended Producers Bowen Estate, Brand's Laira, Hardy's, Hollick, Hungerford Hill, Katnook Estate, Lindeman's Rouge Homme, Mildara, Penfold's, Redman's Redbank, Seppelt's, Wynns.

Riverland

Riverland is a supplier of bag-in-box wines. Simple, commerical wines are produced. If you find yourself in Australia look for Angove's, Berri and Renmano.

Southern Vales

High quality reds and whites come from this region.

Recommended Producers D'Arenburg, Dennis's Daringa Cellars, Chateau Reynella, Fern Hill, Geoff Merrill, Hardy's, Wirra Wirra, Woodstock.

Western Australia

Margaret River, Swan Valley, SW Coastal Plain

Some of Australia's best reds and full-bodied whites come from these regions.

Recommended Producers Alkoomi, Capel Vale, Cullen, Evans & Tate, Houghton, Leeuwin Estate, Moss Wood, Vasse Felix.

Tasmania	The cool climate of the island makes it an ideal location for grape-growing.
	Recommended Producers Heemskerk, Morilla Estate, Piper's Brook.
Sparkling Wine	**Recommended Producers** Chateau Remy, Thomas Hardy, Mildara, Petaluma, Great Western, Seppelt's, Seaview, Wolf Blass, Yalumba, Yellowglen.
Expensive Wines	The most expensive Australian wines are Penfold's Grange Hermitage and Penfold's Cabernet Sauvignon Bin 707.
NEW ZEALAND	The cool growing regions of New Zealand — somewhat similar to Germany though longer in duration — are producing some of the most exciting wines currently being made in the New World. While Loire-style Sauvignon Blancs first

WINE REGIONS OF NEW ZEALAND

captured international attention, the more popular Chardonnay and Cabernet Sauvignon are getting their rightful share of acclaim.

Grape Varieties	**White** Müller-Thurgau, Riesling, Gewürztraminer, Chenin Blanc, Sauvignon Blanc, Semillon, Chardonnay. **Red** Cabernet Sauvignon, Merlot, Pinot Noir.
Recommended Wineries	Babich, Cloudy Bay, Collard, Cook's, Corban's, Esk Valley, Hunter's, Kumeu River, Matua Valley, Montana, Neudorf, Nobilo, St. Helena, Selaks, Te Mata, Vidal, Villa Maria.

Mexico, South America and South Africa

MEXICO

WINE REGIONS OF SOUTH AMERICA

*M*ost Mexican grapes are used for brandy production. But high-altitude vineyards are producing some credible red wines. There are basically nine growing regions, the best of which are Baja California, Aguascalientes and Rio San Juan.

Recommended Producers Domecq, Formex-Ybarra, Casa Madero, Cavas de San Juan, Bodegas de Santo Tomas, Uva de Aguascalientes.

SOUTH AMERICA

Argentina

Perhaps it is fortunate for the local industry based in the Mendoza Valley that Argentinians consume most of the wines produced in their country. The white wines — made from Sauvignon Blanc, Sémillon, Chenin Blanc, Chardonnay and the Muscat-like Torrontes grape — tend to be flat and tired. The beefy reds made from Malbec, Criolla, Cereza, Cabernet, Merlot and Pinot Noir are better and usually are good value.

Recommended Producers Bodegas Bianchi, Humberto Canale, Etchart, Flichman, Penãflor, Bodegas Suter, Pascual Toso, Weinert.

Sparkling Wine Proviar.

Chile

Of all the South American wine-producing countries, Chile is perhaps the only one whose wines have met an international standard of quality. The reds are generally more interesting than the whites and can be the best value you will find. Cabernet Sauvignons are drinkable young, but will age for at least five years.

Grape Varieties

White Sauvignon Blanc, Sémillon, Chardonnay, Riesling, Gewürztraminer (País and Muscatel for Pisco production).

Red Cabernet Sauvignon, Malbec, Merlot, Pinot Noir.

Wine Styles

Chilean whites tend to be full-bodied with lots of fruit and wood character. Reds resemble Bordeaux but with heavier, jammier flavours.

Recommended Producers Canepa, Concho Y Toro, Cousiño Macul, Errazuriz Panquehue, Los Vascos, Santa Carolina, Santa Rita, Torres Santa Digna, Unduragga.

Sparkling Wine Valdiviseo.

SOUTH AFRICA

Port and sherries used to be the staple fare of South African wineries but in the last twenty years exciting Cabernet Sauvignon, Sauvignon Blanc, Chenin Blanc (called Steen here) and Riesling have been produced. A local specialty is Pinotage, a hybrid of Pinot Noir and Cinsault which makes a meaty red wine that can age well. The Cinsault grape of the Rhône is known in South Africa as Hermitage.

Wine Styles	Reds are full-bodied, fruity wines high in alcohol. The whites are full-bodied, fruity and soft with a touch of sweetness.

Recommended Producers Allesverloren, Backsburg, Bertram, De Wetsof, Hamilton Russell, Le Bonheur, Meerlust, Nederburg, Rustenburg, Simonsig, Stellenbosch Farmers' Winery, Stellenryck, Twee Jongegezeelen, Uitkyk, Vriesenhof.

Worth Looking For Nederburg Late-Harvest Edelkeur.

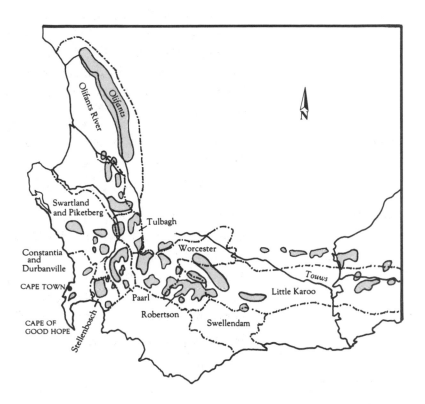

WINE REGIONS OF SOUTH AFRICA

Canada

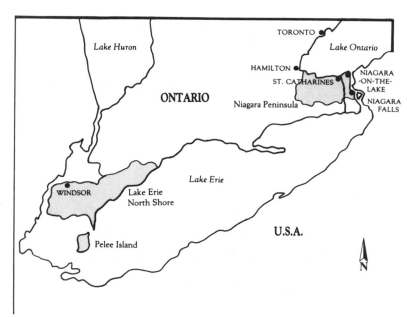

WINE REGIONS OF ONTARIO

*F*our provinces produce wines from *vinifera* and hybrid grapes with Ontario accounting for the lion's share of production. The white wines tend to be better than the reds, with Chardonnay and Riesling proving to be the most adaptable varieties for the cool growing climate. Pinot Noir may eventually be the grape for reds although the industry currently relies on Maréchal Foch and Baco Noir. One of the surprises is the lusciously sweet Icewine made by many Ontario producers from Vidal or Riesling grapes. The trend is for smaller operations with a movement towards farm wineries (small growers who make and market wines under their own labels) producing a maximum of 10,000 gallons.

| ONTARIO | The Vintners Quality Alliance (VQA) is the Appellation of Origin for Ontario and British Columbia wines made from 100 percent locally grown *vinifera* and selected hybrid grapes. The system isolates defined growing areas — Niagara Penninsula, Lake Erie North Shore and Pelee Island in Ontario, Okanagan Valley and Similkameen Valley in British Columbia — and designates minimum sugar levels. |

This appellation appears on the label. A special medallion is a seal of quality for VQA wines which have received fourteen or more points out of twenty from an independent tasting panel. This postage stamp size seal will usually be fixed to the throat of the bottle.

Three growing regions are currently designated in Ontario — Niagara Peninsula, Lake Erie North Shore and Pelee Island.

Ontario producers concentrate on the classic French varieties for their best wines and use white and red hybrids for their blended products.

Wine Style

Crisp, dry whites in French and German style. Light reds.

Recommended Producers By Grape Variety

Ontario wineries produce a bewildering number of varietal wines from hybrid and *vinifera* grapes. Some wines, as a result, are more successful than others.

Chardonnay

Cave Spring, Château des Charmes, Hillebrand Estates, Inniskillin, Stonechurch, Stoney Ridge, Vineland Estates, Marynissen Estate.

Riesling

Cave Spring, Henry of Pelham, Konzelmann, Reif, Vineland Estates.

Gewürztraminer

Konzelmann, Reif.

Cabernet/Merlot

Brights, Château des Charmes, Inniskillin, Marynissen.

Pinot Noir

Château des Charmes, Inniskillin.

Worth Watching For   Ontario Icewine (Riesling or Vidal) — expensive but the wine world's best-kept secret.

BRITISH COLUMBIA

The Vintners Quality Alliance (VQA) is the Appellation of Origin for both British Columbia and Ontario (see under Ontario). There are two designated growing regions — Okanagan Valley and Similkameen Valley.

WINE REGIONS OF BRITISH COLUMBIA

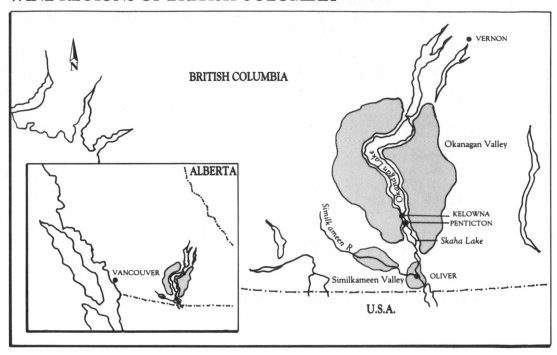

British Columbia winemakers have concentrated on a variety of German grapes, such as Ehrenfelser, Bacchus, Schönburger, as well as Riesling, Gewürztraminer, Chardonnay and Auxerrois.

Wine Style

Whites are Germanic in style with a touch of residual sugar. The reds are light.

British Columbia has six commercial wineries, nine estate wineries and a growing number of farm wineries.

Recommended Producers By Grape Variety

As in Ontario, British Columbian wineries produce a large number of labels as they continue to experiment to find the best varieties to match soil and climate.

German-Style Wines

Gehringer Brothers, Gray Monk, Hainle Vineyards, Andre's (Ehrenfelser).

French-Style Wines

Cedar Creek, Divino, Mission Hill, Sumac Ridge, Bright's Vaseaux Cellars, Hillside Cellars.

WINE REGIONS OF QUEBEC

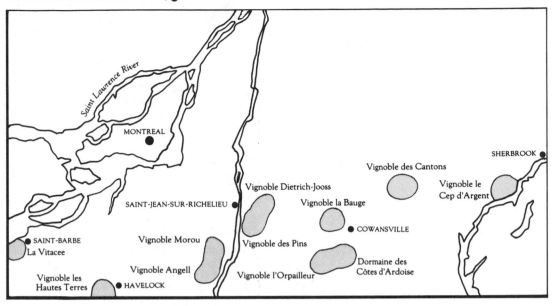

WINE REGIONS OF NOVA SCOTIA

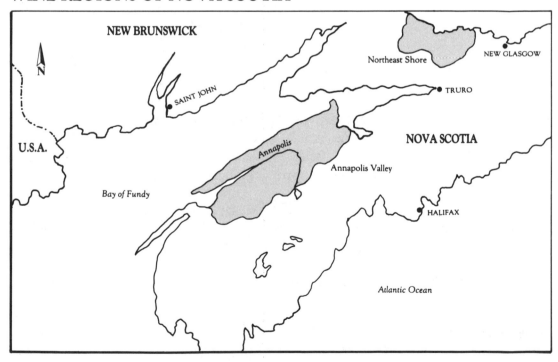

QUEBEC

Apart from imported bulk-wine bottling operations, Quebec has thirteen cottage wineries south of Montreal, along the American border. The grapes are a mix of hybrids and some *vinifera* varieties. In spite of harsh winter conditions (the vines have to be covered with earth in the fall to guard against frost damage) the 100 hectares (247 acres) of vines provide refreshing white wines, mainly from such hybrids as Seyval Blanc and Cayuga and light reds from Maréchal Foch and de Chaunac. Some Chardonnay is also grown.

Recommended Producers   La Vitacée, Vignoble Angell, Société D.C.A. Dunham, Vignoble de l'Orpailleur.

NOVA SCOTIA

Currently there are four wineries in Nova Scotia that make wine from locally grown grapes and bottle off-shore material.

Grand Pré is the oldest and best established, making serviceable whites (L'Acadie Blanc, Seyval Blanc) and full-bodied reds (Maréchal Foch and the Russian variety Michurnitz).

Hans Jost makes German-style whites, including Kerner and Riesling. They make the most expensive Icewine in Canada.

Ste. Famille makes Riesling and Seyval Blanc and bottles imported Chardonnay.

The newest arrival is Ocean Brink Farm Winery.

Old-World Wineries

AUSTRIA

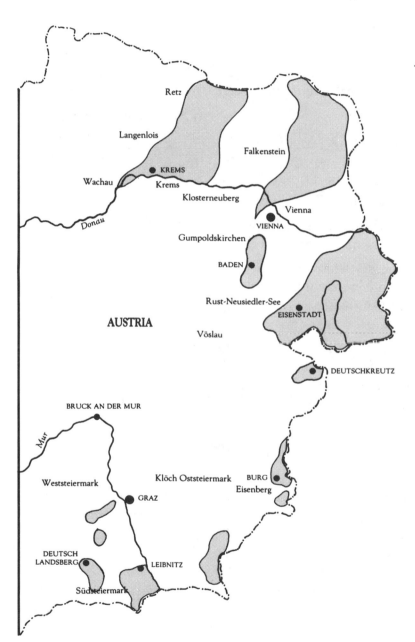

Retz

Langenlois

Falkenstein

Wachau ● KREMS

Krems

Klosterneuberg

Donau

Gumpoldskirchen

Vienna

VIENNA

● BADEN

Rust-Neusiedler-See

AUSTRIA

Vöslau

EISENSTADT

DEUTSCHKREUTZ

BRUCK AN DER MUR

Mur

Weststeiermark

Klöch Oststeiermark

BURG

GRAZ

Eisenberg

DEUTSCH
LANDSBERG

LEIBNITZ

Südsteiermark

WINE REGIONS OF AUSTRIA

ustrian wines can be some of the best bargains around especially in the dessert wine category. Stringent wine laws have been put in place following the "anti-freeze" wine scandal in 1985.

The designations follow the German model — *Qualitätswein, Kabinett, Spätlese,* etc. (see page 198) — although the alcohol levels are generally higher. Austria also has an additional wine category called *Ausbruch,* a level of sweetness between *Beerenauslese* and *Trockenbeerenauslese.* This dessert wine is made entirely from *Botrytis-*affected grapes.

The style of Austrian white wines is more akin to Alsace than to neighbouring Germany whose quality designations they share. The reds tend to be less attractive than the whites except for those of a few producers who use small French oak barrels to ferment and age their wines.

Grape Varieties

White Grüner Veltliner (one-third of production), Neuburger, Muskat-Ottonel Riesling, Gewürztraminer, Welschriesling, Müller-Thurgau, Ruländer, Weissburgunder, Zierfandel, Rotkipfler.

Red Blaufränkisch, Blauer Zweigelt, Blauer Portugieser, Spätburgunder, some Cabernet Sauvignon.

The dry white wines of Wachau, Krems and Langenlois, the fruity wines of Gumpoldskirchen and the dessert wines from Neusiedlersee (especially from the town of Rust) are worth searching out.

Recommended Producers Lenz Moser, Freigut Thallern, Franz Mayer, Florianhoff, M. Müller, Josef Jamek, H. Johann Grill, Karl Grabner, Anton Kollwenz, Weinkeller Siegendorf, Alois Morandell, Sepp Hold, Weingut Elfenhof, Franz Prager.

Sparkling Wines Schlumberger.

SWITZERLAND

Swiss wines are not cheap. Having said that, they can be very refreshing since both whites and reds are light and high in acidity. Wines have been made in Switzerland since the Romans first introduced the vine. The four most important growing areas are the steeply terraced vineyards of the Valais at the headwaters of the Rhône, the northern slopes of Lake Neuchâtel, the steep slopes of the Vaud overlooking Lake Geneva and the area surrounding the city of Geneva.

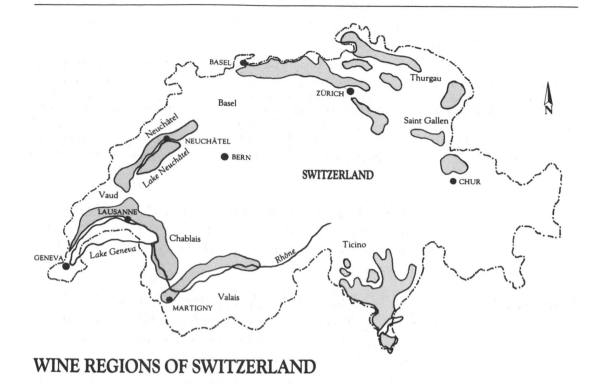

WINE REGIONS OF SWITZERLAND

Grape Variety	**Whites** The principal white grape is the Chasselas, which can masquerade under a variety of names as Fendant, Dorin, Perlan or Neuchâtel. The best is from Dezaley.
	Other Whites Silvaner, Muscat, Malvoisie, Riesling, Marsanne.
	Reds Pinot Noir, Gamay, Merlot.
	Recommended Producers *Valais* — Domaine du Mont d'Or, Charles Favre, Orsat, Vuignier; *Neuchâtel* — Chatenay, Ruedin; *Vaud* — Badoux, Hammel, Schenk, J & P Testuz; *Geneva* — Leyvraz and Stevens; *Zurich* — Schlatter; *Ticino* — Cantine Sociale Meudriso.
GREECE	There is more to Greek wine than the resinated Retsina which to some tastes like turpentine. But it goes wonderfully well with Greek dishes. The red wines of Macedonia age beautifully — look for Naoussa and Nemea — and the whites of the islands can be delightfully fresh if caught young — Santorini and Lindos, especially. The sweet red Mavrodaphne makes an interesting aperitif or dessert wine.

Grape Varieties	**Red** Mavrodaphne, Xynomavro, Agiorgitiko, Mandilari, Liatik, Romeiko, Limnio, Vertzami, some Cabernet Sauvignon.

Red Mavrodaphne, Xynomavro, Agiorgitiko, Mandilari, Liatik, Romeiko, Limnio, Vertzami, some Cabernet Sauvignon.

White Savantino (Retsina), Rhoditis, Assyrtiko, Robola, Debina, Muscat.

Recommended Producers Reds: Boutari, Cava Tsantalis, Château Carras (Cabernet Sauvignon). Whites: Kourtakis.

Worth Looking For Samos Muscat, honey-sweet dessert wine.

TURKEY

Turkish wines are difficult to find but can suprise you. The reds are usually massive. The names can also cause mirth, for example, Buzbag and Dikmen are reds that occasionally appear on the export market. The best wines come from central Anatolia. Sweet whites from the Aegean region are similar to Greek Muscat.

LEBANON

One of the world's great wines comes from the Bekaa Valley — Château Musar — where the imperturbable Serge Hochar manages to overcome wars and political vicissitudes to produce a long-lasting red from Cabernet Sauvignon, Cinsault, Syrah and Merlot. Vintages last twenty years and more.

Retsina

The Retsina comes from Attica, the only appellation for this wine, produced by Kourtakis.

There are many legends how this wine came to be resinated. Some Greeks will tell you that pine gum was originally added to make the wine unpalatable to the Turks. Others will talk about how the amphorae of the ancients were sealed with the sticky substance and the gum was also used to make leather wine-skins leakproof at the seams. Eventually, the Greeks got used to the taste to the point where the resin was added directly to the fermenting wine.

At the Boutari winery in Neo Kordelio I was shown bags of fresh gum that had been collected from pines in Attica. A two-foot strip of bark is stripped from the trunk of the Alep pine to allow the sticky resin to collect in metal cups. It is then dried to crystals and pulverized, ready to be added to the fermenting Savantino grapes. The yellow resin must be added while the substance is still young. If it ages, it will oxidize and give bad flavours to the wine. About one percent of gum by volume is used for a mild taste (usually for export); for the home market more resin is added. There is also — and this was news to me — a rosé Retsina. I tried one made by the Tsantali winery from mature Rhoditis grapes. Orange amber in colour, the nose was piney and medicinal and the taste was very soft, lacking the acidity to clean off the palate. Small wonder it never leaves the country.

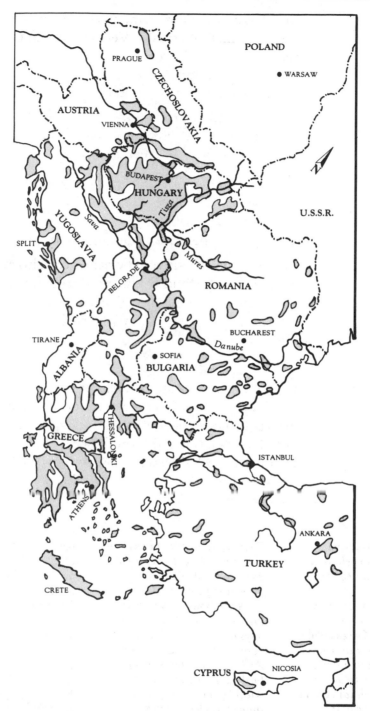

WINE REGIONS OF EASTERN EUROPE

ISRAEL   The Israeli wine industry has improved immeasurably over the products that used to be made at Richon-Le-Zion and Zichron-Yaacov. New wineries in the Galil and on the Golan Heights are making wines from European *vinifera* varieties such as Cabernet Sauvignon and Sauvignon Blanc.

Recommended Producers   Golan Heights, Yarden.

YUGOSLAVIA   Almost as prolific in vines as its Italian neighbour, Yugoslavia offers a bewildering number of grape varieties. Look for the grape variety and place of origin, but don't put too much store by the vintage date since most of the wines are blended. Whites from the Fruska Gora Hills in Serbia and Ljutomer Riesling from Slovenia can be worth looking for. The traditional reds tend to a peasant-like solidity and impenetrability.

Grape Varieties   **Red**   Prokupac, Plavac, Vranac, Gamay, Cabernet Sauvignon, Merlot, Pinot Noir.

White   Welschriesling, Rhine Riesling, Gewürztraminer, Pinot Blanc, Pinot Gris.

HUNGARY   Hungary is best known for its rich dessert wine Tokaji (Tokay) and its fiery reds, Bull's Blood and Szekeszardi. As the largest wine-producing country in Eastern Europe, Hungary is beginning to produce table wines that offer the consumer

---

Tokay — The King of Wines

Hungarian Tokay (also spelled Tokaji) has nothing to do with Alsatian Tokay which is dry and pale straw in colour and named after the Tokay-Pinot Gris grape. The amber-coloured Tokay of Hungary is one of the world's great dessert wines and is said to have magical curative properties. This honey-sweet nectar with nuances of toffee and orange rind is made by adding tubs of Botrytis-affected grape mash to fermenting Furmint and Hárslevelü juice. The tubs are called puttonyos.

The number of puttonyos used in one barrel (gönci) will dictate the sweetness of the final product. This number will be printed on the neck label as 3, 4, 5 or 6 puttonyos.

There are four grades of Tokay ranging from dry to very sweet.

1 **Tokay Szamorodni:** the wine is not sweetened with puttonyos and the style will be dictated by the quality of the harvest. It will either be slightly sweet (Edes) or dry (Száraz). Serve lightly chilled.

2 **Tokay Aszú:** made with Botrytis-affected grapes. The sweetness is determined by the number of puttonyos.

3 **Tokay Aszú Essencia:** made in exceptional vintages, fermented for several years and aged for ten years in oak.

4 **Tokay Essence:** the free-run juice of Aszú grapes pressed by their own weight and fermented slowly over many years. Very rare.

good value in the familiar grape varieties. The poetic names of the traditional grapes are difficult to pronounce but worth investigating, although there is a tendency for the vintners to leave the wines in wood for too long. The whites tend to be a bit flat.

Grape Varieties

White Furmint, Olasrizling (Welschriesling), Hárslevelü (Linden Leaf), Szükebarát (Pinot Gris), Kéknelyü, Juhfark (Sheep's Tail), Mézesfehér (White Honey), Ezerjo (Thousand Delights), Leányka (Young Girl), Gewürztraminer and lately Chardonnay, Pinot Blanc and Sauvignon Blanc.

Red Kadarka, Kékfrankos, Nagyburgundi (Pinot Noir), Médoc Noir (Merlot). Growing amounts of Cabernet Sauvignon and Cabernet Franc are also available.

Recommended Wines Whites from Etyek region. Reds from Eger and Szekszard. Tokaji.

Sparkling Wine Producer Törley.

CZECHOSLOVAKIA

As a northern growing region the main concentration is on white wines. The main production area is Slovakia where the vineyards are planted in a range of aromatic German grapes. The other growing regions are Moravia and Bohemia. The wines tend to be artisanal and somewhat clumsy but are inexpensive.

Grape Varieties

White Welsch Rizling, Rhine Rizling, Grüner Veltliner, Silvaner, Müller-Thurgau, Weissburgunder, Ruländer, Neuburger, Sauvignon, Traminer, Muscat, Pinot Blanc. (Some Tokay is made from Furmint grapes near the Hungarian border but the wine is not in the same league.)

Red Limberger, St. Laurent, Pinot Noir.

RUMANIA

More wine is produced in Rumania than in Germany and much of it is red. Wood ageing in large, old oak vats gives the wine a jammy, slightly oxidized taste. The whites tend to be sweet and powerful designed for their Russian neighbours.

Grape Varieties

Red Pinot Noir, Merlot, Cabernet Sauvignon, Kadarka, Feteasca Neagra.

White Feteasca Alba, Ruländer, Riesling, Sauvignon Blanc, Traminer, Muscat Ottonel, Furmint.

BULGARIA	Surprisingly, Bulgaria has one of the largest plantings of Cabernet Sauvignon in the world. The wines are labelled by variety and tend to have robust flavours. Good values to be found in Pamid and Gamza, light reds usually blended with Cabernet Sauvignon, and the deeply coloured Mavrud.
Grape Varieties	**Red** Pamid, Cabernet Sauvignon, Merlot, Gamza, Melnik, Mavrud.
	Whites Rkatsiteli, Dimiat, Misket (Muscat Ottonel), Laski Riesling, Rhine Riesling, Chardonnay, Sauvignon Blanc, Ugni Blanc, Gewürztraminer, Tamianka.
SOVIET UNION	If Noah planted the first vineyard when his ark came to rest on Mount Ararat, then the Soviets could claim to have invented wine since his landfall was in present-day Armenia. Today the Soviet Union has the largest planting of vines on the planet after Spain and is third, after Italy and France, in terms of production. While eleven of the fifteen republics in the USSR produce wine, the most popular come from Georgia, Armenia, Crimea and Moldavia.
	The whites and reds are generally on the sweet side. Sparkling wine made from Chardonnay and Pinot Noir also tends to be sweet, as does the red sparkler, Tsimlyanskoe.
Grape Varieties	**Red** Saperavi, Khindogny, Black Tsimlyansky, Magaratch Ruby, Magaratch Bastardo, Matrassa, Isabella, Cabernet Sauvignon, Merlot, Pinot Noir.
	White Rkatsiteli, Mtsvane, Terbash, Bayan Shirey, Riesling, Chardonnay.
ENGLAND	By all rights England should not be a wine-growing country at all. It is too far north to enjoy sufficient sunshine for ripening the grapes. But certain German hybrids develop enough sugar in the south to produce delicate, dry wines which are beefed up by the addition of "sweet-reserve" — fresh grape juice which is added to the finished wine before bottling to give it a hit of fruit. The wines tend to be expensive for what they are, but are useful for fooling wine snobs. Vintages are probably more important in England than they are anywhere else. In hot years such as 1989 and 1990 they made excellent wines.
Grape Varieties	Müller-Thurgau, Reichensteiner, Schönburger, Auxerrois, Seyval Blanc, Chardonnay.

Starting
a
Wine
Library

I have nearly five hundred wine books in my wine
library but I must confess I consult only about thirty
of them on a regular basis. Wine books can date very
quickly, especially if you are looking for information on
specific wines in certain vintages. If I had to jettison all but a
dozen of my books for my desert island (where I had a climate-
controlled cellar and an ample supply of wine) I would choose
to have the following with me:

- Hugh Johnson's *The World Atlas of Wines* — detailed maps of
  the world's wine regions and an authoritative analysis of growing and making wines (Simon & Schuster).
- Hugh Johnson's *Modern Encyclopedia of Wine* — very good
  on the best producers around the world (Simon & Schuster).
- Alexis Lichine's *New Encyclopedia of Wines & Spirits* — the
  most comprehensive guide to beverage alcohol, scholarly, authoritative, but dry (Knopf).
- Jancis Robinson's *Vines, Grapes and Wines* — a complete
  guide to grape varieties around the world and the wines made
  from them (Knopf).
- Sheldon and Pauline Wasserman's *Italy's Noble Red Wines* —
  everything you need to know about Italian reds up to 1984.
- David Gleave's *The Wines of Italy* — for the latest on Italy, an
  intelligent assessment of the new directions in Italian winemaking (Salamander).

- Michael Broadbent's *Complete Guide to Wine Tasting and Wine Cellars* — tips from the master on how to do it (Simon & Schuster).
- Tom Stevenson's *Champagne* — how it's made, the history of the region, with profiles of the different houses and their styles (Simon & Schuster).
- Feret's *Bordeaux and Its Wines* — the bible of the trade, descriptions of all the Bordeaux properties, their annual production, with etchings of the châteaux (Editions Feret et Fils).
- Frank Schoonmaker's *The Wines of Germany* (revised by Peter Sichel — a no-nonsense look at German wines (Hastings House). (This book is also published in the excellent Faber and Faber paperback series which also includes terrific studies of *Bordeaux* by David Peppercorn, *Burgundy* by Anthony Hanson, *Rhône* by John Livingstone-Learmonth and *Spain and Portugal* by Jan Read.)

There is one book which is no longer in print but if you can find it in a second-hand store you'll have unearthed a treasure: William Younger's *Gods, Men and Wine*, a history of wine from prehistoric times to the Edwardians written for The Food and Wine Society and published by Michael Joseph in 1966.

For a highly readable book on all technical aspects of winemaking try Philip M. Wagner's *Grapes Into Wine — The Art of Winemaking In America* (Knopf).

And, of course, the book you are reading!

Vintage
Charts

*T*hink of the vintage from a particular wine region as a child. It will bear a family resemblance to all of its siblings, but will have a unique character all its own.

There is an assumption that if a vintage is good in Bordeaux it will be good everywhere else in Europe. There are years when this does happen, as in 1985 and 1989, but weather patterns are not continental. The 1982 vintage, for example, was excellent in Bordeaux but was poor in the Rhine and Mosel. The 1963 vintage was a disaster in Bordeaux, one of the worst years this century, but in Portugal it was a sensational vintage for port.

Climatic conditions in Europe are highly localized even within the same village. A hailstorm might cut a swath through Burgundy devastating one vineyard and leaving its neighbour unscathed.

Vintage charts will give you the overall weather pattern for a particular region but because a given year in, say, Pomerol rates a mere 11 out of 20, does not necessarily mean that all Pomerol wines are little more than mediocre in that year. Rain during the harvest may have diluted the grape sugars, but those growers who happened to pick before the rains came will have made a better wine. Again, 1982 was a great year in Bordeaux for both quality and quantity — so much so

VINTAGE CHART

VINTAGES		'70	'71	'72
RED BORDEAUX	Médoc/Graves	19	17	9
	Saint-Émilion/Pomerol	19	18	9
WHITE BORDEAUX	Sauternes/Barsac	18	15	11
RED BURGUNDY	Côte de Nuits	14	17	16
	Côte de Beaune	14	16	15
WHITE BURGUNDY		16	16	12
BEAUJOLAIS		16	16	12
RHÔNE	North, Côtes-du-Rhône	16	14	14
	South, Côtes-du-Rhône	14	16	14
LOIRE	Muscadet/Touraine/Anjou	14	15	10
	Pouilly-Fumé/Sancerre	14	19	8
ALSACE		15	19	10
VINTAGE CHAMPAGNE		17	15	
GERMANY	Rhine	11	19	8
	Mosel	11	19	8
ITALY	Tuscany	16	20	8
	Piedmont	16	20	4
PORTUGAL	Vintage Port	17		
SPAIN	Rioja	20	11	7
CALIFORNIA NORTH COAST	Red	20	18	14
	White	18	18	14
AUSTRALIA WHITES	South Australia			
	New South Wales			
	Western Australia			
	Victoria			
AUSTRALIA REDS	South Australia			
	New South Wales			
	Western Australia			
	Victoria			
		'70	'71	'72

'73	'74	'75	'76	'77	'78	'79	'80	'81	'82	'83	'84	'85	'86	'87	'88	'89	'90
13	13	18	15	11	18	17	13	17	19	17	15	18	18	12	18	19	(18)
13	13	18	16	11	17	17	13	16	18	17	11	17	15	11	17	18	(18)
13	11	18	16	12	14	17	15	17	13	16	13	18	18	11	18	19	(18)
13	13	5	18	9	18	14	15	12	13	16	12	19	14	15	17	17	(17)
13	12	7	18	9	18	16	13	14	14	17	13	19	14	15	17	16	(17)
16	13	14	16	13	17	17	12	18	18	18	14	17	18	16	16	18	(17)
16	12	13	17	8	19	15	12	16	14	17	14	16	17	12	19	18	(18)
14	12	10	16	12	19	16	15	13	14	19	14	19	16	17	18	17	(18)
13	12	10	16	11	18	16	15	15	12	16	13	18	17	13	16	16	(17)
14	10	16	16	11	16	14	13	15	14	17	14	18	16	14	18	20	(20)
16	14	16	18	12	17	15	15	16	13	15	14	17	16	15	16	18	(19)
17	14	16	18	12	17	16	13	17	14	20	13	18	16	15	18	17	(19)
16		18	16		15	16	14	15	17		13	18	16	14	16	17	(18)
12	5	14	18	8	9	15	8	15	11	18	10	17	15	12	17	18	(19)
13	5	17	18	8	9	15	8	15	11	18	10	17	16	12	17	18	(19)
8	14	16	8	16	20	16	16	12	18	19	13	19	17	13	15	13	(19)
10	18	10	10	10	20	16	14	12	20	17	12	19	16	13	15	15	(20)
		13		19			15		15	17		18			(16)	(18)	
17	13	15	14	8	19	13	15	17	19	15	14	19	16	16	17	18	(18)
16	20	18	18	16	19	18	18	17	15	13	13	19	17	17	16	17	(18)
16	18	18	18	16	17	18	19	17	15	14	15	18	18	17	16	17	(17)
							16	14	15	10	17	19	14	17	15	14	15
							17	14	17	17	16	18	16	16	16	18	16
							17	18	17	17	19	19	17	18	17	16	18
							16	16	17	16	16	18	14	17	17	18	18
							17	14	18	11	19	17	16	15	17	17	18
							17	15	18	17	18	18	16	16	16	17	16
							16	19	18	19	19	18	17	17	17	17	16
							18	18	17	19	18	19	16	17	19	19	17
'73	'74	'75	'76	'77	'78	'79	'80	'81	'82	'83	'84	'85	'86	'87	'88	'89	'90

that some of the smaller producers did not have the capacity to ferment their wines properly. Those who did made excellent wines.

So, vintage charts are merely a rough rule of thumb.

The marginal northern growing areas, such as Champagne, Loire, Rhine and Mosel will have a greater variation of fruit quality from year to year than the warmer growing areas of California, Australia and South America. A good indicator for the quality of the harvest in Europe is vintage champagne — whether the houses actually made one and how it was rated.

I am indebted to Steven Spurrier for the use of his Académie du Vin vintage chart which he uses for his wine courses around the world. His chart is based on a scale of 20 points.

- 0 – 9 Bad wine, avoid this vintage.
- 10 – 11 Acceptable when nothing else available.
- 12 – 13 Not bad. Good enough for large groups when the good stuff has run out.
- 14 – 15 Good. You will not be embarrassed by serving it.
- 16 – 18 Very good. Serve to those who will appreciate it.
- 19 – 20 Exceptional. Keep for the great occasions or share with someone you love.

This chart goes up to 1990. Projections of the quality of the harvest suggest the ratings which are noted in brackets.

Bibliography

Ambrosi, Hans. *Where the Great German Wines Grow.* New York: Hastings House, 1976.

Amerine, Maynard A., and Edward B. Roessler. *Wines, Their Sensory Evaluation,* San Francisco: Freeman, 1976.

Anderson, Burton. *Vino.* Boston: Atlantic-Little Brown, 1980.

Aspler, Tony. *International Guide To Wine.* Scarborough, Ontario: Prentice-Hall, 1986.

Aspler, Tony and Jacques Marie. *The Wine Lover Dines.* Scarborough, Ontario: Prentice-Hall, 1986.

Belfarge, Nicholas. *Life Beyond Lambrusco.* London: Sidgwick & Jackson, 1985.

Benson, Jeffrey and Alastair Mackenzie. *Sauternes.* London: Sotheby, 1979.

Blumberg, Robert S., and Hurst Hannum. *The Fine Wines of California.* (Third Edition). New York: Doubleday, 1984.

Broadbent, Michael. *Complete Guide to Wine Tasting and Wine Cellars.* London: Simon & Schuster, 1984.

Brook, Stephen. *Liquid Gold: Dessert Wines of the World.* London: Constable, 1987.

Clarke, Oz. *New Encyclopedia of French Wines.* New York: Simon & Schuster, 1990.

Duijker, Hubrecht. *The Great Wine Chateaux of Bordeaux.* London: Crescent, Mitchell Beasley, 1983.

247

_____. *The Wines of The Loire, Alsace and Champagne*. London: Crescent, Mitchell Beasley, 1983.

Dussert-Gerber, Patrick. *The Best French Wines*. Paris: Editions Vintage, 1989.

Féret. *Bordeaux and Its Wines*. Bordeaux: Editions Féret (Thirteenth Edition), 1986.

Forbes, Patrick. *Champagne: The Wine, The Land and The People*. London: Gollancz, 1967.

Frumkin, Lionel. *The Science and Technique of Wine*. Cambridge: Patrick Stephens, 1974.

George, Rosemary. *The Wines of Chablis*. London: Sotheby's, 1985.

Galet, Pierre. *A Practical Ampelography*. Ithaca, New York: Comstock and Cornell University Press, 1979.

Gleave, David. *The Wines of Italy*. London: Salamander, 1989.

Hachette. *Guide to French Wines*. New York: Alfred A. Knopf, 1986.

Halliday, James. *The Australian Wine Compendium*. North Ryde, NSW: Angus & Robertson, 1985.

Hanson, Anthony. *Burgundy*. London: Faber & Faber, 1982.

Hazan, Victor. *Italian Wine*. Harmondsworth, Middlesex: Penguin, 1984.

Howkins, Ben. *Rich, Rare & Red, A Guide to Port*. London: Christopher Helm, 1987.

Jan de Blij, Harm. *Wine Regions of the Southern Hemisphere*. New Jersey: Rowman & Allanheld, 1985.

Jeffs, Julian. *Sherry*. London: Faber & Faber, 1982.

Johnson, Hugh. *Modern Encyclopedia of Wine*. New York: Simon & Schuster, 1987.

_____. *The World Atlas of Wine*. New York: Simon & Schuster, (revised) 1985.

Johnson, Hugh, and Hubrecht Duijker. *The Wine Atlas of France*. New York: Simon & Schuster, 1987.

Lichine, Alexis. *Guide to the Wines and Vineyards of France*. New York: Knopf, 1979.

_____. *New Encyclopedia of Wines & Spirits*. New York: Knopf, 1985.

Livingstone-Learmonth and Melvyn C. H. Master, *The Wines of the Rhône*. London: Faber & Faber, 1988.

Parker, Robert M. *Bordeaux*. New York: Simon & Schuster, 1985.

_____. *Burgundy*. New York: Simon & Schuster, 1990.

_____. *The Wines of the Rhône Valley and Provence*. New York: Simon & Schuster, 1987.

Penning-Rowsell, Edmund. *The Wines of Bordeaux.* San Francisco: The Wine Appreciation Guild, 1985.

Peppercorn, David. *The Wines of Bordeaux.* New York: Simon & Schuster, 1986.

Platter, John. *South African Wine Guide.* (self-published) Delaire, 1985.

Read, Jan. *Chilean Wines.* London: Sotheby's, 1988.

————. *The Wines of Portugal.* London: Faber & Faber, 1982.

Robertson, George. *Port.* London: Faber & Faber, 1978.

Robinson, Jancis. *Vines, Grapes and Wines.* New York: Knopf, 1986.

Schoonmaker, Frank. *The Wines of Germany.* (revised by Peter Sichel) London: Faber & Faber, 1983.

Schreiner, John. *The World of Canadian Wine.* Vancouver: Douglas & McIntyre, 1984.

Simon, André. *Wines of the World.* (second edition by Serena Sutcliffe) New York: McGraw-Hill, 1981.

Spurrier, Steven, and Michel Dovaz. *Academie du Vin Wine Course.* London: Mitchell Beazley, (revised edition) 1990.

Sutcliffe, Serena. *Champagne.* New York: Simon & Schuster, 1988.

Stevenson, Tom. *Champagne.* London: Sotheby's, 1986.

Torres, Miguel A. *Wines and Vineyards of Spain.* Barcelona: Editorial Blume, 1982.

Vandyke Price, Pamela. *Alsace Wines.* London: Sotheby, 1984.

————. *The Taste of Wine.* London: Random House, 1975.

Wagner, Philip. *Grapes Into Wine, The Art of Winemaking in America.* New York: Knopf, 1976.

Wasserman, Sheldon, and Pauline Wasserman. *Sparkling Wine.* Piscataway, New Jersey: New Century, 1984.

————. *Italy's Noble Red Wines.* Piscataway, New Jersey: New Century, 1985.

Woutaz, Fernand. *Dictionnaire des appellations de tous les vins de France.* Alleur (Belgium): Marabout, 1986.

Publications

Britain — *Decanter Magazine, Wine Magazine, Wine & Spirit*
USA — *The Wine Spectator*
Canada — *Wine Tidings*
Italy — *Italian Wines & Spirits*
Germany — *German Wine Review*

INDEX